ROMANS

BELIEF

A Theological Commentary
on the Bible

GENERAL EDITORS

Amy Plantinga Pauw
William C. Placher†

ROMANS

SARAH HEANER LANCASTER

WJK WESTMINSTER
JOHN KNOX PRESS
LOUISVILLE · KENTUCKY

© 2015 Sarah Heaner Lancaster

First edition
Published by Westminster John Knox Press
Louisville, Kentucky

15 16 17 18 19 20 21 22 23 24—10 9 8 7 6 5 4 3 2 1

Scripture quotations are from the New Revised Standard Version of the Bible are
copyright © 1989 by the Division of Christian Education of the National Council
of the Churches of Christ in the U.S.A. and are used by permission.

Book design by Drew Stevens
Cover design by Lisa Buckley
Cover illustration: © David Chapman/Design Pics/Corbis

Library of Congress Cataloging-in-Publication Data

Lancaster, Sarah Heaner, 1956–
  Romans / Sarah Heaner Lancaster. -- First edition.
      pages cm. -- (Belief : a theological commentary on the Bible)
  Includes bibliographical references and index.
  ISBN 978-0-664-23261-0 (alk. paper)
  1. Bible. Romans--Commentaries. I. Title.
  BS2665.53.L36 2015
  227'.107--dc23

                                    2015009074

♾ The paper used in this publication meets the minimum requirements
of the American National Standard for Information Sciences—
Permanence of Paper for Printed Library Materials, ANSI Z39.48-1992.

Contents

Publisher's Note

William C. Placher worked with Amy Plantinga Pauw as a general editor for this series until his untimely death in November 2008. Bill brought great energy and vision to the series, and was instrumental in defining and articulating its distinctive approach and in securing theologians to write for it. Bill's own commentary for the series was the last thing he wrote, and Westminster John Knox Press dedicates the entire series to his memory with affection and gratitude.

William C. Placher, LaFollette Distinguished Professor in Humanities at Wabash College, spent thirty-four years as one of Wabash College's most popular teachers. A summa cum laude graduate of Wabash in 1970, he earned his master's degree in philosophy in 1974 and his PhD in 1975, both from Yale University. In 2002 the American Academy of Religion honored him with the Excellence in Teaching Award. Placher was also the author of thirteen books, including *A History of Christian Theology*, *The Triune God*, *The Domestication of Transcendence*, *Jesus the Savior*, *Narratives of a Vulnerable God*, and *Unapologetic Theology*. He also edited the volume *Essentials of Christian Theology*, which was named as one of 2004's most outstanding books by both *The Christian Century* and *Christianity Today* magazines.

Series Introduction

Belief: A Theological Commentary on the Bible is a series from Westminster John Knox Press featuring biblical commentaries written by theologians. The writers of this series share Karl Barth's concern that, insofar as their usefulness to pastors goes, most modern commentaries are "no commentary at all, but merely the first step toward a commentary." Historical-critical approaches to Scripture rule out some readings and commend others, but such methods only begin to help theological reflection and the preaching of the Word. By themselves, they do not convey the powerful sense of God's merciful presence that calls Christians to repentance and praise; they do not bring the church fully forward in the life of discipleship. It is to such tasks that theologians are called.

For several generations, however, professional theologians in North America and Europe have not been writing commentaries on the Christian Scriptures. The specialization of professional disciplines and the expectations of theological academies about the kind of writing that theologians should do, as well as many of the directions in which contemporary theology itself has gone, have contributed to this dearth of theological commentaries. This is a relatively new phenomenon; until the last century or two, the church's great theologians also routinely saw themselves as biblical interpreters. The gap between the fields is a loss for both the church and the discipline of theology itself. By inviting forty contemporary theologians to wrestle deeply with particular texts of Scripture, the editors of this series hope not only to provide new theological resources for the church but also to encourage all theologians to pay more attention to Scripture and the life of the church in their writings.

We are grateful to the Louisville Institute, which provided funding for a consultation in June 2007. We invited theologians, pastors, and biblical scholars to join us in a conversation about what this series could contribute to the life of the church. The time was provocative and the results were rich. Much of the series' shape owes to the insights of these skilled and faithful interpreters, who sought to describe a way to write a commentary that served the theological needs of the church and its pastors with relevance, historical accuracy, and theological depth. The passion of these participants guided us in creating this series and lives on in the volumes.

As theologians, the authors will be interested much less in the matters of form, authorship, historical setting, social context, and philology—the very issues that are often of primary concern to critical biblical scholars. Instead, this series' authors will seek to explain the theological importance of the texts for the church today, using biblical scholarship as needed for such explication but without any attempt to cover all the topics of the usual modern biblical commentary. This thirty-six-volume series will provide passage-by-passage commentary on all the books of the Protestant biblical canon, with more extensive attention given to passages of particular theological significance.

The authors' chief dialogue will be with the church's creeds, practices, and hymns; with the history of faithful interpretation and use of the Scriptures; with the categories and concepts of theology; and with contemporary culture in both "high" and popular forms. Each volume will begin with a discussion of *why* the church needs this book and why we need it *now*, in order to ground all of the commentary in contemporary relevance. Throughout each volume, text boxes will highlight the voices of ancient and modern interpreters from the global communities of faith, and occasional essays will allow deeper reflection on the key theological concepts of these biblical books.

The authors of this commentary series are theologians of the church who embrace a variety of confessional and theological perspectives. The group of authors assembled for this series represents more diversity of race, ethnicity, and gender than any other commentary series. They approach the larger Christian tradition with a critical respect, seeking to reclaim its riches and at the same time to acknowledge its shortcomings. The authors also aim to make available to readers a wide range of contemporary theological voices from many parts of the world. While it does recover an older genre of writing, this series is not an attempt to retrieve some idealized past. These commentaries have learned from tradition, but they are most importantly commentaries for today. The authors share the conviction that their work will be more contemporary, more faithful, and more radical, to the extent that it is more biblical, honestly wrestling with the texts of the Scriptures.

William C. Placher
Amy Plantinga Pauw

Abbreviations

LXX	Septuagint
JDDJ	*Joint Declaration on the Doctrine of Justification*
NASB	New American Standard Bible
NIV	New International Version
NRSV	New Revised Standard Version
REB	Revised English Bible

Introduction
Why Romans? Why Now?

The prominent placement in the New Testament of Paul's Epistle to the Romans—right after the Gospels and Acts of the Apostles and first among the letters—shows its importance to the church that preserved it for future generations. For centuries, Paul's theological reflection in this letter has provided language and ideas that have shaped Christian thinking about how to be faithful to the gospel.

After the Gospels, Paul's epistle to the Romans is probably the most influential New Testament writing for Christian theology. Many foremost theologians wrote commentaries and sermons on this letter, and it inspired new directions for thinking at some pivotal times in Christian history. For instance, Augustine worked out his understanding of the interaction between human free will and divine grace as he interpreted Paul's letter. Although he never finished his formal commentary on the epistle, he continued to ponder in other writings the questions it raised for him. Augustine has had so much theological influence in the West that his wrestling with Paul has also generated many theological issues, on which theologians continue to work.

Martin Luther started lecturing on Romans in 1515, and his preparation for these lectures led up to and formed his thinking for the Ninety-five Theses that he posted on the church door at Wittenberg in 1517. This act is well known to have launched the Protestant Reformation. Like Augustine, Luther's theology has been so influential for Protestants that his wrestling with Romans has set the agenda for theological reflection for the past five hundred years.

Then just over two centuries after Luther's protest, John Wesley

1

had what has been called a "heart-warming" experience when he heard a reading of the preface to Luther's commentary on the Epistle to the Romans in a meeting on Aldersgate Street in London. In that moment, Wesley felt an assurance of God's love that set the direction for the Methodist revival in England. Although Wesley never wrote a commentary on Romans apart from his *Explanatory Notes upon the New Testament,* he was influenced as both preacher and theologian by the vocabulary and vision of Paul's Epistle.

> The object of this Epistle is to destroy all wisdom and works of the flesh no matter how important these may appear in our eyes or in the eyes of others, and no matter how sincere and earnest we might be in their use.
>
> Martin Luther, *Commentary on Romans,* trans. J. Theodore Mueller (Grand Rapids: Zondervan Publishing House, 1954), 28.

More recently, Karl Barth published his first edition of *The Epistle to the Romans* in 1919, and in his preface to the English edition he describes himself at that time as a "young country pastor" in Switzerland who could easily imagine the sound of battle from the Great War that took place just north of him. Writing and revising his commentary between the two World Wars of the twentieth century, Barth was inspired by Romans to insist on the utter transcendence and freedom of God, who stands in judgment on all human power and order.

Each of these prominent interpreters of Romans was reading this letter in light of questions in their own time. Although undoubtedly they thought they understood what Paul meant to say, their understanding was also shaped by their own concerns and contexts. And if the task of theology is not only to hand on belief but also to speak to the time in which we live, then they were doing what theologians do. Lately, concerns have been raised about how easily we mistake what a prominent interpreter of Paul says for what Paul himself says. Equating an interpreter's meaning with Paul's intended meaning does not adequately recognize the way that the interpreter's own contemporary context affects his or her reading. It is important to learn to distinguish Paul's ideas from the ideas of his later interpreters, but it is also important to listen to what those later interpreters themselves have to say to us. The theological legacy of this epistle for the church includes not only what Paul has said but also what has been said about what Paul has said.

Paul's Letter to the Romans has had, then, enduring value for the church. Theologians have found Paul's theological reflection to be useful for their time over and over again. To ask, Why Romans, why now? is to ask what usefulness the letter may have for our time. In part, the answer to the question, Why Romans? is that it has mattered to so many Christians who have gone before. It has repeatedly formed understanding of Christian faith as each generation has turned to Paul for instruction.

Although the legacy of reflection shows that reading Romans is ever timely, this particular period in history gives us a compelling answer to the question, why now? The year 2017 marks the 500th anniversary of Martin Luther's posting of the Ninety-five Theses on the church door at Wittenberg. This anniversary year will be marked by celebration among Protestants around the world. Marking this significant milestone calls for reflection about the meaning of the Protestant Reformation in our time, especially how the ongoing renewal of the church may be sustained. Because Luther formulated his ideas about reform as he was reading Paul's letter to the Romans, observing this anniversary also calls for a consideration of how Paul's letter might speak to us today as powerfully as it did to Luther.

Justification

Although Luther's challenge to the church led to a breach among Christians that has yet to be fully healed, another feature of our time makes it possible to talk about Paul's letter in a new way. Near the end of the twentieth century (1997), an ecumenical breakthrough took place when the Roman Catholics and the Lutherans were able to issue together the *Joint Declaration on the Doctrine of Justification* (*JDDJ*). Since the sixteenth century, the doctrine of justification had been a source of division in the Western church, including mutual condemnations between Catholics and Lutherans. With the signing of this document, those condemnations were no longer in effect and the two communions could see each other in a way that had not

> By appropriating insights of recent biblical studies and drawing on modern
> investigations of the history of theology and dogma, the post-Vatican
> II ecumenical dialogue has led to a notable convergence concerning
> justification, with the result that this Joint Declaration is able to formulate a
> consensus on basic truths concerning the doctrine of justification. In light of
> this consensus, the corresponding doctrinal condemnations of the sixteenth
> century do not apply to today's partner.
>
> *Joint Declaration on the Doctrine of Justification.*

been possible before. A few years later, Methodists demonstrated
their agreement with *JDDJ*. While different interpretations of the
Bible (especially of Romans) had led to the division in the first place,
recent work in biblical studies helped to pave the way for a more
common understanding.

Although the signing of *JDDJ* was not met with universal
approval, the official nature of this document means the doctrine
of justification does not pose the enormous hurdle it once did to
ecumenical relations. Reading Romans now, without the polemic of
the Reformation looming over every text, makes it possible to hear
differently what Paul had to say, understanding better the needs of
his own situation. These new historical insights illustrate that God
can use Paul's letter to say something new to our time.

Old and New Perspectives

Biblical scholarship helped pave the way for ecumenical breakthrough, and the opportunity exists now to listen carefully to further
recent insights of biblical scholarship to understand the power of
Paul's letter for today. To answer the question about the usefulness
of Romans for our time, one must first acknowledge that the reading
of Romans in our time is undergoing a major change in orientation.
Partly because the letter has been such a fruitful resource for theology, theologians have tended to see it as a doctrinal treatise or an
attempt by Paul to make a formal and systematic argument about
a theological principle. Furthermore, his theological argument has

been taken to be about individual salvation, in other words about how persons as individuals are saved, so his interpreters often stress a person's interior life. Taken in this way, the epistle has informed much of the development of Christian soteriology (reflection on salvation) in the Western church, especially among Protestants. The "old" perspective is sometimes called the "Lutheran" perspective because it reads Paul through the concerns emphasized in Luther's theology.

Recently, though, a "new perspective" on how to read Paul has emerged. The horrors for Jews leading up to and during World War II led to a realization that reading Paul apart from, and even opposed to Judaism, had tremendously harmful effects. After World War II, scholars concerned about this problem urged a more fair under-standing of Judaism built not on a "Lutheran" reading of Paul's writ-ings but rather reflective of the sociohistorical context in which Paul wrote. E. P. Sanders's book *Paul and Palestinian Judaism* is respon-sible for much of the shift in perspective. By questioning the widely held assumption that Paul's theology was "the antithesis of Judaism" and looking for a new model for comparative study, Sanders's work opened a new direction for scholarship.[1] What became apparent as scholars adopted a new perspective was that not only had Judaism been treated unfairly under the "old" perspective but Paul himself had as well. Reading him as "Christian" and especially understand-ing "Christian" according to Protestant theology denied his own Jewish identity and concerns. For instance, as Alan Segal points out, Jews besides Paul in the first century were asking questions about whether and how Gentiles not under the law could be saved.[2]

Paul may have encountered this question as a Pharisee even before he was a follower of Jesus. Furthermore, the way he works out this problem is influenced not only by his calling to be apostle to the Gentiles but also by his thinking as a Jew. To do justice to what Paul wanted to say in this letter requires serious attention to the original context. In this commentary, one of the ways that I try to remain

---

1. E. P. Sanders, *Paul and Palestinian Judaism: A Comparison of Patterns of Religion* (Philadelphia: Fortress Press, 1977), 3.
2. Alan F. Segal, "Universalism in Judaism and Christianity," in *Paul in His Hellenistic Context*, ed. Troels Engberg-Pedersen (Minneapolis: Fortress Press, 1995), 1–29.

mindful of that original context is to not call the original recipients of the letter "Christian" but rather Jewish and Gentile followers of Jesus Christ.

Putting Paul back into his context means in part recognizing that his way of answering this question cannot be understood apart from the narrative about God's covenant that the Jews had been telling for centuries. As such, Romans talks about justification quite differently than theologians have often thought. Rather than reacting to and correcting a perceived "works righteousness" in Judaism, Paul understood righteousness as a Jew would, that is as a matter of right relationship and specifically of "meeting the demands of the relationship."[3] Through covenant, God established a relationship with Israel that requires a certain response. As missionary to the Gentiles, Paul was concerned with how Gentiles could also have relationship with God and concerned with what their relationship with God would mean for the relationship between Gentile and Jewish followers of Jesus Christ. This question was for Paul more social and ethnic than individual, even though individuals have to understand their place in what he has to say. Although there are real differences between old and new perspectives, this commentary will attempt to listen to the wisdom of both perspectives, where each has something important to say for Christian life. Acknowledging both perspectives is important for the following reasons.

Proponents of reading with the new perspective remind us of the cost of ignoring Paul's original context for this letter. If we try to make Paul answer questions he never thought of asking, we will never hear what he might have to say to us. Reading Romans now means reading with renewed effort of our time to engage in patient recovery of the argument Paul was trying to make in his own time and place. As part of this recovery, the new perspective makes a conscious effort to pay attention to the Judaism that provided the fertile ground in which his own ideas were shaped.

At the same time, reading Romans now also means reading it as Christians who have been shaped by the readings of the "old perspective." We have learned to care about certain issues that were

3. James D. G. Dunn, *The New Perspective on Paul*, rev. ed. (Grand Rapids: Wm. B. Eerdmans, 2008), 3.

important for theologians who have reflected on this letter. It would be impossible to pretend those issues do not exist for us now, even if they did not have the same kind of centrality for Paul that we have often taken them to have. Reading Romans now also means paying attention to those matters, perhaps with an eye toward whether and how they might look differently in light of Paul's own primary concern. This commentary will include some discussion of those questions that have become traditional even as it also tries to take seriously the reorientation for which many scholars are calling. Doctrines that arose later may not be direct expressions of what Paul thought, but they contribute wisdom for Christian living to the community, so we may appreciate and attend to them alongside Paul.

Theologians and biblical scholars may always read a text with different concerns and arrive at somewhat different conclusions, but it has been my experience in working on this commentary that attempting conversation between the old and new perspectives has yielded a rich understanding of what life before God ought to be like.

Jews and Christians

Reading Paul in his sociohistorical context opens up possibilities for thinking with him about the relation between Jews and Christians. As a Jewish follower of Jesus Christ whose mission was to the Gentiles, Paul stood at the intersection between Jews and Gentiles and had a vantage point for reflecting on the relationship of both groups to God. Although Paul's work was among the Gentiles, he never stopped thinking of himself as a Jew, and he remained concerned for his people. Although the subsequent history between Jews and Christians, with each defining itself over against the other, has produced a different kind of situation than Paul was in, his insight can be useful for reflecting on the legacy that Jews and Christians share as well as the relationship that we may hope for now. For it to be useful, though, we have to do what Paul himself did: namely, interpret Scripture in light of the situation we are actually in. That means Paul's conclusions about the Jews and Jesus Christ may not be our conclusions.

It is sadly incongruous that the letter in which Paul writes so clearly as a Jew has sometimes been used by later Christians to support anti-Jewish ideas. The time is right for reflection that moves us in another direction. After the Shoah, many Christians have become especially aware of the danger of anti-Judaism in some Christian ideas and are concerned to talk about their faith in a way that does not harm or diminish the people of the first covenant. Several church bodies have issued formal statements that intend to promote respect for Judaism. In addition, some Jews are studying the Scriptures unique to Christians as resources for understanding Judaism of the first century CE. A few of these scholars boldly pursue their careers in Christian academic institutions. These factors provide opportunity for more informed and honest dialogue than could take place in the past.

Scholarship in the academy has already begun this kind of dialogue, and some church bodies engage in formal dialogue with Jews at the general level. Insights from study and dialogue, however, have not always reached and shaped worship experiences in local congregations. Although it may be inadvertent, worship sometimes perpetuates misunderstandings. Since Paul's Epistle to the Romans appears often in the lectionary cycle and since it is so rife with possibilities for anti-Jewish interpretation, reading Romans now means reading it when there is still work to be done, but also when there are beginning to be resources for reading differently than our forebears did.

Empire

Paying attention to Paul's context includes not only Judaism but also the Roman Empire, which dominated the lives of people in the first century CE. Since Rome was the seat of the Roman Empire, Paul's letter to the followers of Jesus Christ in Rome had to take into account their situation in the city where the emperors lived. In fact, so much of Paul's theological language is taken from the language of the empire (and given new meaning) that N. T. Wright can even call the introductory verses of the letter a "parody of the imperial cult." Worship of the emperor was a way of uniting the empire and controlling the areas far from Rome without using military force. It "Romanized" people of different cultural backgrounds and allowed them to show their allegiance to the ruler of the known world. In other words, through religion, the empire worked to win the hearts and minds of the people.

> In the Mediterranean world where Paul exercised his vocation as the apostle to the Gentiles, the pagans, the fastest growing religion was the Imperial cult, the worship of Caesar.
>
> N. T. Wright, "Paul and Caesar: A New Reading of Romans," in *A Royal Priesthood? The Use of the Bible Ethically and Politically* (Grand Rapids: Zondervan, 2002), 175.

The notion of empire has been an important category for theological reflection at the beginning of the twenty-first century. Even without the formal structure of the ancient Roman Empire, modern nations can have global influence that extends a form of imperialism. Because the United States has this kind of far-reaching power, reading Romans now invites Christians in the United States to consider, as Paul called the Roman followers of Jesus Christ to do, what it means to follow Jesus near the center of power. The possibility that religion will be coopted for the purposes of imperial control is always present. Reading Romans now can sharpen the distinct vision of Christianity so that by more clearly recognizing its own Lord, it can resist being put in service of another lord.

Disagreement in the Church

With its widespread use and remarkable theological legacy, it is easy to forget that what Paul wrote was not a speculative treatise but rather a letter to particular people. Paul had never visited the churches in Rome, but he knew one thing about them: they had a deep disagreement that was dividing them. This disagreement not only threatened the well-being of the community, but it also threatened to undermine the support he hoped to receive in Rome for his mission to Spain. One way of looking at the theology that Paul develops in this letter is that he was saying what he thought these followers of Jesus needed to hear in order to heal the community.

Certainly, as I worked through the letter, I could see that the theological themes Paul developed throughout came together to support the practical advice he gave to the Roman followers of Jesus about how to live together.

> In other words, there was once ... a body of men and women to whom the Epistle to the Romans could be sent in the confident expectation that it provided an answer to their questions; that somehow or other it would be understood and valued.
>
> Karl Barth, *The Epistle to the Romans*, trans. Edwyn C. Hoskyns (London: Oxford University Press, 1933), 536.

Christians still disagree with one another, and in our time, some of those disagreements (notably over issues related to homosexuality) threaten the well-being of communities and communions as well as the mission of the church. Although in the past, disagreement over Paul's theology of justification divided the church, the time may have come when we can learn how to read Paul's letter to divided followers in order to learn from the advice he gave them about how to live together more faithfully. Reading Romans now, then, means in part reading Romans to learn what Paul would proclaim to us about faith in Jesus Christ that can lead us to welcome one another more fully.

The Situation of the Letter

The Letter to the Romans is agreed to be an authentic letter of Paul: that is, it not only bears the name of Paul but was actually written by him. Of the seven letters in the New Testament scholars agree were written by Paul (Romans, 1 and 2 Corinthians, Galatians, Philippians, 1 Thessalonians, and Philemon), the Letter to the Romans is considered to be the last one Paul sent.

Like his other letters, the Letter to the Romans follows the basic conventions of letter-writing in the ancient world. He begins with a formal salutation and prayer of thanksgiving and ends with courtesies and greetings. Even when following convention, though, as we shall see in the comments, Paul conveys theological meaning. The body of this letter is long, and it develops theological themes, some of which, one can tell from his other letters, he has been thinking about for a long time. This letter contains the fullest and most mature expression of Paul's theology. It is not, though, a theological treatise. It remains a letter, and as such it does not follow a clear and discrete formal outline.

The letter does have a basic structure. After making his formal salutation and prayer of thanksgiving, Paul identifies the theme in 1:16–17 and then works through the theological implications of that theme through chapter 8, covering ideas including the human condition, covenantal faithfulness, justification, and allegiance to a new dominion. Chapters 9–11 address the problem of Jews who do not follow Jesus Christ, a concern not only for Paul himself but also for members of this community. From 12:1–15:13, he draws practical conclusions for how to live in light of the theology he has developed, with chapter 14 and the first part of chapter 15 focusing on specific problems that have arisen among the followers of Jesus Christ in Rome. The end of chapter 15 and the final chapter close the letter with a description of his plans for travel and with formal greetings.

Although this letter follows a pattern that appears in other letters—conventional opening, a body that includes theological development and practical advice, and conventional closing—there is one way in which this letter is not like any of his others. Other letters written by Paul were sent to a group of followers of Jesus in a church that he founded. The letter that Paul writes to the followers of Jesus Christ in Rome is different. Paul has heard of, gives thanks for, and prays for the church in Rome, but he has never been there. At the end of this epistle he states a plan to visit. He is preparing to go to Jerusalem to deliver funds he has collected for the poor. Once this delivery has been made, he plans to go to Spain, by way of Rome. This plan to finally visit Rome may have been an important reason for his letter. Perhaps he was writing to the church in Rome to introduce himself, to prepare them for his visit, and to gain their support for his mission in Spain. Alternatively, because he does address conflict among the Roman followers of Jesus Christ, Paul may be writing to the church in Rome because he has heard of this problem in that community, and he has something to say about it. It may be that he wrote both because of a visit and because of conflict, especially if he could not count on support for his work from a quarrelling community. It is easy to imagine that Paul may have had more than one reason for writing this letter, perhaps also even wanting to correct possible misperceptions of his message.

In Paul's time, followers of Jesus Christ could have either Gentile or Jewish backgrounds. Some scholars argue that those to whom Paul was writing in Rome were all Gentile converts. Others argue that although the majority was Gentile, there also existed in Rome a minority of Jewish followers of Jesus Christ. The list of people greeted by Paul at the end of the letter suggests a mixed community (for more description of the community, see comments on 16:3–16, pp. 260–64). This latter view is the one I will adopt in this commentary.

Because the relationship between Gentile and Jew is such a prominent feature of this epistle, it is important to understand one piece of background history that likely shaped the attitudes of Roman followers of Jesus Christ. Roman historian Suetonius reports that the emperor Claudius issued an edict to expel Jews from Rome (probably in 49 CE) because there had been disturbances about "Chrestos." This report could mean that Jews who followed Jesus as the Messiah (Christ) and Jews who did not were in conflict with one another. Although it is not entirely clear whether this edict expelled all Jews or only those who had been involved in the disturbance, it is clear that the Roman followers of Jesus were affected.[4] Paul's friends Prisca and Aquila had left Rome because of this expulsion (Acts 18:2). When Claudius died in 54, expelled Jews were allowed to return to Rome. Prior to the edict, followers of Jesus Christ with both Jewish and Gentile backgrounds had lived and worshiped together in Rome, but after the edict, the church in Rome became predominantly Gentile. When followers of Jewish background returned to Rome, they and the Gentile followers who had remained may very well have had some difficulty learning how to live and worship together again. Questions about Jewish identity for followers of Jesus may have become especially acute because of the expulsion, adding to the difficulty of reassimilation with Gentile

---

4. Robert Jewett, *Romans: A Commentary*, Hermeneia (Minneapolis: Fortress Press, 2007), 60.

followers. Jewish followers of Jesus expelled by the emperor would have had their distinctive ethnic identity reinforced, and with emphasized distinctiveness, they may have been strengthened in the feeling of being the privileged people of God. Gentiles, on the other hand, who had lived without their Jewish brothers and sisters, may have developed a sense of privilege as the unexpelled majority. The timing of the return of the expelled Jews to Rome helps to establish that Paul probably wrote this letter some time in the mid to late 50s.

Theological Commentary

Other authors in this series have acknowledged, as I must, lack of expertise in biblical studies. The situation of the letter that I have described above is based on my evaluation of the work of others, and the whole commentary is written with such limitation. My judgments are affected largely by what helps to illumine for me the theological issues that I want to address.

It is good to be reminded that Paul's Epistle to the Romans was not a theological treatise in the way it has often been imagined to be, but it also should not be missed that this letter to specific people in a specific time and place is theological. Paul's concerns are God and our lives before God. He is instructing this specific group of people about what their faith means for their life together. It is because his instruction is theological and not merely pragmatic that this letter has had such enduring value. Christians may not have shared the details of the particular situation of the Roman followers of Jesus, but they have shared for centuries the concern about what faith means for life, and they have turned to Paul to understand what it means to be faithful to our faithful God. The job of a theological commentary is to highlight precisely these matters.

I am deeply indebted, then, to all the biblical scholars that I have read as I have worked on this commentary (I turned especially often to Robert Jewett, Leander Keck, and Katherine Grieb). They have educated me richly. I can only hope that as I have done my work as a theologian, I have not distorted their work in the process. I am also indebted to the theologians who have commented on this letter in centuries past. Even if they have sometimes gone in directions that biblical scholars now see need correction, they have also had insights for their own time that add to the wisdom Paul himself shares.

Paul's message that we may trust our trustworthy God is always timely. How we enact that trust in the twenty-first century is the question we must explore in preaching, teaching, and worship. Listening to what Paul had to say about that question in the first century is surprisingly helpful for beginning to think about it in the twenty-first century.

1:1–17

Salutation, Thanksgiving, and Theme

1:1–7

The Salutation

The opening verses of Romans follow the standard form for a letter of the time, giving first the name of the person sending the letter and then stating to whom the letter is directed. In this letter, Paul says much more about himself in the salutation than he does in his other letters, probably because unlike his other letters, this epistle is not to a church that he founded. He has not yet even visited it. He needs to say more about himself than he does in other letters. What does he say? He does not give details of his life that many of us would give if we were introducing ourselves to someone new: for instance, where we come from, something about our families, or how we make a living. Instead he introduces himself theologically, that is, he tells who he is in the context of the task he has received from God. He is a "servant of Jesus Christ," "called to be an apostle," "set apart for the gospel of God." These are all descriptions that show his role as one who has responsibility to proclaim the gospel. His introduction also sets this gospel in the context of the Jewish Scriptures; the good news was promised by the prophets, and it concerns the Son descended from David. Paul has been given the task by God to proclaim Jesus Christ in order to bring Gentiles to faith and obedience. This is what Paul thinks important to say about himself.

As a theological interpreter of Romans, Luther finds more than information in Paul's introduction of himself. Reading Romans as a professor lecturing to theology students shortly before he posts his famous Ninety-five Theses, he sees a model for the proper understanding of ministry in the church. Luther notes that the two chief sins, from which all pastoral offenses flowed, were self-indulgence and tyranny. He ponders how Paul's introduction reflects a self-understanding that can guard against these problems. Luther sees both "modesty and majesty" in Paul's self-description as "servant of Jesus Christ." There is modesty in seeing himself as a servant, but there is majesty in serving Jesus Christ.[1] In former times the respect due to a servant was in proportion to the importance of the servant's master. So even as Paul is showing personal humility in calling himself servant, he is also calling attention to the importance of his office by noting the one he serves. Paul again stresses the importance of his office by calling himself "apostle." Luther concludes from the way Paul introduces himself that every minister of the church should distinguish between his (or her) own person, which should be regarded humbly, and the office that he (or she) occupies so that "he with dignity and love might administer his office with the sole object in mind to promote the welfare and salvation of his parishioners"[2]

The example Luther saw in Paul is certainly still relevant for reflecting on ministry in the church today. The way Paul introduces himself applies not only to those who hold a specific office in the church but also to all Christians. Every Christian would do well to consider the kind of theological introduction she or he would give. For what task has God set each of us apart? And how can we learn to approach that task with a combination of personal humility but also high regard for what we have been called to do?

Paul writes this letter to "all God's beloved in Rome, who are called to be saints." Who are these beloved? Paul gives much more information about himself at the beginning of the letter than he does about those to whom he was writing. After all, they knew who they were! Paul's greetings at the close of the letter indicate that he had met some of the members of the community to which he was writing, probably during travel, so he knew something about the followers of Jesus in Rome even though he had never been there. From the list of the people he greets at the end of the letter, the beloved seem to be a mix of Gentile and Jewish followers of Jesus Christ,

---

1. Martin Luther, *Commentary on Romans*, trans. J. Theodore Mueller (Grand Rapids: Kregel Classics, 1974), 31.
2. Ibid.

who come from different stations in life.[3] The population of Rome included a large number of slaves, and many of the Jews in Rome had been brought there as slaves. It is likely that many of the followers of Jesus who received this letter were slaves or former slaves. Others, though, may have been wealthy. They did not constitute a single congregation in the way we think of congregations today. Rather, they probably met in several small groups around Rome. The groups were necessarily small because they met in space available where they lived. The wealthy followers could provide a room in a house, but those of lower station undoubtedly lived in crowded tenements in the city where space for meeting would be more difficult to arrange.

Paul does not address his audience as "Christians" because that term had not yet gained widespread use, and I will avoid the use of that term for the original readers of the letter. Instead, he says of all of them—no matter what their life situation or where they meet—that they are "called to be saints." Christianity had not yet developed a system of identifying particular, outstanding people as saints; so Paul frequently uses the term "saints" to address the followers of Jesus Christ. The word translated in the NRSV as "saints" means "holy" or "set apart as sacred." When Paul addresses Jesus' followers as holy ones he is reminding them of their status as set apart for God, the Holy One. Karl Barth explains that being called to holiness means Christians no longer belong to themselves or the world that is passing away. They belong to the one who called them, to God.[4] Luther is quick to point out that they are not saints or holy because of their merit but because of God's "love and calling."[5] Any holiness that a Christian has is a sharing in God's holiness.

Writing to God's beloved in Rome means writing to the followers of Jesus Christ in the city that is the seat of the empire. Recently, scholars have begun to point out how much imperial language is employed in Paul's letters but with very different effect than when employed by the empire. We have already seen that Paul understands

---

3. Leander E. Keck, *Romans*, Abingdon New Testament Commentaries (Nashville: Abingdon Press, 2005), 370.
4. Karl Barth, *The Epistle to the Romans*, trans. Edwyn C. Hoskyns (Oxford: Oxford University Press, 1933), 31.
5. Luther, *Commentary on Romans*, 37.

himself to be set apart to proclaim the gospel. The Greek word *euangelion*, which we translate into English as "gospel," was already in use in the empire to talk about the "good news" of military victory and dynastic succession. When Paul introduces himself as set apart for the gospel, he gives a short summary of what this good news is about. Paul is preaching that Jesus is descended from David (a king) and has been declared through resurrection to be Son of God (a title used by emperors) and Christ our Lord. People living in Rome probably recognized reference to dynastic succession.

Part of what made military victory and dynastic succession good news for citizens of the Roman Empire was that they were enjoying an unprecedented period of peace (what we call the Pax Romana) that began under the emperor Augustus and was secured by a strong military presence. The empire promised "peace and security" to its people, but when Paul wishes grace and peace to the beloved in Rome, he does not mean peace gained through military victory. He means the peace of Christ (rooted in the Jewish idea of *shalom*), which is very different good news indeed. Christians who were living in Rome, the seat of the empire, could not have missed the way he was using imperial language but giving it a very different meaning.

1:8–15

Thanksgiving

Giving thanks to someone at the beginning of a letter was a common convention in the ancient world. The thanksgiving often served to introduce a major theme of the letter. Origen noticed that even though in other letters Paul often gives thanks in general for a community to which he writes, he rarely says "for all."[6] With this phrase, Paul underscores the way he addresses the letter to "all God's beloved." Robert Jewett points out that the word "all" appears in Romans sixty-four times, more than in any other of Paul's letters.[7] It

---

6. Origen, *Commentary on the Epistle to the Romans, Books 1–5,* The Fathers of the Church, vol. 103, trans. Thomas P. Scheck (Washington, DC: The Catholic University of America Press, 2001), 77.

7. Robert Jewett, *Romans: A Commentary,* Hermeneia (Minneapolis: Fortress Press, 2007), 113.

may be that Paul uses this word so often to stress inclusivity in the community and God's impartiality, both themes that come up later in the letter.

Paul gives thanks for all of them "because your faith is proclaimed throughout the world." Why would the faith of the Roman Christians be proclaimed? It does not seem to be the case that they have some special kind of faith that is newsworthy to other followers of Jesus Christ, but rather what makes their faith a matter of proclamation to others is that their faith shows the gospel has reached into Rome, the seat of the empire. There is need for the power of the gospel to confront the power of the empire, so its arrival in Rome is indeed a cause for giving thanks.

Paul is not directly responsible for their acceptance of the gospel because he has not yet been able to preach in Rome; but he is connected to them through prayer, and he hopes to be among them eventually for mutual encourage-

> **The Resurrection has proven its power: there are Christians—even in Rome.**
>
> Barth, *The Epistle to the Romans*, 32.

ment in faith. Although separated by distance and also strangers to one another, Paul and the Roman followers of Jesus are connected through their faith in Jesus Christ. Because of that connection, Paul refers to them as *adelphoi* (NRSV: brothers and sisters). That relationship can deepen and strengthen all of them if they get the opportunity to be face to face, but the relationship already exists through Christ. Such connections still exist among Christians who are scattered throughout the world. They may never meet one another, but sometimes they get to know one another's stories and can give thanks and pray for one another.

Paul wants to visit the Roman followers of Jesus in order to "reap some harvest" among them. Many have looked to chapter 15 of this letter to help explain this phrase. There, Paul explains he is going to Spain, and he uses the same word (*karpon*) in 15:28, translated here as "harvest," in relation to the collection for the saints in Jerusalem. It may be that the harvest he hopes to reap is financial support by the Romans for his mission in Spain. If this is correct, then the reminder of how the followers of Jesus Christ are united through Christ might serve a double purpose, not only Paul's introduction to Roman followers but also the harvest he hopes to receive from them to bring more into relationship in Christ in Spain.

By saying he is a "debtor" (*opheiletēs*) to Greeks and barbarians, Paul is indicating that he has obligations of relationship both to the civilized (Greeks) and uncivilized (barbarians). This common way of grouping people would have covered the Gentile world. Similarly, wise and foolish would be categories that cover a wide range, more focused on individuals than groups. Together, the two pairs of terms stress the breadth of Paul's indebtedness.[8] Because he is apostle to "all the Gentiles," as he says in verse 5, he has an obligation to proclaim the gospel to everyone, whether cultured or not.

1:16–17

The Theme

These two verses are packed with ideas that run through the whole epistle. Some initial orientation to these ideas is important, although each will become clearer as they are employed through the argument of the letter.

Readers often wonder why Paul says he is "not ashamed" of the gospel. Honor was a high value in the Roman Empire, as well as in the Mediterranean world. Shame (the counterpoint to honor) was felt keenly. Given the importance of honor and shame, it is not surprising that Paul would use this language as he addressed the Romans. It is possible that when Paul says he is "not ashamed," he is using a manner of speaking called litotes (affirming something by denying its opposite), for instance when a person says "that's not bad" to mean "that's good." If that is the case, then Paul is saying he is proud of the gospel. It is also possible that Paul's point is more straightforward. There are several reasons why people might think he does have reason to be ashamed, for instance because his "good news" seems preposterous compared to the "good news" of the

---

8. C. E. B. Cranfield, *The International Critical Commentary on the Holy Scriptures of the Old and New Testaments: The Epistle to the Romans*, ed. J. A. Emerton and C. E. B. Cranfield, 2 vols. (Edinburgh: T. & T. Clark, 1973), 1:84–85.

empire, or because the preponderance of Gentile followers of Jesus may make some wonder whether God has abandoned the covenant with Israel in favor of Gentiles, or even because the proclamation of salvation through crucifixion seems sheer foolishness (as he says in 1 Cor. 1:22–25). Paul may be seriously denying the shame some might expect him to feel for any of these possibilities, thereby affirming the value of the gospel. Regardless of whether he is using litotes or speaking more straightforwardly, Paul is expressing confidence in the good news he has been set apart to proclaim.

And what is that good news? It is "the power of God for salvation to everyone who has faith." The power of God (not the power of the empire) saves (not just establishes temporary temporal peace and security) for everyone who has faith (not for those who submit to Roman rule). The gospel is not simply telling us about God's power, rather God's power *is* good news. If Paul proclaims the gospel, and the gospel is the power of God, then Paul proclaims the power of God. To see how radical this message was, consider that the emperors were sometimes called "savior." They legitimated their use of power by calling themselves divine, and they required citizens to worship in the imperial cult. Paul's gospel would be an affront to those imperial claims. This strong affirmation of Paul calls us to consider the ways that the gospel is an affront to the claims of our time and place.

Paul affirms in verse 16 that God's power to save extends to everyone, "the Jew first and also to the Greek." This phrase not only reinforces the inclusivity he has already established by using the word "all," but also sets up the reflection that he carries out in the first three chapters, as well as through chapters 9–11. In this verse, Paul uses the term "Greek" instead of "Gentile." Jews tended to see the world as Jew/Gentile, and Greco-Roman culture tended to see the world as Greek/barbarian. Those who organized the world in these ways considered the first term in each of those pairs to indicate the privileged group. By mixing "Jew" and "Greek," Paul refers to both groups with their preferred term. He thus avoids the usual dichotomies and does not encourage one group to feel superior to the other.

Verse 17 introduces "the righteousness of God," a major theme of Paul's letter and a major concern for theologians who reflect on how humans can be saved. Martin Luther, for instance, interprets verse 17 in this way: "The righteousness of God is the cause of our salvation. This righteousness, however, is not that according to which God Himself is righteous as God, but that by which we are justified by Him through faith in the Gospel. It is called the righteousness of God in contradistinction to man's righteousness which comes from works."[9] Although the matter of righteousness for our salvation is not unimportant, many biblical scholars are drawing attention back to the question of God's own righteousness. It is precisely God's righteousness that is revealed through Paul's proclamation of the gospel. God's righteousness is not revealed as a point of information (Is God righteous? Yes or no.), and in this way Luther is right that the verse is not simply making a point about the nature of God. Rather God's righteousness becomes evident when one understands the gospel concerning Jesus Christ. The word translated as "righteousness" can refer to rectifying what is wrong or making right.[10] It can also refer to fidelity in a relationship.[11] It is language of the lawcourt (being declared "in the right"), but it is also language of covenant (to be righteous is to fulfill the promises of a covenant).[12] If the success of Christianity among the Gentiles had caused many to wonder about God's faithfulness to God's covenant with the Jews, then God's righteousness may not have been evident. Paul needs to explain the gospel concerning Jesus Christ in order to show that God's righteousness has not been compromised by the Gentile mission.

> "Righteousness" carries the overtones both of "justice"— the Creator's passion to put things right—and of "faithfulness"—YHWH's faithfulness to the covenant which he established so that through it he might indeed put all things right.
>
> N. T. Wright, *Justification: God's Plan and Paul's Vision* (Downers Grove, IL: IVP Academic, 2009), 164.

The remainder of verse 17 brings out the important theme of faith that has been so central for the theological understanding

---

9. Luther, *Commentary on Romans*, 41.
10. Keck, *Romans*, 56.
11. A. Katherine Grieb, *The Story of Romans: A Narrative Defense of God's Righteousness* (Louisville, KY: Westminster John Knox Press, 2002), 21.
12. N. T. Wright, *Justification: God's Plan and Paul's Vision* (Downers Grove, IL: IVP Academic, 2009), 63.

of Romans. The righteousness of God is revealed "through faith for faith." This little phrase looks simple, but the translation of the prepositions from Greek to English allows for many options. The most simple would be "from (*ek*) faith to (*eis*) faith." Not only the translation but also the interpretation of the meaning of the phrase can differ greatly. Origen took "from faith to faith" to mean going from the faith of the old covenant to faith of the new covenant.[13] Luther acknowledges this interpretation, but because he recognizes one faith in both Testaments, he prefers to say, "The believer grows more and more, so that he who is justified becomes more and more righteous."[14]

In addition to the problems of the prepositions, the interpretation of "faith" itself is a huge question. The Greek word "*pistis*" can be translated into English as "faith," "faithfulness," "belief," or "trust." It also can take the form of a verb (*pisteuō*) that is difficult to render into English because we do not say "to faith." To display the verb's connection to the noun, English translation could read "to have faith," or "to put faith in," but it may also be rendered "to believe" or "to trust." As an adjective (*pistos*) the Greek can mean "faithful," "believing," "trusting," or even "trustworthy."[15] The possible range of meaning must be kept in mind throughout Romans, but it makes this little phrase in verse 17 even more difficult to understand. Is Paul talking about believing something to be true, about trusting, or about faithfulness? Whose faith or faithfulness is he talking about? Luther took Paul to mean the faith by which a human being is justified. Karl Barth took this verse to mean that God's faithfulness to us is what reveals God's righteousness to us. God remains faithful to us even when we have forgotten God.[16] Because Paul's words "from faith" (*ek pisteōs*) call to mind the Greek translation (LXX) of Habakkuk 2:4, a book that presents a dialogue between the prophet and God about why the righteous suffer, Paul may be thinking both about the faithfulness of God, who will eventually make things right,

---

13. Origen, *Epistle to the Romans*, 83, 87.
14. Luther, *Commentary on Romans*, 41.
15. Grieb, *Story of Romans*, 11.
16. Barth, *Epistle to the Romans*, 41.

as well as the faithfulness of the righteous who keep trusting in God until God does so.

FURTHER REFLECTIONS
Faith as Believing and Trusting

Because "faith" can mean several things, theologians have developed a tradition of using special terms in Latin to talk about some of its complexity. The most basic distinction in these terms is between *fides quae creditur* (the faith that is believed) and *fides qua creditur* (the faith by which it is believed). This distinction calls attention to the importance of the content of what is believed (sometimes called objective faith) as well as the attitude of believing it (sometimes called subjective faith). When someone asks the question, "What do Christians believe?" she or he is asking about objective faith, in other words the content of Christian faith. When someone asks, "Are you a faithful (or a believing) Christian?" she or he is asking about subjective faith, in other words the attitude a person holds toward that content.

These basic distinctions may be further subdivided into the categories of *notitia* (knowledge or information), *assensus* (assent) and *fiducia* (trust). *Notitia* is simply the informational content of what Christians believe. *Assensus* is the acceptance of that content as true. *Fiducia* is trusting that truth in such a way that it shapes and directs one's life. These further distinctions are helpful for showing that not all three necessarily go together at all times. Atheists would be able to make a statement about content, "Christians believe there is a God," (*notitia*) without accepting the truth of that statement themselves (*assensus*) or trusting in it (*fiducia*). Referring to James 2:19, the theologians of previous centuries could say "even the demons believe" that there is a God (*notitia* as well as *assensus*), but they shudder at this knowledge rather than trust in it (*fiducia*).

> Faith is a living, daring confidence in God's grace, so sure and certain that a man would stake his life on it a thousand times.
>
> Luther, *Commentary on Romans*, xvii.

The recognition that it is possible to intellectually assent to doctrines without trusting one's life to that knowledge has sometimes led to a distinction between "head" (intellect) and "heart" (emotion). Using this distinction usually is meant to encourage Christians to go beyond intellectual assent to a deeper trust. Some have stressed "heart" faith even to the point of saying that only *fiducia* justifies us or makes us right with God. The stress on "heart" is probably a useful corrective to an exclusive focus on intellectual assent alone, but an overemphasis on "heart" can have the unfortunate effect of leading to anti-intellectualism in faith, a problem that also needs to be corrected. The fullest expression of faith involves "head" and "heart," and they should not be opposed to one another.

Faith is neither simply intellectual nor simply emotional. When we feel, we feel "about" something. A person does not get angry in general; a person gets angry about some action or situation. Similarly, a person does not simply trust; a person trusts someone or something. So the emotional is rooted in some understanding of the intellect. The content and attitude of faith are closely related to one another.

Because faith necessarily implies some understanding, theology has often had to work through questions regarding the relationship between faith and reason. Having a category for faith as assent to the truth of a body of knowledge has sometimes placed faith in conflict with reason (when reason is also taken to require assent to a body of knowledge). Several options for resolving the conflict between faith and reason have been explored by theologians and philosophers. One option is to side with faith over reason when the two conflict with one another. In other words, I must believe X to be true despite what reason shows me to be evidence to the contrary. Alternatively, one could side with reason over faith. In other words, I simply cannot believe X to be true in the face of evidence that disproves X. In both these options, faith and reason are taken to be competing on the same level, and one must win out over the other. Some avoid a win/lose situation by working to find a way that faith and reason may be shown to be compatible (for instance finding a scientific explanation for a miracle). Others, though, avoid putting faith and reason into head-to-head confrontation in the first place by saying the two operate in different spheres. Faith and reason do not compete because they are talking about fundamentally different things.

Believing faith, though, is not simply about matters of information. Even though believing and trusting do not have to go together (as in the case of the demons mentioned in Jas. 2:19), they often do. We may first come to believe information because it is told to us by someone we trust, such as a teacher. But information is not all that we learn from people we trust. We also come to know, believe, and trust in a certain way of viewing the world that includes values, attitudes, and expectations by participating in communities where such things are shared. Believing is not simply a matter of accepting the truth of assertions (statements of fact) but also accepting a way of going through life. This kind of acceptance is very much a matter of trust. I can count on people reacting to who I am and what I do in a certain way because we have a shared way of seeing the world. Believing is not simply a matter of true and false; it is also a matter of committing oneself to values that will guide one's life.

1:18–2:16

The Human Condition and God's Judgment

1:18–32

God's Judgment on Humankind

The popular image of God's wrath is that of an angry God throwing thunderbolts from heaven or otherwise smiting with destruction those who have made God uncontrollably angry. This picture of vengeful anger does not fit well with what theologians have said about God. Although the ancient world did have stories of angry gods, even then philosophers understood the highest divinity to be undisturbed by passions (such as anger), and this idea was accepted by theologians in Christian reflection. Still preserved in the Articles of Religion of the Church of England is the affirmation that God is "without body, parts, or passions."[1] Whatever God's wrath is, it is not an explosive fit of anger.

To say that God's wrath is not a fit of anger does not mean that it has nothing to do with displeasure. God's wrath is a negative

---

Before we reject the idea of God's wrath, we need to reflect on how we can express God's relation to the horrors of history that result from human refusal to worship God or to serve the inclusive whole. To say simply that God loves the world, while true and supremely important, can also be a way of sentimentally turning attention away from the appalling reality of genocidal, and sometimes suicidal, practices on the part of those who are in power in the world. We ourselves feel deep anger about much of what is happening today. Perhaps God shares such feelings.

John B. Cobb Jr. and David J. Lull, *Romans* (St. Louis: Chalice Press, 2005), 41.

---

1. "Of Faith in the Holy Trinity," Article 1, in *The Book of Common Prayer with the Additions and Deviations Proposed in 1928* (Oxford: Oxford University Press, 1928), 688.

The violation of human beings is an outrage. When consciences and hearts awaken to this, then energy for resistance is born. . . . To be sure, some forms of anger are destructive, escalating hostility that quickly leads to hate and violence. This is not the anger that we are speaking about here. But there is also righteous anger which waxes hot because something good is being violated. This is a genuine form of living care. It gives birth to courage and humor and unleashes energy for change.

Elizabeth A. Johnson, *She Who Is: The Mystery of God in Feminist Theological Discourse* (New York: Crossroad, 1993), 257.

judgment against something, and it is sometimes felt as punishment. Paul can use the word fury with wrath to indicate intensity of feeling (2:8), even if God does not lose control and throw a fit. Pamela Eisenbaum explains that the Jewish understanding of God's wrath, which Paul would surely have shared, was known in the context of covenant. When calamitous events befell Israel, they were seen as signs of God's displeasure at Israel's disobedience, and they acted as a kind of disciplining to bring Israel back into proper covenantal obedience. Seen this way, God's wrath is actually an exercise of God's faithfulness to God's promise to be in covenant with the people.[2] It is something like a parent's continual discipline of a child, to help the child learn and behave as she or he should. That kind of discipline occurs within a relationship of love.

It is not surprising that Paul would say that like the righteousness of God, the wrath of God is "revealed," that is, God makes it known to us. Righteousness and wrath are related to one another. God's wrath is revealed "against all ungodliness and wickedness." The Greek word translated in the NRSV as "wickedness" (*adikian*) shares the same root in Greek as the word translated in 1:17 as God's "righteousness" (*dikaiosynē*) The "wicked" are the "unrighteous." Human unrighteousness is constituted by not living in right relationship with the righteous God. The unrighteous know the truth, but they suppress it. God has shown them the truth about God's self, and although they know God, they do not honor or give thanks to God. Because they do not live rightly in light of what they know,

2. Pamela Eisenbaum, *Paul Was Not a Christian: The Original Message of a Misunderstood Apostle* (New York: HarperOne, 2009), 81–82.

their own judgment is clouded and they foolishly give honor and glory to creatures instead of to the creator. They worship images of things in nature rather than God.

In a time and place with many temples where sacrifice to idols was a common practice, Paul's words about worshiping images had concrete relevance. Katherine Grieb points out that followers of Jesus living in Rome would have known that emperors erected statues of themselves in the colonies to manifest their power in locations where they were not present. To replace the emperor's statue with another statue "would be an act of treason."[3] Treason is an act of rebellion against the order of the state that makes a person an enemy of the state. Directing honor to someone other than the emperor who deserved this honor had serious consequences. Roman followers of Jesus could easily draw a comparison between that kind of civic disruption and Paul's description of the human problem before God. Putting a creature in the place of God to receive honor and glory that are due to God would be a violation of God's rightful position and would disrupt the proper order of the creation.

As actual worship of images became less common, theologians preserved this point but began to express it in a different way. They talked less about worshiping creatures and more about loving them. If we are commanded to love God with all our heart, soul, mind, and strength (Mark 12:30)—in other words, to devote ourselves utterly to God—then devoting ourselves to something other than God violates this command. The desire for material things (or even immaterial things, such as status) is a constant threat to right relationship with God. It can distort our thinking and lead us away from God. The wrath of God stands in judgment against this unrighteousness.

Karl Barth extends this insight about idolatry to say all human effort stands under the constant judgment of God. In the context of what was happening in Germany in the early twentieth century, Barth

> To him alone our heart is due.
> . . . And to give our heart to any other is plain idolatry.
>
> John Wesley, Sermon 78, "Spiritual Idolatry" I.3, in *The Works of John Wesley* (Nashville: Abingdon Press, 1986), 3:104.

---

3. A. Katherine Grieb, *The Story of Romans: A Narrative Defense of God's Righteousness* (Louisville, KY: Westminster John Knox Press, 2002), 28.

knew how easy it was for humans to take themselves and their accomplishments as having ultimate value, and he saw in Paul's letter a reminder that only God is ultimate. Suppressing the truth about God means also suppressing the truth about ourselves: namely, that we are not of final importance but are only temporary and limited creatures. We usurp God's place when we take our own ideas (even our ideas about God) as the standard of truth. Whenever we make ourselves and our efforts the measure of how things are or ought to be, God says no. This negation of our pretended ultimacy is God's wrath.

> The wrath of God is the judgement under which we stand in so far as we do not love the Judge; it is the "No" which meets us when we do not affirm it; it is the protest pronounced always and everywhere against the course of the world in so far as we do not accept the protest as our own.
>
> Karl Barth, *The Epistle to the Romans*, trans. from the 6th ed. by Edwyn C. Hoskyns (London: Oxford University Press, 1968), 42.

Paul moves from a description of how humans turn away from God to a description of the consequences of turning away. Verses 24 and 26 begin with words that indicate a causal connection between human dishonoring of God and activities that dishonor ourselves as human beings. In both Mark 12:28–31 and Matthew 22:34–40, the commandment to love God is followed by the commandment to love one's neighbor as oneself. Neither self nor neighbor are loved properly in the acts of wickedness that Paul lists at the end of chapter 1, where he uses a common device in the Greco-Roman world of listing "vices." The causal connection that is indicated in verses 24 and 26 means that there is a deeper problem than just the activities themselves. To focus on the activities themselves would be to miss the way they grow out of forgetfulness of God. Breaking right relationship with God leads to breaking right relationship with others and with oneself.

Paul says God "gave them up" to the consequences of their idolatry, which Paul names in verse 24 as the desires (*epithumia*) of their hearts and "degrading passions." (Paul will say more about *epithumia* in 6:12). The "them" to whom Paul refers are not specified as Gentiles, even though many of the examples of unrighteousness are associated with Gentiles of the time. God directs wrath against unrighteousness, not against Gentiles per se, and as we shall see, Paul insists that all are unrighteous. For Paul to say that God "gave up" all humankind to the consequences of their unrighteousness does not mean that God abandoned humankind. Rather, it means that God's wrath is expressed in forbearance—that is, letting us undergo the effects of our forgetfulness of God to learn how that way leads to harm and futility instead of well-being and meaning.

Paul reinforces the causal connection between turning away from God and harmful behavior as he begins the list of "vices," but his way of doing so is hard to see in English. In the NRSV, verse 28 reads "And since they did not see fit to acknowledge God, God gave them up to a debased mind and to things that should not be done." The words translated in English as "see fit" (*edokimasan*) and "debased mind" (*adokimon*) sound similar in Greek and have a more similar meaning than one would guess from this English translation. To make the point clearer, one could say that because they did not "see fit," the mind has become "unfit," that is, the mind is not competent to make good moral decisions. Suppressing the truth about God is a way of rationalizing unrighteousness (dishonor and ingratitude), which leads to behavior that also has to be rationalized.[4] The mind that did not "see fit" to acknowledge God then becomes "unfit" to make good decisions about how to behave. The more unrighteous the behavior is the more rationalization it requires, and the mind becomes even less fit to know God. Doing and thinking go together. This connection shows why the revelation of wrath matters. Humans need to know God's judgment in order to regain the mind's fitness to be a moral guide.

The point of showing this causal connection is that the fundamental sin is human failure to honor God and setting something else up in God's place. Focus on the list of activities could easily deflect attention from that point.

With this in mind, something must be said about one kind of activity Paul names that is of particular interest in our time: same-sex relations. Even in a culture that was often tolerant of same-sex

---

4. Leander E. Keck, *Romans*, Abingdon New Testament Commentaries (Nashville: Abingdon Press, 2005), 71, 73.

sexual behavior, Paul seems to assume that a group of mostly Gentile Christians will agree with him that same-sex relations belonged in his examples. He does not seem to need to defend its inclusion. Study of the period has discovered a common world of ideas that Paul and the followers of Jesus in Rome would no doubt have shared.[5] First, although sexual behavior between people of the same sex was known and commented on, the ancient world had no idea of homosexual identity in the way we do today, that is, as a way of understanding oneself in relation to the gender to which one is attracted. Second, what was known in Paul's time and place was same-sex sexual conduct, primarily pederasty, and this behavior was often portrayed as an expression of unrestrained, excessive desire. Sometimes compared to hiring a prostitute, this behavior was thought to exhibit desire that is out of control. With these assumptions, this behavior exemplifies letting a creaturely experience control one's life, and so it displaces God.

Regulating desire was a high value in Greco-Roman culture, so much so that reflection on sexual desire often took the form of describing the proper "use" of the object of desire. Attention to this matter opens up a new possibility for understanding Paul's inclusion of same-sex behavior as an example of an activity that follows from dishonoring God—not as a condemnation of homosexuality per se but rather to underscore the problem of passion. David Frederickson shows how the word "use" indicates the way the ancient world thought of intercourse: not as mutual pleasure, but as the desiring subject using the desired object. "Use" described heterosexual behavior as well as same-sex behavior. In that world, it was natural for a husband to use his wife for pleasure. What made the use of a sexual partner natural or unnatural was whether or not desire was controlled or excessive. Uncontrolled, excessive desire was desire that could not be sated, and it was culturally dishonorable to be controlled by one's passions rather than to be in control of them.[6] To be given up to one's own passions, then, was to be left dissatisfied

---

5. Victor Paul Furnish, *The Moral Teaching of Paul: Selected Issues*, 3rd ed. (Nashville: Abingdon Press, 2009), 55–93.

6. David Frederickson, "Natural and Unnatural Use in Romans 1:24–27: Paul and the Philosophic Critique of Eros," in *Homosexuality, Science, and the "Plain Sense" of Scripture* (Grand Rapids: Wm. B. Eerdmans Publishing Co., 2000), 197–222.

and disrespected. The problem of uncontrolled passion leads to the opposite of a fulfilled human life.

Even if condemnation of homosexuality is not Paul's main point, same-sex behavior provided him with an easily understandable example under the assumptions of the time for how failing to give God honor disrupts the order of God's creation. Apart from the question of what constitutes natural "use," same-sex intercourse could be considered "unnatural" partly because it did not produce children. Equally important was that when it occurred between two men, it required one of the men to assume the role of a woman. One of the men had to adopt an "unnatural" gender role. Because women were not considered the equals of men, this role necessarily placed one of the men in an inferior position. In addition, unrestrained, excessive sexual desire could express itself in sexual conquest and domination, therefore degrading the other person. The act was not simply unnatural but also exploitative. Robert Jewett points out that slaves or former slaves who made up a large number of the followers of Jesus in Rome may have been subject to sexual exploitation by their masters or patrons, so Paul's words might have confirmed their experience of wrongful exploitation.[7] Through the example of same-sex behavior as he knew it in the ancient world, Paul could link the problem of dishonoring God with experienced injustice. The consequence of suppressing the truth about God is to live in an unrighteous world, where many are hurt.

Although Paul could presume agreement among his hearers regarding same-sex conduct, such agreement cannot be presumed in our time. In fact, homosexuality is one of the most hotly debated issues in the church today. What can be said about Paul's inclusion of same-sex sexual conduct when he talks about unrighteousness? First, Paul is not an unerring guide regarding what is natural and unnatural. He says in 1 Corinthians 11:14 that nature teaches that it is degrading (and Paul uses the same word here he uses in Romans 1:26 to describe "degrading passions") for a man to wear long hair. The dominant philosophical view of the world in Paul's time used the idea of "essence" to talk about why things are what they are. In

7. Robert Jewett, *Romans: A Commentary*, Hermeneia (Minneapolis: Fortress Press, 2007), 181.

other words, we are what we are because of some kind of substance or nature that makes us so. This view shaped common assumptions of the time and made it easy to connect common cultural norms with what is "natural." Paul shared that tendency with others of his time. In our time, though, we have come to recognize how much of who we are and what we know is constructed in a social context. So it is far less obvious that cultural norms are simply "right" and that deviation from those norms is "degrading." Christians today cannot simply accept Paul's assumed connection between culture and nature but must think for themselves about what a fitting life before God should be.

Second, if Paul's main point is that dishonoring God leads to dishonoring and harming our neighbors, then listening to Paul means using this point for the basis of the reflection we must do in our own time. The "vices" Paul lists are not a precise, timeless diagnosis but only examples. The list cannot possibly be exhaustive (as we can be endlessly creative in how we dishonor each other) but can only point us toward many ways that we fail to love one another properly. Paul himself recognizes his list only provides examples when he says "such things" in 1:32 and 2:2 and 2:3. Guided by Paul's fundamental question about how we honor God and each other properly, we can consider many ways relationships bring wholeness or damage. In that light, Paul could not imagine committed homosexual relationships. But we can. To make good use of Paul's most important point, we must look at all relationships and ask whether they honor God and the persons involved or not.

Furthermore, it is important to recognize that something on this list of "vices" is likely to touch every reader in some way. Perhaps few who read this letter as Christians would include murder in their sins, but envy? An honest appraisal of one's life will surely allow one to find one's place somewhere in what Paul has said. To use Paul's remarks about homosexuality to condemn others of sin would be to miss Paul's caution about passing judgment,[8] which becomes clear in the next section.

8. Beverly Gaventa, "Romans," in *Women's Bible Commentary*, ed. Carol A. Newsom and Sharon H. Ringe (Louisville, KY: Westminster John Knox Press, 1998), 407.

FURTHER REFLECTIONS
General and Special Revelation

Paul's observation that all humans know something about God even if they suppress it has provided a basis for the distinction in theology between general and special revelation. The fundamental idea of the theological understanding of revelation is that of unveiling: something that has been hidden from sight is now revealed to sight. Revelation has the character of being a gift, of knowledge given by the one who does the unveiling. For Christian revelation, the one who does the unveiling is God, and the knowledge that is given is knowledge of God's own self. This is knowledge to which we would not have access if God did not make it known to us.

Protestant theologians have used language of general and special revelation (Catholic theologians are more likely to treat these issues under the term "natural theology") to distinguish means of access. The category of general revelation acknowledges that God makes some knowledge of God's self generally available to all human beings. This knowledge is available through the ordinary faculty of human reason as it considers nature (including all creation itself as well as human nature). For instance, the observation of an orderly universe can lead humans to understand that there must be a maker who gives creation this order. Such an insight is generally available to all human observers, but it has the character of revelation because it is knowledge about God that is given by God (the Creator uses the order in creation to call our attention to the orderer, who is God). In addition, contemplation of our own human nature can give us some knowledge of God. For instance, the human conscience gives some guidance to what is right and wrong, so this awareness can lead humans to understand that the universe has a moral order instituted by God.

Theologians who acknowledge general revelation have usually also acknowledged the need for further special revelation. General revelation by itself is incomplete and may be ambiguous. For instance, does the order of the universe imply only one Creator, or could there be several? Even if an observer concludes there is one

Creator, how would the observer know anything about that Creator, such as whether God has a loving nature? In addition, human
conscience does not always guide us unerringly to the same moral
judgments. There is need for some more particular, special act of
God to give us clarity about those things God wants us to know.
Special revelation is special both because it takes place in a special act not generally available to everyone and because it provides
knowledge above and beyond what humans can know by reason
alone. This revelation is more obviously "giftlike" than general revelation is. Paul's letter to the Romans also talks about knowledge
of God that belongs to this kind of revelation. Both the law given
to the Jews and the gospel concerning Jesus Christ are instances of
God's special acts to reveal something humans should know.

Because all humans have some knowledge of God, Paul says
all humans are "without excuse" (1:20) when they deny what they
know about God. In our time of global interaction with other religions, some have drawn a more positive point from this recognition
that some knowledge of God is available to all. The policy statement
on interfaith relations of the National Council of Churches in Christ
in the U.S.A. encourages churches to reflect on Paul's affirmation in
Romans 1:20 without denying the special revelation given in Jesus
Christ.[9] In a similar spirit, the Vatican statement *Nostra Aetate* recognizes (without giving up the need to proclaim Jesus Christ) that
some teachings in other religions "often reflect a ray of that Truth
which enlightens all men."[10] Acknowledging that God commu-
nicates something of God's truth to all does not in any way settle
important questions concerning interreligious dialogue, but it does
give Christians encouragement to be in conversation with persons
of other faiths.

Although postmodern epistemologies that identify how knowledge is constructed put pressure on these traditional categories, it may yet be useful to find a way to talk about what kind of

9. National Council of Churches of Christ in the U.S.A., "Interfaith Relations and the
Churches", ¶34.
10. Paul IV, *Declaration on the Relation of the Church to Non-Christian Religions (Nostra Aetate)*,
October 28, 1965, The Holy See, §2.

knowledge of God we share and what kind of knowledge belongs
to specific communities.

2:1–16
God's Righteous Judgment

Up to this point, Paul has been speaking in third person about the
ungodly and the unrighteous. God gave *them* up to their passions
and lusts, but now Paul changes to *you*, using the rhetorical style of
diatribe, where the "speaker" imagines a conversation with another
person to make his point. Because Paul controls both sides of the
conversation, he is able to advance an argument he wants to make.[11]
In 1:20 he says, "so they are without excuse" for dishonoring God,
but in 2:1 he says, "therefore you have no excuse" for passing judgment on others. With this shift to second person, a discussion about
God's wrath in general becomes an address of accountability. In a
situation where Jewish followers of Jesus Christ were having trouble
being reassimilated after their expulsion from Rome by Claudius
(see "The Situation of the Letter" above in "Why Romans, Why
Now?," pp. 10–13) among mostly Gentile followers, there may have
been feelings of superiority on the part of both groups. Gentile followers may have thought their situation to be better than that of Jewish followers. After all, the Gentile mission was flourishing while the
Jewish mission met with resistance. Gentile followers of Jesus may
have considered themselves to be favored by God. In the face of that
kind of confidence in a favored status, Paul's use of Gentile idolatry
to describe unrighteousness would be sobering.

Paul also has sobering words for the Jewish followers. James D.
G. Dunn describes the attitude expressed in some Jewish writings of
the time, and the Jewish followers of Jesus newly returned to Rome
may have had this attitude reinforced. Because of their identity as the
chosen people of God, Jewish self-understanding of being favored
over Gentiles included the expectation of different treatment: "they
do not sin like the Gentiles, or if they do, their sin is not so serious.

---

11. Keck, *Romans,* 23.

Thus, Israel is disciplined, but others are punished; Israel is chastised, but others are scourged; Israel is tested, but the ungodly condemned; Israel expects mercy, but their opponents can look only for wrath."[12] If Jewish followers of Jesus thought themselves superior to Gentile followers because they were the original people of the covenant and claimed to know what God's judgment would be, Paul reminds them they will not escape God's judgment, particularly because judging others brings the person doing the judging under God's judgment.

Because Paul did not specify Jew and Gentile in his description of unrighteousness, he presents a shared problem. All humans suppress the truth in some way, so every one of us is unrighteous in some way. Using the list of vices to point fingers at someone else instead of recognizing your own responsibility simply shows how effectively you are able to suppress the truth about yourself. So using the list of "vices" to judge others actually demonstrates your own unrighteousness. This problem is a reminder that the only fair and competent judge is God.

> The righteous invariably try to see their own faults and overlook those of others. Again they are eager to recognize the good things in others and to disregard those of their own. On the other hand, the unrighteous look for good in themselves and for evil in others.
>
> Martin Luther, *Commentary on Romans*, trans. J. Theodore Mueller (Grand Rapids: Kregel Classics, 1976), 52.

While we are quick to judge others, we hope to escape judgment ourselves. Although we may think that judging others according to what we think is God's truth puts us on the side of God, God sees how we fall short. We certainly are capable of fooling ourselves about our righteousness, and we may even be able to fool others, but we are not able to fool God. We should not suppose we are escaping the judgment of God simply because we have so far escaped direct punishment for the life we live. God's patience does not mean absence of displeasure. It is not the case that God has somehow missed our ingratitude and idolatry or our behavior or that God thinks these things unimportant. Rather

---

12. James D. G. Dunn, *The New Perspective on Paul*, rev. ed. (Grand Rapids: Wm. B. Eerdmans Publishing Co., 2008), 219.

it is that God is giving us time to repent of them (2:4). Paul has made the point in 1:24 that God "gave up" the unrighteous to their lusts. By delaying judgment on those who judge, God is similarly allowing the one doing the judging to undergo the effects of his or her own sins. God's wrath, or displeasure, does not need to impose an added penalty, because it leaves that person to experience the consequences of damaged relationships produced by his or her attitudes and behavior. God gives a person time to see that the behavior does not bring wholeness but rather brokenness, so the person can repent. This forbearance is, in its own way, also a kind of judgment. Too few of us, though, take this opportunity to repent. Instead, we live in the illusion that God is not displeased, and we carry on as if all is well.

Because denial of sinfulness is so easy and so common, Christian tradition has known the importance of self-examination. Worship services include time for confession, and the liturgical year devotes the entire season of Lent to introspection. In recent years, theologians have been pointing out how intense interest in one's own standing before God leads to an understanding of Christianity as primarily individualistic. The gospel calls us not only to recognize our individual sinfulness but also to act in the world to bring God's justice to all. We are sinful not only in our thoughts, hearts, and individual behaviors but also in the way we participate in structures of injustice that harm the vulnerable. It may be even easier to deny our participation in sinful structures than our sinful thoughts. Self-examination needs to be broad enough to include reflection about what we do or fail to do that contributes to injustice instead of encouraging the kingdom of God. Although we may be blind to injustice in the world, God is not; and God's judgment and forbearance for repentance extends to this sinfulness, too.

Meanwhile, Luther points out, we continue to enjoy health and safety, the use of God's creation, and many blessings for which we should be grateful.[13] Because the beginning of our problem is ingratitude, though, the riches God bestows on us that ought to bring us to repentance may fail to do so. Not only are we given blessings

---

13. Luther, *Commentary on Romans*, 54.

for which we are ungrateful, but we also continue in behaviors that dishonor God as well as ourselves and others. Because God's wrath is revealed against unrighteousness, and we continue, and in fact increase, our unrighteousness through complacency toward God's forbearance, God's wrath is stored up until the future day when God reveals full and final judgment.

Barth describes the situation of human unrighteousness for which God's wrath is revelation in this way. If all humans are without excuse, then all are unrighteous. There are no saints and sinners; there are only sinners. God is the standard of truth and righteousness, and God's transcendence over human beings is so great that every human falls short. God's standard negates every human achievement because no matter what humans do that seems good to us, God's standard shows how far from true goodness it actually is. God's wrath is this judgment that all human effort fails to measure up. Even human effort to improve the world falls short of God's standard and is finally then unrighteousness. God's "no" to every human effort is judgment, but those who recognize it as the truth about themselves and who realize that being measured by God—even when falling short—is an encounter with God also see it as grace. In seeing the truth about one's negation, one is also seeing truth about God's transcendence. For those who receive this judgment with awe and humility of being in the presence of God, the judgment is revelation.

This revelation of wrath as grace leads to the repentance of abandoning every security in oneself or the world and honoring God alone. Those who do not receive God's negation of human effort in this way experience God's judgment only as wrath.[14] Barth's description of the completeness of human unrighteousness is in keeping with the traditional Protestant

> The ungodly do not realize that the goodness of God should lead them to repentance. The righteous, on the contrary, know that even the severity of God must redound to their good.
>
> Luther, *Commentary on Romans*, 54.

14. Barth, *The Epistle to the Romans*, 55–60.

commitment that there is no human righteousness, so humans must depend entirely on God's righteousness for salvation.

As Barth recognized, God's wrath is being revealed already for those who have eyes to see, but Paul also speaks of a "day of wrath" that is yet to come. It has been very common to think of a day of wrath as a day of destruction. The word "apocalyptic" in popular use has been almost reduced to this idea. But the real meaning of "apocalypse" is "revelation," so the appropriate question to ask is not when and how the world's destruction will take place but rather what will be revealed? If the day of wrath is a full revelation of God's displeasure against ungodliness (see comments on 1:18–32, pp. 27–37), then it will look very different from how it has been popularly conceived.

Paul understood the gospel as offering a quite different apocalypse. Instead of inflicting mass destruction, God would disarm the powers of sin and death and give those who had been faithful the power to resist, through Jesus Christ and the Spirit, the enticement to do and be evil. Instead of the world's destruction, Paul wrote of the world's liberation and transformation (see Rom. 8).

Cobb and Lull, *Romans,* 57.

Considering the day of wrath as a day of revelation may help with a problem of how to interpret Paul's comments about deeds (2:6) in light of the traditional Protestant commitment to being saved by grace through faith. If no human works can possibly be good when judged by God's standard for goodness, then no works can contribute anything to salvation. This insight about human standing before God has been important and helpful in the Protestant tradition. This commitment is sometimes thought to be difficult to reconcile, though, with Paul's description that on the "day of wrath" to come, God will "repay according to each one's deeds." This problem is amplified in 2:13 where Paul says that the "doers of the law" will be "justified" (for more on this discussion, see comments for 3:9–20, pp. 57–64).

This tension between traditional Protestant theological emphasis on thorough human unrighteousness and Paul's ideas about repayment for deeds is one of the reasons biblical scholars caution theologians against making Paul fit a system. It should be noted, though, that theologians of the "old perspective" have not been unaware of this tension and have tried to find ways to resolve it. Melanchthon, for instance, acknowledges that this verse makes clear that the righteous will be rewarded according to works and the unjust will be punished. This acknowledgment, though, may be made while still holding that works are not what make one righteous.[15] Rather, it is God's imputation that does so. Melanchthon manages his resolution in part by distinguishing between law and gospel, a distinction that has in history too easily served anti-Judaism by being interpreted to provide the basis for supersessionism. There is good reason to pay attention to new possibilities for how to talk about this matter that do not depend on this distinction. Paul's conviction about God's impartiality is one such possibility.

Biblical scholars recommend listening to Paul in his entirety and in his context. As a Jew, Paul had learned about God's judgment from the prophets and from apocalyptic literature. The motif of a day of judgment modeled on courtroom judgment is the framework for Paul's discussion of repayment according to deeds. What we have learned so far from what Paul has said is that no one who appears before God in this courtroom has any excuse. We have also learned that the only rightful judge in the courtroom is God.

So what kind of judge is God? God is an impartial judge, not basing judgment on the category in society one occupies (as Jew or Greek, or on the honor that society has bestowed) but on the way one has lived one's life. The idea that all humans stand before God without excuse is accompanied by the idea that God judges all humans who stand before the court without partiality. In his argument thus far, Paul has not explicitly distinguished Jew and Greek (Gentile) apart from 1:16 in his thematic statement. Even though the description of unrighteousness in chapter 1 might imply Gentile behavior, Paul does not name it as such. Katherine Grieb suggests that Paul presents this description as basic human unrighteousness because Gentiles and Jews are all the descendants of Adam and Eve, where (as we learn in chapter 5) the problem began. The story starts with a basic human problem, before God's covenant made a distinction between

---

15. Philipp Melanchthon, *Commentary on Romans*, trans. Fred Kramer (St. Louis: Concordia Publishing House, 1992), 87–88.

Gentile and Jew, so Jews and Gentiles share some of the same story.[16] It should also be remembered that even though the Jews were not idolaters, the people of Israel had their own story of the unfortunate incident with the golden calf recounted in Exodus 32, which served as a warning about the forgetfulness of God that Paul is talking about. All humans live together in this world gone wrong. At the point of talking about the day of wrath to come, though, Paul begins making explicit reference to the situations of Jews and Gentiles.

His reason for making the distinction between Jew and Greek in chapter 2 is not to reinforce ethnic division; rather it is to show that before this impartial judge, neither group will be privileged over the other. On this day, they will be paid according to their deeds. If this idea that deeds (or works) would have a place in determining how God judges us is only considered on the surface, then it is not an easy one to reconcile with the traditional Protestant position of being saved by faith apart from works. Let us consider, though, whether Paul's deeper concerns are really incompatible with the concerns of the Reformers.

Paul explains that deeds will be repaid according to whether persons do good or instead obey unrighteousness. Especially unfitting to the Protestant position, Paul says those who receive eternal life are seeking "glory and honor and immortality." Surely seeking these things is a sign of sinful pride and desire—not to be rewarded with eternal life. Paul is using language that would have been very familiar in the context of the empire that held honor and glory in high regard, and where it could be awarded by the emperor. At this point in the letter, Paul seems to be getting the attention of the Romans with language they would be used to hearing in their social context: namely, that God will give "glory and honor" to those who do good. John Chrysostom points out that these are, after all, what people strive for.[17] But this familiar language will come under some intense scrutiny and redefinition as the letter continues. Paul is not misleading his hearers by using this language. God's judgment and deeds are

16. Grieb, *The Story of Romans*, 25–26.
17. John Chrysostom, *The Homilies of S. John Chrysostom, Archbishop of Constantinople, on the Epistle of St. Paul the Apostle to the Romans*, 3rd ed., trans. members of the English church (Oxford: James Parker and Co. and Rivingtons, 1877), 59.

connected to each other, but not in the way that those who live in Rome have come to expect. God does not ascribe glory and honor to them because of social position or ethnic identity, nor is it acquired through winning competition, and it certainly is not for boasting. The deeds that will receive glory and honor from God on the last day are those that have demonstrated allegiance (or faithfulness) to God, deeds that follow from the way they have honored God. We make our trust in and loyalty to God evident through our actions, and this enacted trust and loyalty is faithfulness.

The Protestant concern about being saved by works has been intended to prevent humans from thinking God owes them something or from taking credit for their own salvation. This commitment, though, does not exclude works entirely. In Reformation theology, the quality of a work that follows faith (motivated by love for God rather than self-interest) is quite different from that of a work done apart from faith. Works that follow from faith show the kind of faithfulness to God that Paul cares about. Even Luther can talk about deeds that are pleasing to God, although they are not likely to be seen as pleasing to the world. For instance, it may be very unpopular to act according to God's values rather than the values of the dominant culture—to stand with the marginalized, to call for changes in political and economic systems to protect the weak, to criticize the use of human power. God judges these deeds differently than the world does, so the only glory and honor they will receive is from God.

No one knows exactly what will happen on the day of retribution, but it will be unfavorable for some and favorable for others, as Paul says in verse 9: "anguish and distress for everyone who does evil, the Jew first and also the Greek, but glory and honor and peace

---

But there is not so much difficulty in this verse, as it is commonly thought. . . . he will also crown their good works, but not on account of any merit: nor can this be proved from this verse; for though it declares what reward good works are to have, it does yet by no means show what they are worth, or what price is due to them. It is an absurd inference to deduce merit from reward.

John Calvin, *Commentaries on the Epistle of Paul the Apostle to the Romans,* trans. and ed. John Owen (Grand Rapids: Wm. B. Eerdmans Publishing Co., 1959), 89–90.

for everyone who does good, the Jew first and also the Greek." There are no details about the misery the ones who have done evil will experience, but it would seem likely that when people who have suppressed the truth about themselves for a lifetime are confronted fully and unmistakably with that truth on that Day of Judgment, the disclosure itself would be agonizing. Those who have lived in God's truth

> But when our good work is followed by persecution, let us rejoice and firmly believe it is pleasing to God; indeed, then let us be assured that it comes from God, for whatever is of God is bound to be crucified by the world.
>
> Martin Luther, *Commentary on Romans*, 55.

will instead be confirmed in their course of life. Theologians in the Protestant tradition have generally accepted the idea that different judgments await different lives, but that those different judgments would be assigned according to deeds has been harder for many to reconcile with traditional Reformation theology.

N. T. Wright tries to explain the meaning of this repayment in the following way. He notes that those things we are to do as Christians are not merely duties; they are things that please God. The point is not to total up tasks fulfilled but rather to show our love for God by doing things that please God. Recognizing this difference is important to help us avoid thinking about God as cosmic accountant and put in its place thinking about God as the parent who smiles at the children's offerings. The Holy Spirit who sets us free not only frees us *from* sin but also frees us *for* joyful work. Being able to choose responsible living is a gift of grace, and our cooperation with God in doing the work of God should not be discounted as worthless. God's response to our deeds on the day of judgment is not to say, "You have earned your reward" but rather to say, "Well done, good and faithful servant."[18]

Of course, Reformation theologians have not been insensitive to the concern about being freed for responsible living. The matter is not simply important for interpreting Paul but also for giving an adequate description of a faithful Christian life. To avoid denying that

18. N. T. Wright, *Justification: God's Plan and Paul's Vision* (Downers Grove, IL: IVP Academic, 2009), 187–93.

we are justified by faith alone, though, Protestant theologians have talked about works as "fruits" of faith. They are not the ground of human righteousness before God, but they do follow from the faith that is the ground of righteousness. As Melanchthon says, "It is necessary that a person first have forgiveness of sins and justification. Afterward, the obedience which has been begun is found pleasing, and is worship of God."[19] More will be said about the relationship of faith and works in "Further Reflections: Faith and Good Works." At this point we can note that Protestants are not against deeds. Their concern is to keep deeds from usurping the role of grace. It would not seem to threaten grace to acknowledge that deeds express our faith, that God views our deeds with pleasure or displeasure, or that the way God judges those deeds to be pleasing or not pleasing will eventually become known to us.

Paul, of course, is not thinking about the relation of faith and works as he writes about the day of wrath. He is thinking about the relation of Jews and Greeks. The point of saying that we are repaid according to our deeds is to show that God's judgment is not made with partiality toward a group but rather with regard to how human members of either group have actually lived their lives. There is one sense, though, in which the group does affect the judgment. When Jews are judged on how they have lived their lives, they will be judged according to the law because God gave it to them as their guide. Gentiles, on the other hand, will not be judged by the written law because God did not give it to them. Instead, they will be judged by "what is written on their hearts." In other words, God has provided for them knowledge to guide their lives in a different way. Whether written on stone tablets or on hearts, God has provided understanding of the divine will to guide how we live, and this will determine how we are judged. God's impartiality does not imply God's insensitivity to their different situations. Judging them according to their deeds allows God to consider what they know and how they know it. God's impartiality does imply that whether one is Jew or Greek, one will be judged according to whether one has made good use of the

19. Melanchthon, *Commentary on Romans*, 109.

knowledge God has provided or whether one has suppressed that knowledge and followed one's own path.

When Origen wrote his commentary on Romans, he was concerned about various gnostic groups who claimed that human beings had different natures. According to these gnostic groups, some humans had natures that were able to be saved, and other humans had natures that could not be saved. Origen opposed this idea that people were different by nature and therefore some had no chance to be saved at all. To his mind, Paul's reflections about conscience showed that God had placed a guide in every person and that God would judge each person "not by the privilege of possessing a certain nature, but by his own thoughts, accused or defended by the testimony of his own conscience."[20] In Origen's interpretation, Paul's message of equality before God was played out in an important affirmation of universal human nature. This message continues to be important because it is so easy for one group of people to see another group of people as less than human. In the face of that problem, it is important to say that no group has a privileged nature that sets it above another group, but rather all human beings are equally human.

In our time, though, theologians have begun to recognize that we also face a different kind of problem. Lately, theologians have become more aware that majority groups have often maintained their privilege by insisting their group's own cultural norms represent universal human nature. For instance, as missionaries took the gospel around the globe, they sometimes acted as though being Christian meant being Western. This assumption led to imperial and colonial imposition of values and customs that is now being studied and repented of in theology. Although the message of equality before God that Origen cared about is still relevant, it may be equally important now to recognize Paul's affirmation that God understands our different situations and judges us accordingly. Such a recognition guards against making falsely universal claims that guard human privilege rather than enable people to live honestly and honorably before God.

20. Origen, *Commentary on the Epistle to the Romans, Books 1–5,* The Fathers of the Church, vol. 103, trans. Thomas P. Scheck (Washington, DC: The Catholic University of America Press, 2001), 135.

2:17–3:20

Law and Covenant

2:17–29

The Jews and the Law

It has been all too easy for interpreters of Romans to use this portion of Paul's letter to criticize Jews as legalistic hypocrites and elevate Christians as having a superior understanding of God's law. Reading the previous section as a caution against group privilege (whether through Origen's denial of special natures or a more current affirmation of diverse situations) should make problematic any reading of this section to reinforce superior attitudes.

In fact, superior attitude is exactly what Paul is confronting when he talks about "boasting." He is again using the rhetorical style of diatribe, which serves as a device to allow Paul to instruct through the responses he gives to an imaginary dialogue partner. The imaginary dialogue partner that Paul creates is a Jew who seems to feel superior to Gentiles because of the covenant God made with the people of Israel through the law. Paul does not use the word "covenant," but the story of God's special relationship with Israel lies behind the things Paul is talking about. The attitude of this imaginary Jew in the dialogue Paul constructs is a device to further an argument, and Paul takes the device to the point of being ludicrous to show how damaging this attitude is. It should not be seen as an attitude held by all Jews. Furthermore, one should remember that the diatribe in this letter serves to address Jews in Rome who are already following Jesus.

When the imaginary Jew boasts of being special because God made the people of Israel a "guide," a "light," a "corrector," and a "teacher" (2:19–20), Paul points out that the teacher has something to learn. The list of descriptions Paul uses reminds the hearers of the letter that even though the law was given to the Jews alone, it was given so that the nations would see the greatness of Israel, the greatness of Israel's God, and the greatness of the law itself (Deut. 4:5–8). Isaiah understood that the people of Israel were supposed to be a light to the nations (Gentiles) for the salvation of the world (Isa. 49:6). By using the law to establish a special relationship with one people, God intended to become known to all people. The law established this relationship and gave identity to the people of God, but at the same time it created a boundary between Israel and the nations. By celebrating this "special relation" the imaginary Jew emphasizes the difference and focuses on ethnocentrism rather than God's universal purpose for the law.[1] In the context of the church in Rome, ethnocentrism can only serve division. Paul uses this imaginary conversation to highlight how boasting in Jewish distinctiveness could overwhelm the ability of a particular people to point others to the one, true God of all. If this happens, they cannot be the light God intended them to be. A church divided by ethnocentrism cannot effectively shine the light of God in Rome. This is not only a problem in Paul's ancient world. Christians today can be prone to celebrating specialness to the point of failing to be the light we are supposed to be. In fact, some Christians have taken this problem to the point of sometimes claiming that one church has a more special relationship with God than another. Christians ought to lead their individual and corporate lives so that we point to Jesus Christ, but all too often the pride we take in who we are leads away from the light instead.

As he lists the way the imaginary teacher breaks the very law he teaches (2:21–23), Paul is returning to the point he made at the beginning of the chapter that no one escapes judgment. Instead of making this point by using a list of vices (a device he has already used that would be especially familiar to Gentiles among his hearers) he makes the point by using the law (which would be of concern to the Jews among his hearers). Paul is not making specific accusations of this group or suggesting that Jews flagrantly violated the law; after all, this is a diatribe with an imaginary partner. Rather, he is showing that having (or teaching) the law is not a guarantee of following

---

1. Daniel Boyarin, *A Radical Jew: Paul and the Politics of Identity* (Berkeley: University of California Press, 1994), 52–56.

the law. For instance, having a law against stealing does not prevent all stealing. Having the law does not guarantee proper honoring of God. We all dishonor God in some way, and so we all stand together under God's judgment. None of us ever stands outside of the condition shared by all humanity, so no one is ever in a position to judge others.

Of course, any actual instance of breaking the law would make the failure to be a light to the nations worse. Gentiles would see disobedience, not something pointing to God. They would not be encouraged to live differently or to see the truth about God they have suppressed. Instead of leading Gentiles to God, such behavior would lead Gentiles to ridicule God (2:24). Because God's judgment considers whether deeds demonstrate living a life of faithfulness to God, the failure to convince Gentiles to honor God in faithfulness would be especially serious if, as Paul thought, the day of judgment was near.

Any Christian who might be inclined to gloat over Jews upon reading what Paul says about their failure to be a light to the world would do well to reflect on Christianity's own failure to present a convincing witness to the world. Christian leaders who have broken trust—for instance, in sexual or financial scandals—have damaged the witness to God, often for their own parishioners and certainly to the world. Indeed the church's history of violence against the Jews (fueled in part by attitudes of Christian superiority) has led many to doubt the truth of Christian faith. Christian boasting over Jews is a rather striking example that in passing judgment on another, you condemn yourself.

Paul shifts from diatribe to talking about circumcision in verse 25. Circumcision was the physical sign of the covenant God made with Abraham, and Jews regarded it as a sign of their chosenness and obedience to the law.[2] The boasting Jew of the diatribe would surely have regarded circumcision as important for calling himself a Jew. Paul points out, though, that the sign of obedience to the law does not guarantee actual obedience to the law (circumcision can become uncircumcision). Paul has already shown that those who

---

2. Leander E. Keck, *Romans,* Abingdon New Testament Commentaries (Nashville: Abingdon Press, 2005), 85.

have been given the law may not always follow it, and now he allows that those who have not been given the law (the uncircumcised Gentiles) may in fact live in a way that pleases God. Being a Jew, he says, is not merely a matter of bearing in one's flesh the sign of the covenant but rather manifests itself when one lives according to the covenant (2:28–29). In this reasoning, Paul echoes his earlier claim that God judges according to deeds in the sense that what we do reveals our true loyalty. He calls real circumcision "a matter of the heart," an idea that has roots in the Hebrew Scriptures (for instance, Deut. 10:16).

The question of whether Gentiles needed to be circumcised to become followers of Jesus had been an important one as Paul began his mission to the Gentiles, and Paul's Letter to the Galatians had taken up the topic directly. In this Letter to the Romans, Paul is not dealing with the problem of Gentiles who wonder whether they need to be circumcised. Rather he is dealing with the problem of Jewish and Gentile followers of Jesus who do not seem to be integrated well into a single community in Rome. His comments about circumcision come in the context of "boasting" groups to which he proclaims God's impartiality as a response to the desire for favored treatment. God sees through those external things that we think make us special and that separate people from one another and looks deeply at what directs our lives.

Long after Paul, Christians began to see similarity between the rite of circumcision and the rite of baptism because both initiated people into a covenant and a way of life. This connection became particularly important for Protestants who practiced infant baptism when other Protestants claimed baptism should be deferred until a person was old enough to make his or her own commitment of faith. Protestants who practiced infant baptism could point out that infants were brought into Israel's covenant with God through circumcision even though the infants did not yet have full understanding of what that meant.

Because theologians understood this connection between baptism and circumcision, some could also make the connection between Paul's admonition about being an outward Jew without an inward commitment to the law and the situation of many in their

time who were outward Christians without an inward Christian
faith (*fiducia*). Calvin warns against those who are "satisfied with
the empty shadow of baptism" but do not care about the holiness
to which it calls them.[3] In a sermon that took Romans 2:29 as its
text, John Wesley describes the right inward state of "a true follower
of Christ" as being marked by "humility, faith, hope, and charity."[4]
These, rather than any outward form, constituted the circumcision
of the heart. Much of Wesley's ministry was spent calling people
from a nominal Christianity to "real" Christianity.

Although this text is not as prominently used as it was at one time,
every generation needs to ponder that being a Christian is about
more than going to church or living a conventionally decent life or
even holding certain beliefs. Many theologians have held that being
a Christian is about having a heart that beats for God. When we can
say that desire for God comes before all else and shapes the way we
desire other things, then we will have grasped one of the most significant theological insights that the tradition of the church has to offer.

3:1–8
Entrusted with the Law to Bless the Nations

Now that he has argued that a Gentile can be obedient without being
circumcised, Paul must consider what it means to be a circumcised
Jew. He puts forth a series of questions, continuing his conversation
with the imaginary Jew he began in chapter 2, that allows him to
develop his thoughts. He begins with the question of whether there
is any "advantage" to being a Jew. If many Hellenistic Jews expected
the advantage of more lenient judgment on account of special relationship, Paul has just dismantled that expectation by arguing for
God's impartiality.

The answer he gives, though, to the stated question is that there is
much advantage, albeit a different one: namely, "the Jews were

---

3. John Calvin, *Commentaries on the Epistle of Paul the Apostle to the Romans*, trans. and ed. John
Owen (Grand Rapids: Wm. B. Eerdmans Publishing Co., 1959), 109.
4. John Wesley, Sermon 17, "The Circumcision of the Heart," *The Works of John Wesley*, ed. Frank
Baker, vol. 1, Sermons I, ed. Albert C. Outler (Nashville: Abingdon Press, 1984), 402–3.

entrusted with the oracles of God." The word translated as "oracles" is used also in Acts 7:38, and there it refers specifically to the law given to Moses on Mt. Sinai. The law does not *belong* to the Jews; it has been "entrusted" (the word in Greek has the same stem as *pistis,* or "faith") to them. God has put faith in them regarding the oracles.

To entrust someone with something is both a privilege and a responsibility. It is an honor to be chosen to guard or do something that is important, but it also means giving proper care to this important thing.

Paul moves quickly from the question of advantage to a question of faithfulness. God put faith in the Jews, but they have not all been faithful. Some have suggested that the faithlessness under discussion in verse 3 is lack of faith in Jesus Christ. If this is so Paul's answer here anticipates his longer discussion in chapters 9–11. The way the root *pistis* appears not only in verse 3 but also in verse 2, though, suggests a link with entrusting the oracles and provides a clue about the kind of faithlessness Paul has in mind. The word translated as "oracles" is *logia.* When used outside the Bible, this word often referred to a divine communication, along with which the receiver took on a duty. In the Septuagint (the Greek translation of the Hebrew Scriptures), the word is used for God's commands and promises.[5] Perhaps the problem for Paul is that God entrusted the oracles (God's commands and promises) to Israel, but Israel did not completely fulfill the task God had in mind when entrusting the oracles to them.

N. T. Wright explains the situation in this way, taking Paul to be speaking about Israel as a whole. God's plan to make right a world gone wrong began with God's covenant with Abraham, through

> To use a contemporary example, if I entrust my money to a bank in a trust fund, that does not mean that the bankers can do whatever they want with it: it is for the benefit of the person for whom I am intending it, for my beneficiary, although the bankers use it and benefit from it as well.
>
> A. Katherine Grieb, *The Story of Romans: A Narrative Defense of God's Righteousness* (Louisville, KY: Westminster John Knox Press, 2002), 33.

5. Keck, *Romans,* 90.

which God will bless the whole world (Gen. 12:3).[6] Paul's argument is rooted in this narrative, so when he talks about entrusting the oracles of God to the Jews, he means that Israel was chosen by God "for the task of bringing his healing message to the world."[7] Wright's suggestion of this large narrative structure has not been universally accepted, but it is possible that Paul had some idea that the oracles given to the Jews were not for the benefit of Jews alone. The law was entrusted to them for the purpose of benefitting not only themselves but also for blessing the nations. In the Hellenized ancient world, the Jews did attract some Gentiles to their way of life. There were "God-fearers," viewed by Jews as righteous Gentiles, and other Gentiles admired the Jewish way of life.[8] But clearly there was also still much idolatry and much immorality among Gentiles. The task of Israel had not been completed. Why was the task still undone? The problem may be that instead of understanding itself to be entrusted with the oracles for the sake of the nations, Israel understood the oracles to be its own possession. It is not that Israel failed to take seriously the oracles entrusted to it, but its concern for maintaining identity deflected attention from the task of healing the world. Paul is continuing the reference to the problem of Jewish distinctiveness that he began in the previous chapter.

Keeping in mind that Paul's instruction is intended for a particular community of mixed Jewish and Gentile followers of Jesus, Paul's concern about fulfilling the task of the oracles may be even more specific. Certainly among the followers of Jesus, the limitation of the boundaries set by the law had become problematic as Gentiles became followers, and throughout his mission Paul had to contend with the question of how to include Gentiles among the followers of Jesus who were Jewish. In Rome, this problem had manifested itself around two matters that Paul addresses at the end of the letter: how to eat together and how to observe sacred days. In this context, Paul's point may be that the Jews in this community, who have been entrusted with the law, should not use the law to keep themselves

6. N. T. Wright, *Justification: God's Plan and Paul's Vision* (Downers Grove, IL: IVP Academic, 2009), 67.
7. Ibid., 198.
8. Pamela Eisenbaum, *Paul Was Not a Christian: The Original Message of a Misunderstood Apostle* (New York: HarperOne, 2009), 108–15.

apart from the Gentiles. They have been entrusted with the law to bless the Gentiles, and both their actions toward their brothers and sisters in Christ and their witness to Gentiles who do not yet follow Christ is compromised by focusing on Jewish identity over blessing the nations.

With Paul's understanding that Jesus' resurrection meant that the day of judgment would soon come, the uncompleted task of bringing the nations to worship the true God would have very serious consequences. The question Paul considers is whether having made this covenant with Israel to be a light to the nations (Isa. 42:6), God would abandon the covenant because Israel had not completed its task. Some (he does not claim all) had been unfaithful (3:3), but the unfaithfulness of some dims the light of the whole. Paul asks, "Will their faithlessness nullify the faithfulness of God," and he answers, "By no means!" Paul is posing a question about God's righteousness (as faithfulness to covenant promises). And, of course, his answer is that God continues to be trustworthy in the covenant, and is therefore righteous. Even if everyone else is false, God is still true.

The quotation in verse 4 comes from Psalm 51:4 (LXX Ps. 50), and the superscription of that psalm explains that its occasion is when Nathan confronts David about his sin with Bathsheba. In the psalm, the quoted lines express David's acknowledgment that God is right to judge him. This quotation sets up Paul's further questions. Whether Israel's faithlessness is not following Jesus or not succeeding in lighting the way for the nations to come to the true God, the problem is the same. If by their faithlessness, God is shown to be in the right to judge them, then isn't that a good thing for God? If their unrighteousness (*adikia*) has brought glory to God by showing that God is in the right, then why should they deserve God's wrath?

Human unrighteousness allows God's righteousness to become apparent by contrast—God's glory shines when God is faithful despite Israel's faithlessness. If the contrast with human unrighteousness helps us see God's faithfulness better, then is God's wrath against that unrighteousness unjust (3:5)? It is a very human tendency to cry "unfair" when one is judged negatively for doing something that results in a positive benefit. If God's faithfulness is confirmed, then it does not seem fair to punish the very thing that brought that confirmation. Paul, though, denies that thinking this situation is unfair is the right response. Human unrighteousness will always stand in contrast to God's righteousness, and the contrast will always make God's righteousness more apparent, the way that dark colors in a painting make the light colors stand out. The contrast in itself cannot make judgment unfair. God could never judge anything at all if God were not permitted to judge those human failures that highlight God's righteousness and truth and goodness (3:6).

Furthermore, it would be exactly the wrong lesson to draw from this situation to think we ought to do wrong so God's glory may be enhanced in contrast (3:8). If we do think that way, we rightly deserve God's judgment. Not only is God righteous with regard to keeping covenant promises, but God is also "in the right" to act as judge.

The contrast between human unrighteousness and God's righteousness occupied the attention of Luther and Barth. They generalize beyond Israel's situation to make a point about the unrighteousness of all humans. Luther understands human unrighteousness to highlight God's righteousness because human unrighteousness shows "how necessary and beneficial" God's righteousness is for us. According to Luther, "God's righteousness humbles us, casts us down before His feet and causes us to long for His righteousness" because we cannot rely on our own merit and must depend on God's righteousness alone. As soon as we receive it, we glorify God.[9] Luther's reading of Paul underscores Luther's understanding of justification by faith.

Barth calls attention to the transcendent God as judge. Only God determines whether our actions are "lies or obedience." We are not in a position to see as God sees, so we cannot second-guess God's judgment. He says, "Whatever my fate may be, I can only give honour to Him." It is precisely in giving glory to God even when God judges a person to be a sinner (which we all are) that she or he is truly "upright before God" in "free and joyful subjection to God."[10]

---

9. Martin Luther, *Commentary on Romans*, trans. J. Theodore Mueller (Grand Rapids: Kregel Classics, 1974), 68.
10. Karl Barth, *The Epistle to the Romans*, trans. Edwyn C. Hoskyns (Oxford: Oxford University Press, 1933), 83.

Barth's reading of Paul highlights God's judgment on any human enterprise.

These examples demonstrate why theologians have been criticized for imposing readings onto Paul. Instead of seeing how Paul's argument is meant to defend God's righteousness (in being faithful to the covenant God made), Luther and Barth use Paul's words to emphasize human unrighteousness. To be sure, there is a difference between what Paul and these theologians are doing. All three, though, were speaking to issues in their own time. Paul's reflection came out of the acute problem of what to make of God's covenant with Israel. Luther's reflection came in the context of long debate in the church over the conditions a person needed to meet in order to be saved. Barth read Paul in circumstances that had already led to one world war and would soon lead to another. Paul's point that God is faithful may have been muted, but it has surely not been lost when Luther claims we must depend on God alone, because we ourselves are unable to do anything to save ourselves. Nor has Paul's point that God is in the right been completely lost when Barth insists that God is above all human achievement, and so God alone may be trusted to judge that achievement for what it is. God's righteousness is essential to the reflection of Luther and Barth, although they do concentrate on individual (Gentile) humans. Certainly they make different points, and it is too much to claim that Paul actually says the things they say. But in their own way and in their own time, Luther and Barth have listened to Paul as well as to what Christians needed to hear. Their insights can still be helpful for reflecting on Christian life, even if we must learn to distinguish them from Paul's own thoughts. Seeing these differences highlights the need to bring God's righteousness to the forefront even when we talk about human unrighteousness.

3:9–20

Universal Sin

The question that the NRSV translates in verse 9 as "Are we any better off?" is only one word in Greek. The NRSV translation echoes the question of advantage in verse 1. It is possible, though, to read the one word in Greek to refer not to advantage but to disadvantage. Because the Greek verb can be read in the passive, the question could be asking something like "Are we bettered?" (surpassed by someone else).[11] In other words, "Are we worse off" (than someone else)? Taking the passive into account, Paul is raising a different kind of question than he did in verse 1. When asked if there is any advantage to being a Jew, Paul says yes, but then he goes on to point out the vulnerability of that advantage, namely that by not fulfilling the task entrusted to them, the Jews are open to God's judgment. Considering that vulnerability, one might well ask if Gentiles are better off not having the law because they neither have to obey it nor be held accountable by it. If Paul's question is read as "Are we bettered?" he is taking the situation to the next logical step, asking if there is disadvantage to being Jewish (if the Gentile situation is better than theirs). To this question, Paul says no.[12]

Even though the one-word question is open to quite different translations, the matter Paul introduces with it is strikingly clear. Whether talking about advantage or disadvantage, Paul insists that neither Jews nor Greeks are in a better position than the other. Both groups alike are "under the power of sin." To support this claim that all are under sin, Paul offers a series of quotations taken from different materials (many of them psalms) in the Septuagint. Paul is citing texts that are considered holy and authoritative for all followers of Jesus Christ, whether Jewish or Gentile. Neither group could possibly have an advantage over the other because Scripture is quite clear

---

The expression "all are under sin" must be taken in a spiritual sense; that is to say, not as men appear in their own eyes or in those of others, but as they stand before God. They all are under sin, those who are manifest transgressors in the eyes of men, as well as those who appear righteous in their own sight and before others.

Luther, *Commentary on Romans*, 69.

---

11. Robert Jewett, *Romans: A Commentary*, Hermeneia (Minneapolis: Fortress Press, 2007), 256–57.
12. Ibid., 257.

that "no one" is righteous. The evidence from Scripture is overwhelming and could leave neither group in doubt.

Paul moves from this chain of scriptural evidence for the universality of sin to return to the law. The law speaks to those who are "under" it (3:19), namely, the Jews. Paul has already said that those who are under the law will be judged by it, and he has said that those who do not have the law will be judged according to their consciences, where what God requires has been written internally. So no one can beg to be excused from judgment; no one can escape being held accountable by God.

It is perplexing that Paul next (3:20) says no one will be justified in God's sight by "deeds prescribed by the law" (*ergōn nomou*: works of the law) when he said in 2:13 that the doers of the law will be justified. This is a complicated theological problem, and there are several things to keep in mind in trying to work out what Paul may have meant. Leander Keck points to the different contexts for each of these statements to offer one way through this problem. Paul's point in chapter 2 is about *who* will be justified. God's impartiality ensures that Jews and Gentiles alike can be justified, even though one group has the written law and the other does not. Because God justifies Jews and Gentiles alike, members of both groups are then capable of doing what the law requires (whether known from tablets or in hearts). They may all do the deeds they know are faithful expressions of their knowledge of and relationship with God. In this way they honor God as they should and are righteous rather than unrighteous (in the way Paul describes in 1:18–23). In chapter 3, Paul is working on a different matter: namely, *the basis for* justification.[13] His main point in this part of chapter 3 is the universality of the power of sin: Jews, who have the law, and Gentiles, who do not, dishonor God. Paul has already pointed out to both Gentiles (using the list of vices) and Jews (using the law) that no one can stand in judgment of another. God must act to break the power of sin so that we may honor God as we should. Doing the deeds prescribed by the law cannot break this power of sin, so those deeds cannot be the basis for justification. Paul, then, is not contradicting himself in 2:13

13. Keck, *Romans,* 99–101.

and 3:20; he is rather talking about matters that serve his argument in different ways.

It also bears reflection that one aspect of the different contexts in which Paul makes these statements is that chapter 2 talks about being "repaid" according to deeds on the Day of Judgment. The deeds prescribed by the law may not be able to acquit us before God, but they may very well represent how our lives have been lived. God's pleasure (Well done, good and faithful servant) or God's displeasure (wrath) may be expressed commensurate to deeds. This is not the same as an acquittal, but it is a kind of judgment in that it is an assessment of our lives.

Another important consideration in making sense of this apparent contradiction is that Paul's phrase *ergōn nomou*, works of the law, used in 3:20 but not in 2:13, may have had a much more restricted meaning than the "good deeds" that many today consider to be "works." James Dunn shows that some Qumran writings use a phrase like this to refer to those particular deeds that set off the community as distinctive.[14] The general obligation to follow the law becomes focused in specific laws. For many Jews of the first century, that focus would be dietary laws and the observance of Sabbath.[15] These laws could be influencing the problems among the Roman followers of Jesus that Paul addresses at the end of his letter, so he may be using this phrase in the way Dunn has found. Because Paul uses this phrase after his discussion of circumcision and boasting in a special relationship, Paul's point may be that the faithfulness (*pistis*) by which we are acquitted does not come to expression simply by following these distinctive laws, so it is not restricted to those who identify themselves with the community marked off by those laws. None is righteous, no one has an advantage, no one can boast. All are justified by another kind of faithfulness (*pistis*). In this way, God is the God of the Gentiles as well as the Jews.

In considering these two statements about justification in 2:13 and 3:20, it is important to find a way to hold a number of ideas together: namely, that Paul has a favorable view of "doing" the law,

---

14. James D. G. Dunn, *The New Perspective on Paul*, rev. ed. (Grand Rapids: Wm. B. Eerdmans Publishing Co., 2008), 462–63.

15. Daniel Boyarin, *Radical Jew*, 53.

but that Jews and Gentiles please God by "doing" the law in different ways. He recognizes all, Jew and Gentile alike, are under the power of sin and that all will be judged.

It may be easier for many people to grasp the idea that people should be judged according to their deeds than it is to grasp the scope and depth of sin as it has been portrayed in the Christian tradition. It is not hard to imagine that all people do some things they shouldn't do, but Christians have taken the claim that sin is universal to be more than a claim that everyone occasionally does something wrong. Christian theologians have used Paul's earlier point that idolatry and ingratitude give rise to unrighteous behaviors to examine what goes wrong internally before sin is manifested in actions. (See "Further Reflections: Original Sin," below). The scope and power of this internal problem has received a great deal of attention from theologians.

This kind of reflection on a person's interior life takes us, of course, into the realm of individual salvation, which new perspectives often warn against. It may not be entirely inappropriate, though, that theologians have gone in this direction. After all, Paul talks about how Gentiles are circumcised inwardly and how their consciences both guide them and accuse them of sin. As Christianity became an essentially Gentile religion, it is not surprising that these inner standards would become important for thinking about relationship to God.

So Luther is drawn by Paul's letter to examine the motives for our actions. He explains how the law brings knowledge of sin in two ways. First, the law informs us of what sin is. Second, our experience of trying to fulfill the law shows us how much we love sin, because when we obey the law not because we want to but because we have to, we show that we love something more than God's law. We recognize how our inclinations direct us away from the good that God's law intends.[16] The attraction to sin is so strong that when we are told to give sin up, we resist. Even if we do avoid the sinful behavior, we still want it, so we are only grudgingly obedient. When we obey the law to avoid punishment or to gain the approval of others, we are not

16. Luther, *Commentary on Romans*, 76.

obeying out of a sincere desire to please God. Because we still long for what the law denies us, we participate in some level of rebellion. By becoming an occasion for rebellion, the law brings to our attention that sin still exercises power in our lives.

Barth's understanding of the universality of sin is equally serious. The lesson Barth gains from Paul's words is not about motive, though, but about inadequacy. The advantage of having the law is that it puts us in a position to recognize our ignorance of God. The law removes all "romantic sentimentality" about God and gives us genuine awe. No human can be justified by deeds prescribed by the law, because all human work is inadequate when we stand before God. Deeds can give us "no security or rest or excuse." Once deprived of every security, we know we depend utterly on God's favor or disfavor. The law, then, does not give us security in what we have accomplished but rather directs us to God alone and shows God to be judge.[17]

Although these reflections go beyond what Paul has said, they add dimensions that have been important for Christian understanding of the human problem. Not only is sin universal, but humans can overcome neither their sinfulness nor their inadequacy before God. This realization ought to make humans turn to God as their only help. Grace can be recognized more fully as gift when we understand how seriously we need it.

FURTHER REFLECTIONS
The Power of Sin

Paul does not actually use the Greek word for "power" in verse 9 and simply says that we are "under sin." Beverly Gaventa has argued that it is not inappropriate to infer "power" in this text, because Paul talks throughout the letter of sin as a force that needs to be defeated, often characterized as the subject of active verbs.[18] Sin is not simply behaviors (specific transgressions) but is also the influence behind

---

17. Barth, *Epistle to the Romans*, 88–91.
18. Beverly Roberts Gaventa, "The Cosmic Power of Sin in Paul's Letter to the Romans," in *Our Mother Saint Paul* (Louisville, KY: Westminster John Knox Press, 2007), 125–36.

the behaviors. As we saw in the comments for 1:18–32, there is some fundamental problem that gives rise to the actions we call sins.

Christian theologians have long recognized that people need not only to be forgiven but also need to be set free, and so they have talked about both the guilt and power of sin. Although the power of sin is seen as enslaving and needs to be defeated, theologians often describe it as working on us not by coercion but by attraction. One of the mysteries of sin is that we so often want things that turn out to be bad for ourselves and others. So desire has become an area much discussed by theologians.

One word that has been used much in the discussion of desire is "concupiscence." That word is commonly taken to be about sexual desire, but it is more than that. Sexual yearning is a good (maybe premiere) example of this desire, but we can also yearn for other things that lead us into sinful behavior. Whether or not desire itself is sinful has been debated in Christian theology, and the *Joint Declaration on the Doctrine of Justification* between Lutherans and Roman Catholics had to work through this issue carefully. Roman Catholics do not see desire that is controlled as sinful while Lutherans refer instead to "'controlled sin' (*peccatum regnatum*)."[19] Both agree, though, that the struggle with desire is lifelong, and so Christians are "continuously exposed to the power of sin" and in need of forgiveness.[20]

Christians rejoice that Jesus Christ breaks the power of sin and by doing so allows us to live in a way that is pleasing to God. It is Christ's breaking of the power of sin that allows Christians to rule or control their desires rather than be ruled or controlled by them. When they are not consumed by desire for things that are less than God, they are also free to love God above all else.

> **He breaks the power of canceled sin, He sets the prisoner free.**
>
> Charles Wesley, "O for a Thousand Tongues to Sing" (1739), *The United Methodist Hymnal* (Nashville: Abingdon Press, 1989), #57.

19. *Joint Declaration on the Doctrine of Justification*, appendix commentary for 4.4, http://www.vatican.va/roman_curia/pontifical_councils/chrstuni/documents/rc_pc_chrstuni_doc_31101999_cath-luth-joint-declaration_en.html.
20. Ibid.

The weight of Christian tradition has talked about the power of sin over individuals, but more recently, theologians have begun to recognize how sin exerts power through social systems. Even when thinking about the sin of individuals, sin always affects more than the sinner. We live in community, and sin ripples through relationships to harm many who are not directly involved. The network of relationships that constitutes a community is affected by individual behaviors, but it is also affected by common practices, social conventions, and institutional structures.

These impersonal systems take on and perpetuate sinfulness that originated with the actions and ideas of individual persons: for instance, prejudicial stereotypes and positions of privilege first gained by exploitation. Even after the individuals who originated the sin are gone, the identities of people in subsequent generations are formed in these social systems, and so they become complicit in those systems. For instance, later generations may benefit from privilege that was gained by earlier generations through explicit oppression. The people in later generations are not making individual choices that seem sinful to them, but they enjoy the benefits of their position. Especially if their position contributes still to exploitation of others, their participation in the system involves them in the sin of the system. The power that sin exerts through systems is particularly effective because people may not even be aware of the power that sin is exercising. It just seems the "way things are," and maybe even the "way things should be." Nonetheless, harm is done, both to humans and to relationship with God.

Because the situation Paul addressed in his time included systemic issues, such as questions of ethnic privilege and imperial exploitation, the letter to the Romans ought to be read with attention to what it may have to say to these subtle forms of sin's power in our time as well.

3:21–5:11

Sin and Justification

3:21–31

Justification

New and old perspectives often clash over interpretation of justification, which is a central idea in these verses. The courtroom scene that Paul uses to talk about the day of judgment in 2:1–11 is reinforced by language in 3:19–20 that brings to mind a speechless defendant being held accountable.[1] This forensic image has given theologians, especially Protestant theologians, a rich metaphor for imputed righteousness in justification. The traditional view of this courtroom scene is that individuals stand before God in order to receive a decision about guilt that will determine their personal ultimate destinies—who will be saved and who will be damned. New perspectives that pay close attention to the sociohistorical context in which Paul writes call attention to other aspects of the text that a traditional theology of imputed justification often ignores. For instance, they remind us that for Paul, one of the most important things that needed to be put right was the relationship between Jew and Gentile among the followers of Jesus in Rome.

Justification in the old view has always been about right relationship, but it has focused on that relationship so much in terms of guilt and pardon that it has lost sight of other dimensions of right relationship. N. T. Wright calls attention to the covenant background of right relationship that Paul would have known. God is righteous in being faithful to the covenant promises, and God's promises were not only to Israel. Yes, God chose Israel and gave this nation a special

---

1. C. E. B. Cranfield, *The International Critical Commentary on the Holy Scriptures of the Old and New Testaments: The Epistle to the Romans*, ed. J. A. Emerton and C. E. B. Cranfield, 2 vols. (Edinburgh: T. & T. Clark, 1973), 1:196–97.

commission. It is favored and blessed to have been chosen by God for this purpose. God made covenant with Israel and those promises will be fulfilled, but one of the promises was that Israel would be a blessing to all the other nations. God has not only made promises *to* Israel, God has made a promise *through* Israel: that the nations will be blessed. This promise, too, needs to be fulfilled.[2]

A courtroom may seem an unlikely place for fulfilling a covenant, but Wright explains that one way of understanding the verdict of the judge is as a pronouncement that puts one "in good standing in the community."[3] Questions that are raised by matters such as circumcision and works of the law have to do with who is in the community and how one can tell who is in it. In the situation that Paul knew, circumcision and obligation to follow the requirements of the law divided Jew and Gentile. If God's intention was to create one community (Wright says a single family), then these divisions had to be overcome. God's righteousness is shown in how God creates this single community and thereby honors God's promise.

Paul's conviction is that these divisions have been overcome in Jesus Christ. To see how, it is important to recognize a particularly troublesome translation difficulty in the Greek text. The phrase in 3:22 that the NRSV translates "faith in Jesus Christ" could also be translated "faithfulness of Jesus Christ." Two things explain how these translations could be so different. First, the word *pistis* has a range of meanings (see comments for 1:16-17, pp. 20-26) that includes both "faith" and "faithfulness." Second, the Greek does not have a preposition between the word *pistis* and the name Jesus Christ. The text uses a form (the genitive) of the name that means simply "of Jesus Christ." Even in English, one can see that the word "of" can function in different ways. The phrase "love of God" can mean both love for God (God is the object of someone's loving) or the love God has for someone else (God is the subject doing the loving). The NRSV has translated "of Jesus Christ" to make Jesus Christ the object of faith. But what if Jesus Christ was the subject doing the "faithing"? Then Jesus would be the one who is faithful—best understood as a

2. N. T. Wright, *Justification: God's Plan and Paul's Vision* (Downers Grove, IL: IVP Academic, 2009), 211-16.
3. Ibid., 213.

faithfulness that includes trusting obedience to the point of death on a cross, not simply belief but enacted trust and loyalty.

It is not clear from syntax which translation of this phrase is preferable, so exegetical and contextual issues must also be considered.[4] To take those matters into consideration is to become involved in questions about what matters for interpretation, so those issues may not yield a clear-cut answer either. We do well to keep the ambiguity of the phrase in mind. To continue to develop the idea of covenant that Wright believes is important for understanding righteousness, let us read the Greek as the faithfulness of Jesus (keeping in mind that the ambiguity allows us also to think about our own faith/faithfulness). For Wright, Jesus is central to how God fulfills God's covenantal promise. He is the "faithful Israelite" through whom God acts to fulfill God's plan to bless the world through Israel.[5] Giving Israel the law was intended for this blessing as part of the way God would work through Israel, but as we have seen, in 3:9–20, the law also served to mark off Jews as a distinct community. Jewish distinctiveness was in tension with the idea of a universal community, so God is working apart from the law to fulfill part of the covenant promise. God will bless the nations through Jesus Christ. The faithfulness of Jesus Christ is for (the benefit of) all who believe—or taking into account the range of meaning of words based on *pistis*, for the benefit of all who are faithful. The word "faithful" has the advantage in English of covering a broader range of response than "believe" does, including the way we enact our trust and belief. Keeping in mind that Paul introduces his gospel in 1:3–4 by clearly speaking of Jesus in terms of being king and Lord, the appropriate response of believing what Paul says about Jesus would be to give him allegiance, that is, faithfulness and obedience.

This revised way of fulfilling the plan is "apart from the law." This could be both because the nations do not put themselves under the law—that is, they do not live as Jews—to be blessed and because even for the Jews under it, the law has not kept them from being

---

4. Arland J. Hultgren, "*Pistis Christou*: Faith in or of Christ?" appendix 3 in *Paul's Letter to the Romans: A Commentary* (Grand Rapids: Wm. B. Eerdmans, Publishing Co., 2011), 623–61.

5. Wright, *Justification*, 204.

under the power of sin (see comments for 7:7–13, pp. 122–26). But it is attested by the law and the prophets because these Scriptures point to the Messiah, who Jesus is. God's righteousness is disclosed for all who are faithful, whether Jew or Gentile ("For there is no distinction," 3:22). This echoes the theme as it is stated in 1:17. The righteousness of God is revealed through the faithfulness of Jesus for those who are faithful. Followers of Jesus Christ, whether they are of Jewish or Gentile origin, are justified by grace through the redemption that is in Jesus Christ.

This reading of Paul raises christological issues that the church spent centuries developing but that were not yet decided in his time. Much later, councils would settle on an understanding of the person of Jesus Christ in a doctrine of incarnation that was closely connected to the doctrine of the Trinity. Together, these doctrines would indicate that Jesus was not a subordinate, separate agent from God. Paul could have no knowledge of such conciliar decisions, but this reading does connect God and

> **Jesus Christ is God's own covenant righteousness shown in his faithful obedience to death on behalf of the lost world.**
>
> A. Katherine Grieb, *The Story of Romans: A Narrative Defense of God's Righteousness* (Louisville, KY: Westminster John Knox Press, 2002), 38.

Jesus quite closely. The righteousness of God is revealed, and God's righteousness is God's faithfulness to God's covenant promises. If God's righteousness is revealed through the faithfulness of Jesus, then God's faithfulness is revealed through Jesus' faithfulness. In other words, through Jesus' faithfulness, God is revealing God's own faithfulness. It is through Jesus' faithfulness in carrying out the covenant on behalf of Israel that God fulfills God's covenant promises. In this way, Jesus' actions are God's actions. Although not stated in traditional incarnational or Trinitarian terms, this close association suggests that Jesus is sharing in God's agency. The commitment that Jesus reveals God will be developed doctrinally in later theology.

The other major area of Christology, the study of the work of Christ, is also anticipated in these verses. Unlike questions about the person of Christ, atonement questions were never settled by councils, and many atonement understandings have existed alongside one another in Christian history. Paul does not provide a fully articulated explanation of atonement, but he does firmly hold that it takes place "in Christ Jesus." For anyone familiar with Jewish practices, the language that Paul uses (*hilastērion*, 3:25) would have called to mind the ark of the covenant and the Day of Atonement.[6] Paul has made a clear and compelling argument that sin is a universal problem, and it is this problem that God must address in order to make the world right. God dealt with Israel's sins through "sacrifices, prayers, and repentance,"[7] and Paul, by calling to mind the ritual in which the priest sprinkles blood on the lid of the ark on the Day of Atonement, is claiming that in some way Jesus' death was a sacrifice, a means used by God to deal with sin by forgiving the one who sinned so that she or he may regain uprightness before God.

The word *hilastērion* was also used in 4 Maccabees 17:22 to refer to voluntary martyrdom, and if Paul knew of this use, it would have made the word particularly apt for talking about Jesus' death.[8] Paul does not seem concerned with explaining how a sacrifice of atonement works—in fact he would hardly have needed to, since the pervasiveness of sacrifice in the culture ensured that people grasped the idea that sacrifice changed situations. Instead, his point is that this sacrifice shows God's righteousness. The sins that God has previously "passed over" in patient forbearance are now forgiven, so God may rightly justify sinners: that is, pronounce them to be in right standing before God and in the community.

Another translation issue affects the way one understands the sinners who are justified. The old perspective has influenced the NRSV translation of 3:26 to say that God justifies "the one who has faith in Jesus." As in 3:22, though, it is possible that this phrase refers to Jesus' faithfulness, so Leander Keck suggests this translation: "the one who lives out of [or on the basis of] the faithfulness of Jesus."[9] In this reading, the sinners who are justified are the ones who live by faithfulness to the faithfulness of Jesus.

6. Leander E. Keck, *Romans,* Abingdon New Testament Commentaries (Nashville: Abingdon Press, 2005), 108.
7. Pamela Eisenbaum, *Paul Was Not a Christian: The Original Message of a Misunderstood Apostle* (New York: HarperOne, 2009), 221.
8. Keck, *Romans,* 109.
9. Ibid., 113.

Paul sees Jesus Christ as the means through which God works in order to accomplish what God has intended all along: the making right of a world gone wrong. Sin exerts power in the world gone wrong, but Jesus Christ is the means of dealing with that sin. This means is "effective through faith" so it is available to Gentiles as well as Jews who follow Jesus. Atonement is reconciliation, making "at one" those who have been torn apart. God's lawcourt pronouncement of justification restores right relationship with God, and because it has been made on the basis of Jesus Christ rather than the law, it forms a new community for those who follow Jesus that makes no distinction between Jew and Gentile. Through this sacrifice, they are made "at one" with God and also with one another. This acquittal has relevance for more than individual salvation; it also matters for how the community is able to live together.

Developing a reading that highlights *pistis* as faithfulness may at first raise concerns about violating the longstanding distinction between faith and works (especially where faith is taken primarily to be assent to doctrine). But if one remembers that faith is not only believing but also trusting (see "Further Reflections: Faith as Believing and Trusting"), then the difference between saying we are justified by faith or by faithfulness is not so large. It is hard to see how a Christian could be faithful to Jesus' own faithfulness without some belief that Jesus is indeed the means through which God deals with sin and makes the world right. The lack of clarity about the meaning of *pistis* may at first seem daunting and even frustrating, but the wide range of what Paul might mean by faith (*pistis*) offers an opportunity to reflect on how our beliefs about the world and about God shape the way we actually lead our lives.

Paul begins another conversation with the imaginary partner in 3:27–31 to work out some implications of what Paul has said. The leading question is about boasting, which had a more prominent place in the ancient world than in ours. Our society can encourage and reward humility (even people who are proud may display in public a false modesty when they know that is expected). In the Roman Empire, though, honor was greatly desired, and people competed for honor by boasting about their accomplishments. Boasting was an expected part of life because pursuing honor was a noble goal.[10] In addition, Rome was "the boasting champion of the ancient world."[11] The question arises naturally, then, for this group of followers. If the one advantage that Jews can claim is having been entrusted with the law, but Jesus Christ discloses God's righteousness apart from the law, then what becomes of the honor they could claim? It is excluded.

Why is boasting excluded? The "law of works" is not what excludes boasting. It is the "law of faith" that does so. The language that Paul uses is not at all clear and has prompted much reflection about what he could mean in using "law," "works," and "faith" in this way. *Nomos* can mean "principle" as well as "law," and Paul seems to be capitalizing on this double meaning. What law/principle excludes boasting? Not the law/principle of works, and Paul reminds the reader he has already said a person is justified apart from the "works prescribed by the law" (*ergōn nomou*). Because this phrase could at times refer to distinctive markers of the community (see comments on 3:9–20, pp. 57–64), Paul may be pointing out that the very works that lead to boasting of distinctiveness among the Jewish followers in Rome cannot be the grounds for excluding boasting. It is, rather, the law/principle of faith/faithfulness that excludes boasting. Because the atoning sacrifice of Jesus Christ makes forgiveness available to Gentile and Jew alike, faithfulness to Jesus does not allow either group to boast over the other.[12] If we accept that God is justifying Gentile as well as Jewish followers in Jesus Christ, so that the one God is not the God of the Jews only, then no superior position can be gained over the other. Whether circumcised or uncircumcised, they are all justified by their faithfulness to the faithfulness of Jesus Christ.

Because he has been using the word *nomos* in a dual sense, the next question that arises is about what happens to the law that established covenant with the Jews. Has it been abolished or rendered ineffective by faith? Paul's answer is that this law is upheld (3:31). God acted in Jesus Christ to demonstrate faithfulness to the covenant, and the instrument that established the covenant is the law.

10. Robert Jewett, *Romans: A Commentary*, Hermeneia (Minneapolis: Fortress Press, 2007), 49–51.
11. Ibid., 295.
12. Ibid., 291, 298.

It is not the law that is excluded but boasting. Jew and Gentile alike are called to respond faithfully to the way of life that is established by covenant relationship with God. Because Jesus is our Lord, he deserves our faithfulness, and we show ourselves truly to be his followers by following him faithfully. If we are indeed faithful followers, our lives will be lived in accordance to our allegiance to this Lord, who has summed up the law for us as loving God with everything that we are and loving our neighbor as ourselves (Matt. 22:34–40). We show our allegiance by following these commandments. What we do, then (our deeds), will display the measure of our faithfulness. On the Day of Judgment, how faithful we have been will come to light, and we will then be repaid accordingly. Christian faithfulness does not "overthrow" the law but "upholds" it.

Since Christianity has become essentially a Gentile religion, it is easy to interpret Jew and Gentile in verses 29–30 as Jew and Christian and so take Paul's words to indicate the need for Jews to have the same faith as Christians. In reading this letter we need to keep in mind how different was the context for the original recipients than for us. In Paul's time, Jews and Gentiles could both follow Jesus Christ, and in Rome the special problem was how they could function together as a single community. To do so, the followers of Jesus, whether Jewish or Gentile, certainly needed to share the same faith. After Paul's lifetime Jews and Christians went through a time of defining themselves over against one another and developed into distinct religions. Now that Christianity is thought of as a Gentile religion, Paul's description of God's disclosure apart from the law is especially apt for those who read his letter as Scripture. It has been easy for Christians to take Paul to be supporting Gentile faith and discounting the law for Jews. This way of reading him is the "de-Judaizing" of Paul that the new perspective warns against. As recent scholarship shows how much Paul's Jewishness influenced his ideas and how he never intended to diminish Judaism in any way, Christians should take care not to use this text to diminish Judaism now.

Christians may be able to learn something from Paul regarding the relationship between Judaism and Christianity, if we take the time to understand him in his own Jewish context. To use his insights appropriately we will have to be alert to when his observations best fit the situation of Jewish followers of Jesus in the first century rather than the Judaism that we encounter in the twenty-first century. Perhaps the most important insight we should listen to is the one he speaks about throughout his letter. Christians exist because God has been faithful enough to take the situation of Gentiles into account and find a way to bless the nations apart from the law. Christians should fully expect God to be faithful enough to find a way to bless the people of Israel in their own situation.

FURTHER REFLECTIONS
Christians and the Law

The first Scriptures that Christians used were the Jewish Scriptures (read by many in Greek instead of Hebrew). This was the case both because the first followers of Jesus Christ were Jews and because it took some time for the materials that we call the New Testament to be written, collected, and considered part of the Bible. As these new materials were gaining the status of Scripture among Christians, theologians had to consider the status of the Jewish Scriptures as Christian texts. When Marcion (ultimately deemed a heretic) denied that the Jewish Scriptures were to be included among Christian holy, authoritative texts, the reaction against his bold move helped to solidify Christian commitment to retain the Jewish Scriptures in the Christian canon. Although Irenaeus used the categories of old testament (covenant) and new testament (covenant), his opposition to Marcion shows he would deny vigorously any attitude that distinguishes and contrasts the God of the Old Testament and the God of the New Testament (an attitude that is unfortunately expressed by some Christians today). It was and is crucial for maintaining the integrity of the revelation of the Bible to understand that all these texts bear witness to the one God.

The Jewish Scriptures have three basic categories of texts: Law, Prophets, and Writings. In this categorization, the first five books (Genesis, Exodus, Leviticus, Numbers, and Deuteronomy), known as the Pentateuch or Torah, constitute the Law. These books certainly contain prescriptions and instructions of the Sinaitic law, but they also contain many narratives. The narratives belong together with the Sinaitic law in the sense that they give guidance for how to live in relationship to God, but they do so by inviting us to imagine the consequences of our actions for relationship with God rather than by specifying duties. Living according to the law (torah, meaning instruction) can be considered to be more than simply following rules. It can also mean learning the stories well enough that we allow them to shape us to be people of God.

Because the law (torah), though, does specify many duties, Christians have had to reflect on their obligation to the laws in the Law (Torah). The early decision that Gentiles who followed Jesus should remain uncircumcised meant that Christians were not bound to follow every regulation written in the Torah (for instance, regulations regarding clean and unclean food). But surely other duties, prominently the Ten Commandments, did still apply to Christians. Thomas Aquinas distinguished between moral, ceremonial, and judicial precepts. With these distinctions, it was easy for Christians to see that they were bound to moral duties in Scripture but not laws regarding things such as manner of worship or civil matters.

With the Reformation and the Protestant affirmation that we are saved by faith and not by works, even obligation to the moral law became a matter for further reflection. Both the Lutheran and Reformed traditions developed ways of talking about the use of the law for Christians that did not imply being saved by works. In the Lutheran tradition, the Formula of Concord (1577) speaks of three uses of the law: (1) to restrain sinful people and maintain discipline, (2) to bring sinful people to recognize their sins, and (3) to guide justified believers. Calvin also spoke of these three uses, although he transposed the first two in his list.[13] In this way, the Reformers could speak of the usefulness of the law without claiming that obedience to it would be salvific. These Reformation traditions that looked to Scripture as the rule of faith and practice could honor the importance of the law without compromising their conviction about salvation by faith.

13. John Calvin, *Institutes of the Christian Religion*, 2.7.6–12; ed. John T. McNeill, trans. Ford Lewis Battles, 2 vols., Library of Christian Classics (Philadelphia: Westminster Press, 1960), 354–61.

One of the dangers that has always accompanied the conviction that Christians are free from obedience to the law is antinomianism (no obligation to follow laws), and although this danger existed even before the Reformation, it became a more attractive tendency after the Reformation. John Wesley, who lived long enough after Luther and Calvin to have seen this tendency express itself regularly in neglect of moral and spiritual discipline, taught that saving faith "established" the law.[14] He maintained the commitment that we are justified by faith, not by works, but he also maintained that God actually expects us to obey the moral law. He dared to talk about following the discipline of living a holy life, not to gain God's favor, but as a response to God's justification and as an expression of love for and gratitude to God.

It may be helpful to Protestants who have difficulty affirming obedience to the law to remember that the Torah is more than regulations. If living according to the law includes living according to the narratives, then what we do as Christians is not simply obey but find our place in the story of the people of God. It takes a certain kind of life to live appropriately in that story, and we are warned by poor examples in the narratives as well as encouraged by good ones as to what kind of life is expected by God. Even with our freedom in Christ, Christians can delight in the law of the Lord and meditate on it day and night (Ps. 1:2).

4:1–12

Abraham

After Paul affirms upholding the law, he does not talk about Moses, through whom God gave the law to Israel, but rather about Abraham. By doing so, Paul reminds the reader of God's covenant with Israel even before the law was given. Paul does not use the word "covenant," but he is making use of the covenant stories in Genesis 15 and 17. Abraham is the ancestor of the circumcised, and the covenant God made with Abraham initiated the practice of

---

14. John Wesley, Sermons 35 and 46, "The Law Established through Faith," Discourses I and II, *The Works of John Wesley*, vol. 2, Sermons II, 20–43.

circumcision as the sign of that covenant (Gen. 17). So Abraham is clearly the ancestor of the Jews, but God also promised Abraham would be the father of "nations" (Gen. 17:5–6). Because "nations" is the word commonly used by Jews to refer to Gentiles, Abraham serves to support not only what Paul wants to say about Jews but also about Gentiles. Paul will explain how God's covenant with Abraham extends to *all* his descendants, Jew and Gentile alike.

> God's purpose in calling Abraham was to bless the whole world, to call out a people from Gentiles as well as Jews.
>
> Wright, *Justification*, 118.

Abraham is the Jews' ancestor "according to the flesh," a phrase Paul used in 1:3 to refer to Jesus' descent from David. Jews can claim direct physical descent from Abraham, and they share with him the sign of the covenant in their flesh (circumcision). Abraham also has something in common with Gentiles. At the time that Abram was called by God to leave his kindred and go to Canaan, Abram could have been considered among the "ungodly" (4:5, *asebē*—without reverence for the true God), the same word used in Romans 1:18 to describe the situation of those who know God to some degree but worship images.[15] In other words, before his call, Abram would have been just another human being in the same situation as all the rest, which also means he was in the same situation the Gentiles were in at the time Paul wrote. But Abram became Abraham, the one whom God promised to bless as the "ancestor of a multitude of nations" (Gen. 17:4–5).

If Abram/Abraham had been justified (put in right standing with God) by his works, then he could boast, that is he could claim honor due to his achievements. But he cannot boast before God. He can claim no honor as his due because he has no achievement to count as his own. When Paul explains that God "reckoned" (4:3), he uses a word (*logizesthai*) that was often used in mathematics and commerce that means to calculate or credit. This word can also be extended to thought processes (to count as, or consider or regard).[16]

15. Wright, *Justification*, 220.
16. Keck, *Romans*, 123.

Paul expands this image of commerce by talking about wages. In normal business, a person works a number of hours or fulfills a contracted order or task and then expects to be paid. Wages are not paid as a gift but rather as compensation for services rendered. It is easy for us to think in such contractual terms. The way God justifies the ungodly, though, is different. The one who trusts has that trust counted as righteousness.

The difference between earned wages and a gift has been essential to the way that Christians think about how God saves us. The word Paul uses in 4:4, translated in the NRSV as "gift," is *charis*. This is the Greek word also used by Paul for what we now call "grace." Grace is a gift. To say that we are saved by grace is to say that our salvation is a gift. God does not owe it to us the way an employer owes an employee a wage for labor. God saves out of God's freedom to offer salvation, not because of any obligation. Paul is committed to understanding God's salvation as gift, but, as we have seen in comments on 2:1–16, he does not understand this commitment to rule out the place of deeds as our response to this gift. It is faith to which he draws attention here. Specifically, he needs to explain that faith can be counted or reckoned as righteousness.

> **Grace is something you can never get but only be given. There's no way to earn it or deserve it or bring it about any more than you can deserve the taste of raspberries and cream or earn good looks or bring about your own birth.**
>
> Frederick Buechner, *Wishful Thinking: A Theological ABC* (New York: Harper & Row, 1973), 33.

Because the law had not yet been given to Moses, Abraham could not possibly have been justified by works prescribed by the law. He obeyed God, but he did not do so by following the written prescriptions that were to come. In this, too, he is like the Gentiles about which Paul is concerned, who obey by following something unwritten rather than something written. Abraham was in right standing with God because he was faithful in his trust of God, so his faithfulness justified him.

Paul connects this idea to the opening verses of Psalm 32 (LXX 31). By quoting this psalm, he introduces the idea of forgiveness, an idea central to the traditional doctrine of justification. Forgiveness

fits within the image of commerce called to mind by the verb translated as "reckon" because debts can be forgiven. This image of can-
celing a debt has been used often in traditional theology to talk
about how God forgives sins. This view holds that because of our sin,
we owe something to God to put us back in good standing with God,
but we are unable to pay what we owe. Jesus pays the debt for us so
that we may be restored to right
relationship with God. We owe
God a righteous life, but the power
of sin is so strong that we cannot
live righteously, so Jesus' righteousness is counted as (reckoned as)
our righteousness. The image of
commerce becomes also a forensic
image when the forgiveness of jus-
tification is understood as pardon; we are acquitted of the charge of
sin because Jesus' righteousness has been counted as our own. This
is the idea of imputed righteousness. It is counted as our own when
we have faith, but faith is not the cause of our forgiveness. Our pardon is an act of God's grace. It is a gift, and not even our faith should
be seen as a work that earns pardon.

> **The plain scriptural notion of justification is pardon, the forgiveness of sins.**
>
> John Wesley, "Justification by Faith," II.5, in *The Works of John Wesley* (Nashville: Abingdon Press, 1986) I:189.

The idea of imputed righteousness has long raised the concern
that there is some undue "creative accounting" involved in simply
transferring Jesus' righteousness to sinful humans. It has also been
feared that it will lead to the mistaken impression that because
Jesus' righteousness is freely credited as not for anything people
have done, they do not have to think about or change how they live.
Such questions arise from an exchange mentality that stays close to
the commercial origin of the term Paul uses. The way the word gets
extended into thought processes may be more helpful for understanding something other than a transaction. Rather than trying
to make accounts balance without actual funds, God is "regarding"
something real in Abraham as the response that will put him in good
standing.[17] Seen in this way, Paul is not talking about transferring
righteousness into an empty account but rather is expressing an

17. John B. Cobb Jr. and David J. Lull, *Romans* (St. Louis: Chalice Press, 2005), 78.

understanding about what God regards as righteousness. What God "regards" as righteousness is also "imputation"—that is, a counting as—but it is not as exclusively about guilt as traditional theology has held. In the case of Abraham, God regards trust as righteousness rather than merely following commands. Abraham trusts God, and he even enacts that trust by doing what God has told him to do. Obedience, then, may be included in this idea, but Paul puts focus on something other than the act itself, much like Protestant theologians did when they talked about "good" works (see "Further Reflections: Faith and Good Works"). God's grace comes first in the gift of relationship that God offers to Abraham, then Abraham trusts and displays that trust in obedience. This is not a righteousness gained by obeying legal prescriptions, but God considers it righteousness. To be like Abraham, we also have to exhibit a trusting faithfulness in our own lives. Under this view, even though Abraham's trust is real, grace is still gift. Nothing Abraham does comes before God has acted, so it does not "earn" anything from God. God's recognition of his faith and God's willingness to understand it as righteousness is a gift. God considers as righteous whomever God wants and on whatever basis God decides.

The blessedness of forgiveness of which David speaks (4:6–8), Paul says, is not restricted to the circumcised but extends to the uncircumcised. Abraham's faithfulness was counted as righteousness before he was circumcised, and then circumcision became the sign and seal of what had already happened (4:10–11). By being justified before being circumcised, Abraham became the ancestor not only of the circumcised but also of all those who are faithful without being circumcised (4:11). The uncircumcised Gentiles have righteousness counted on their behalf by their faithfulness just as Abraham did. But this faithfulness is not restricted to the uncircumcised. When the circumcised live with the kind of faithfulness that Abraham had, they have Abraham as their ancestor not only in the flesh but also in the manner that the Gentiles do.

Protestant theologians have often seen Paul's description of Abraham as serving as a weighty example, even a pattern, of how Christians are justified by faith, not by works. His example is taken to illustrate the traditional Protestant understanding of the theology of justification, in particular to show how Jesus Christ's righteousness is imputed (reckoned) to us or counted on our behalf. As such, Abraham has become the model for how every individual sinner is accepted by God. These interpretations of Paul's letter have served to stress the graciousness of God's saving action toward us, and so they have played an important role in reminding us of the unearned gift of God's love and favor. In doing so, the traditional theological reading has had value.

Exclusive focus on this matter has obscured an insight that new perspectives want to bring out: namely, that Abraham is not simply a pattern for justification but the common father of Jew and Gentile. This is surely a point that Paul would have wanted the original recipients of this letter to hear. By showing the similarities between Abraham's situation and that of the Gentiles, Paul is showing the way that God is faithful to God's covenant promise to Abraham about being the father of a multitude of nations. The faithfulness of Gentile followers of Jesus to the faithfulness of Jesus shows them to be the spiritual descendants of Abraham. Gentiles share in Abraham's ancestry.

Paul intends to stress not uniformity, but unity in diversity. The pluralistic diversity of peoples in their ethnic and cultural variety is maintained, although in Christ this pluralism becomes nevertheless a unity.

J. C. Beker, "The Faithfulness of God and the Priority of Israel in Paul's Letter to the Romans," *The Harvard Theological Review* 79, nos. 1–3 (1986): 13.

For the Roman community to which Paul writes (in which Jews and Gentiles are having trouble living in unity), it is equally important to show (as Paul does) that even if a Jewish follower of Jesus is circumcised, he can also share in Abraham's faithfulness as well as his ancestry (4:12). So again, there is no distinction between Jew and Gentile because they both share Abraham in ancestry and faith.

FURTHER REFLECTIONS
Faith and Good Works

The way Paul distinguishes being justified by works from being justified by faith and his contrast between earning wages and receiving a gift has led to much theological reflection about what we do and whether we contribute anything to our salvation.

In Western Christianity, the question of how to regard the value of good works has a long and controversial history. In the early fifth century, Augustine and Pelagius argued over how to understand what human beings could do to be saved. Pelagius was alarmed by the moral laxity of many Christians, and he argued for human accountability. In order to be accountable, a person had to be able to choose between good and evil, and that choice would have consequences regarding salvation—a person affects her or his status before God by the choices she or he makes. Although this position has a "common sense" attraction, Augustine opposed it because he saw that it attributed the power to do good to natural human ability rather than to God's grace. Through his response to Pelagius, Augustine formulated positions (notably, on original sin and human freedom) that have shaped Christian thinking in the West for centuries. When a church council held at Carthage condemned Pelagius, the church clearly affirmed its commitment to God's grace as the source of good works.

Much later, with the Protestant Reformation, the question of what humans could do in order to be saved arose again in a divisive way. The Roman Catholic Church had adopted language of "merit," which suggested to some that humans were rewarded by God for doing something. Luther's reading of Paul's Epistle to the Romans, supported by his understanding of Augustine that we are utterly dependent on grace, led him to reject any suggestion that humans earn their salvation by anything that they do. As the two sides in the Reformation conflict worked out their positions in opposition to each other, this issue caused a breach that remained for centuries.

During this period of disagreement, Protestants have not denied that good works have a place in the life of a Christian, but they have given particular attention to what makes a work "good." Because it is possible for people to perform beneficial deeds even if they do not have hearts that are right with God, Protestant theologians have insisted that to be truly good, a work must be more than simply beneficial to someone. It must be done with the doer's will aligned to God's will, so that the only motivating desire is to please God. With this understanding, works can only be truly "good" when they follow from faith (from a complete trust in God), not when they are performed apart from faith. Only when we respond to God's grace in faith do we follow God's guidance with the joyful gratitude that transforms our actions into genuine offerings to God. Protestants have stressed the order of faith first, then works in order to preserve the dependence on grace that Augustine argued for. In doing so, they have not been as far from Catholic thinking as was once thought, and which twentieth-century ecumenical dialogue has been able to demonstrate.

> ". . . for God does not accept the person on account of his works, but He accepts the works on account of the (believing) person. He first accepts the person who believes in Him and then the works flowing from faith."
>
> Martin Luther, *Commentary on Romans*, trans. J. Theodore Mueller (Grand Rapids: Kregel Classics, 1976), 83.

Recently, with the signing of the *Joint Declaration on the Doctrine of Justification,* Roman Catholics and Lutherans have been able to speak together on this matter in a way that was not previously possible. This document states as their common understanding of justification, "Together we confess: By grace alone, in faith in Christ's saving work and not because of any merit on our part, we are accepted by God and receive the Holy Spirit, who renews our hearts while equipping us and calling us to good works."[18] Roman Catholics have not given up the language of merit, but they have clarified, "When Catholics affirm the 'meritorious' character of good works, they wish to say that, according to the biblical witness, a reward in heaven is promised to these works. Their intention is to emphasize the responsibility of persons for their actions, not to contest the character of these works as gifts, or far less to deny that justification always remains the unmerited gift of grace."[19] For their part, Lutherans have clarified, "When they view the good works of Christians as the fruits and signs of justification and not as one's own 'merits', they nevertheless also understand eternal life in accord with the New Testament as unmerited 'reward' in the sense of the fulfillment of God's promise to the believer."[20]

18. *Joint Declaration on the Doctrine of Justification*, 3, ¶15, http://www.vatican.va/roman_curia/ pontifical_councils/chrstuni/documents/rc_pc_chrstuni_doc_31101999_cath-luth-joint -declaration_en.html.
19. Ibid., 4.7, ¶38.
20. Ibid., 4.7, ¶39.

Christianity in the West has been deeply marked by the struggle to think about how to understand the role of works in Christian life. Because Christianity in the East has so often been isolated from Western developments, it has not been touched in the same way by these controversies. Eastern Christians share, though, a concern that the role of works can be misunderstood. Christoforos Stavrapoulos explains,

> The Christian life comes into being with the sacraments and with holy works, those virtuous works which are done with a pure and holy motive in the name of Christ. At this point there is the need for special attention, because many Christians believe that good works and virtues are what save us and unite us with God. We must understand this point very well. The purpose of our struggles, our efforts, the purpose of the Christian life is not good works and virtues. This is so because they do not of themselves grant us theosis. The true purpose of the Christian life is that we receive the Holy Spirit as our own, which in turn divinizes our existence.... A work is good insofar as it is a means for a purpose, insofar as it serves to unite us with God, and insofar as it leads us to the reception and personal acceptance of divine grace.[21]

With Paul, we need to be clear that salvation is a gift. Although there may be different emphases in Christian traditions regarding human participation in God's saving work, it is God who saves. Our response to God's saving grace, however, is that in thanksgiving, we demonstrate our faithfulness to God by doing what God would have us do.

4:13–25

God's Promise Fulfilled

Paul shifts his argument from ancestry to inheritance. Genesis clearly states that Israel was promised land, but Paul says in 4:13 that Abraham and his descendants (literally "seed," *spermati*) will

---

21. Christoforos Stavrapoulos, "Partakers of Divine Nature," in *Eastern Orthodox Theology: A Contemporary Reader*, 2nd ed., ed. Daniel B. Clendenin (Grand Rapids: Paternoster Press, 2003), 189–90.

inherit "the world" (*kosmou*). To make such a claim at the time the
Roman Empire was conquering the known world was quite remarkable. Neither "world" in English nor *kosmos* in Greek simply indicates geography, though, and interpreters have extended its meaning
to other ideas. John Wesley takes "the world" to be another way of
talking about "the nations."[22] So for him, the use of this word underscores the inclusion of the Gentiles as heirs, as well as pointing to
Christ's rule of all things. John Calvin connected this word to the
expectation that in Christ "the fallen state of the whole world should
be repaired."[23] Both interpreters also infer from the text that Jesus
Christ is Abraham's descendant ("seed") according to the flesh, as
he was David's, so Jesus Christ is Abraham's heir (1:3). They closely
connect to Jesus Christ the fulfillment of the promise made to
Abraham.

Even if "seed" refers to Jesus Christ, though, the inheritance is not
restricted to a single person. The followers of Jesus who share in the
faithfulness of Abraham may claim Abraham as spiritual ancestor,
so through Jesus, the inheritance is shared with all Abraham's spiritual descendants, Jew and Gentile alike. In this way, God's covenant
promise is fulfilled. The many nations (Gentiles) who can claim
Abraham as their ancestor can also claim his inheritance.

Both Wesley and Calvin have seen that this inheritance has something to do with a change in the status quo of the world—a rule or
repair. In Greek, *kosmos* signals order, and as the Roman Empire
extended itself geographically, it was also extending its rule and
order. Because of this association with order, Robert Jewett connects the use of *kosmos* in 4:13 with the expectation that Christians
had for the kingdom of God.[24] When the will of God is done on the
earth, a new social order will be established. What the descendants
of Abraham inherit, then, is the rule of God.

Becoming an heir of this new reality is not a matter of adhering to laws but of faith. Paul gives two reasons in 4:14–15 why this
inheritance cannot be tied to legal adherence. If inheritance were

22. Wesley, *Explanatory Notes upon the New Testament* (repr., London: Epworth Press, 2000), 534.
23. John Calvin, *Commentaries on the Epistle of Paul the Apostle to the Romans*, trans. and ed. John
    Owen (Grand Rapids: Wm. B. Eerdmans Publishing Co., 1959), 169.
24. Jewett, *Romans*, 326.

determined by adhering to the law given at Sinai, then both the promise made to Abraham and his faithfulness in response to that promise (both of which occurred before the law was given to Moses) would be empty. Furthermore, by stating prescriptions and pro-scriptions, the law specifies rules that can be violated. When trans-gressions occur, God's wrath is invoked. Although the direct cause is transgression and not the law itself, the law, as Wesley says, which is intended for blessing, "becomes to us an occasion of wrath."[25]

Barth saw this potential to be the occasion for wrath not only with the law, but with any religious endeavor.[26] Religious ideas and prac-tices are intended to point beyond themselves to the reality of God, but instead of seeing them as a means to the transcendent, all too often people become attached to the ideas and practices themselves. When that happens, people seek security in their religion and expend energy trying to justify it. Because they seek security in religion instead of in the living God, they transgress. Although people can seek security in any activity, religion is more likely than any other activity to be mis-used in this way, so it has particularly dangerous potential for harm. Barth warned, though, against responding to that danger by replac-ing religion with anti-religious activities because they, too, offer false security. No human endeavor can offer true security, so we must depend on faith. Barth's reflections serve as an important reminder not to think that only the law is a problem, and they call us to self-examination about how we regard our own religious commitments.

This inheritance of which Paul speaks, then, depends on faith, which itself depends on grace. Inheritance is clearly a gift. It is not something owed because of adherence. Because this inheritance is not a matter of legal adherence, all Abraham's descendants (Jew and Gentile) can receive this gift because the faithfulness of Abraham is a possibility for all of them.

The promise to and faith response of Abraham, which originated the possibility of this inheritance, took place "in the presence of the God in whom he believed." Paul makes an affirmation about the God who evokes the kind of faith that Abraham and his heirs have. God is

25. Wesley, *Explanatory Notes*, 534.
26. Karl Barth, *The Epistle to the Romans*, trans. Edwyn C. Hoskyns (Oxford: Oxford University Press, 1933), 135–37.

the one who "gives life to the dead and calls into existence the things that do not exist." This description of God clearly references resurrection and the creation of the world in the beginning. The God who creates is the same God who resurrects. This God has power over death and nothingness, and so this God is worthy of our hope. At a time when Abraham and Sarah were childless, God promised to make Abraham ancestor of many nations—an outrageous promise that only a God who can make something out of nothing could deliver on. In the NRSV (4:18), the English phrase "hoping against hope" is used to translate the Greek, which is phrased a little differently. The original Greek has two prepositions, and Jewett translates it as "beyond hope in hope."[27] In other words, when the situation seemed beyond hope, Abraham nevertheless continued in hope. Because this hope is a trust that this God could fulfill even an outrageous promise, hope is also faith. This faith did not depend on his own situation (his age or Sarah's barrenness) but rather depended on the God who made the promise. So Abraham's faith did not weaken when he was confronted with the limitations of his existence (4:19). He continued to trust God because he was convinced of God's ability to do what he himself could not do. Furthermore, he "gave glory to God" (4:20) the opposite of the "ungodly" who do not honor God in 1:21–23.[28] Because he cannot boast in his own achievements, Abraham is in a position to honor God alone, as God should be honored. God reckoned Abraham's faith as righteousness not because of Abraham's own glory, but because Abraham glorified God.

> **Hope is trusting God in spite of all the evidence, then watching the evidence change.**
>
> Jim Wallis, *Faith Works: How Faith-Based Organizations Are Changing Lives, Neighborhoods, and America,* rev. ed. (New York: Random House Trade Publishing, 2001), 1.

When people hope and trust in the God who creates, faith becomes creative. Faithfulness sees and acts on God's possibilities in situations where no possibilities seem to exist. Relying on God to help us face the challenges we could never face by ourselves, Christians can follow Jesus wherever he leads. The things

---

27. Jewett, *Romans,* 335.
28. Grieb, *The Story of Romans,* 52.

that come about because of this faithfulness bring glory to God, and the faithful see them as God's achievements, not their own.

It was Abraham's hopeful, glorifying trust in God's ability to overcome a seemingly hopeless situation that was counted as righteousness (4:22). Paul asserts that just as this faith was counted on Abraham's behalf, our faithfulness to the same God (who did another outrageous thing by raising Jesus from the dead) will be counted as righteousness for us.

If being counted righteous makes us heirs of God's rule, it also calls us to live according to the rule that is our inheritance. Living according to God's order rather than the order of the present world will often put us at odds with the generally accepted way

> Let us then also glorify Him by faith as well as by works, that we may also attain to the reward of being glorified by Him.
>
> John Chrysostom, Homily VIII, *Homilies of S. John Chrysostom, Archbishop of Constantinople, on the Epistle of St. Paul the Apostle to the Romans,* 3rd ed., trans. by members of the English church (Oxford: James Parker and Co. and Rivingtons, 1877), 125.

of doing things. No wonder so many tasks God calls us to do seem hopeless! Trust in God, though, gives us the hope we need to persevere, glorifying God all the while.

As he has worked through a way of showing Jewish and Gentile followers of Jesus how they ought to regard one another as belonging to a common family, Paul has also left enduring insight for Christians of later generations about faithfulness, grace, and hope.

5:1–5

Peace, Hope, and Glory

The first eleven verses of chapter 5 serve both to draw a conclusion from what has already been said and to introduce the themes of the next chapters. I will treat these verses in two sections. These transitional verses have the tone of confession rather than argument, that is, they express deeply held conviction rather than build a case for that conviction. Paul uses rhetorical devices that would have been well known and effective in his time, such as using a term at the end of one phrase and then again at the beginning of the next phrase.

The use of heightened rhetoric in this section would have caught the attention of those who heard the letter read aloud and would have invited their affirmation.[29]

The first verse of this section contains a textual problem. Where the NRSV (5:1) translates "we have peace," the ancient manuscripts do not all have the same word. Some have *echomen*, which is the indicative assertion that the NRSV uses, but some have the subjunctive *echōmen*, which would be translated "let us have peace." The difference of one Greek letter in the word makes a considerable difference in meaning. The former is a statement of a present condition, the latter is an exhortation, encouraging the community to live peacefully. Because there is no further exhortation in this passage and recognizing the theological conviction that peace is a gift of God, most commentators prefer the simple statement of fact (we have peace). Jewett points out, though, that given the situation in Rome, with difficult relationships between Jewish and Gentile followers of Jesus, the exhortation "let us have peace" makes sense. Paul in fact clearly encourages peace in 14:19.[30] The ideas conveyed by the two translation possibilities, as different as they seem, may not necessarily be in conflict. If indeed we are justified and have the peace of God as gift, then we ought to live in peace with one another. There are social implications for the theological reality that we claim. How many times do the people who follow the Prince of Peace have to be encouraged to live in peace among themselves?

Peace was an important idea in the Roman Empire, which promised peace and security to its citizens. The empire gained peace through military victory, so peace was very explicitly related to war. Battle ended when Rome defeated its opponent and thereby established a relationship of domination between the conqueror and the conquered. Peace established a hierarchical relationship that fit well within the highly hierarchical social structure of the empire. Maintaining this kind of peace required a continual vigilance against attack, readiness of armed forces to respond, and suspicion of those who might use violence to throw off domination.

The Jewish understanding of *shalom*, which informs Paul's

---

29. Keck, *Romans*, 134–35.
30. Jewett, *Romans*, 348–49.

understanding of peace for Christians, goes far beyond this understanding. The word *shalom* certainly means in some contexts the absence of war or violence, but it also conveys a much wider range of ideas, including well-being, justice, and safety.[31] With this expansive meaning in mind, *shalom* describes a world that is not made up of conquerors and conquered but rather a world in which all have an equal opportunity to thrive. Peace that is gained when all have their needs met is quite different than a situation in which overt violence may be absent, but some are still exploited by others. The peace that *shalom* points to is informed by the eschatological vision of God's intent for all creation.

Whether we read "we have peace" or "let us have peace," it is this *shalom* peace we should have in mind. Both the peace that God gives and the peace that we are called to work for is the peace of wholeness and justice. Theologians have not always grasped this point. Luther understood the peace referred to in this verse to consist "properly in an appeased conscience and in confidence in God," so it referred to inner peace of an individual. Origen interpreted Paul's words to refer not only to peace within the individual but also to peace in the community. With regard to the individual, Origen points out that there can be no inner peace as long as we struggle against the law of God.[32] As long as we know what God wants but we continue to seek something else, we will be internally conflicted. Community dissension can also produce this kind of internal conflict. As long as we wish ill for another when we know God wants us to wish her or him well, neither the community nor

> A church that prays for peace, serves its community, uses money ethically, cares for the environment and cultivates good relations with others can become an instrument for peace.
>
> World Council of Churches, *An Ecumenical Call for Just Peace,* ¶ 29, http://www.overcomingviolence.org/fileadmin/dov/files/iepc/resources/ECJustPeace_English.pdf.

31. Daniel L. Smith-Christopher, "Shalom," in *The New Interpreter's Dictionary of the Bible,* vol. 5 (Nashville: Abingdon Press, 2006), 211–12.
32. Luther, *Commentary on Romans,* 89; Origen, *Commentary on the Epistle to the Romans, Books 1–5,* The Fathers of the Church, vol. 103, trans. Thomas P. Scheck (Washington, DC: The Catholic University of America Press, 2001), 281.

the individual will live in God's peace. Given how often Christians fight among themselves, it would certainly be a step in the right direction for Christians to stop quarrelling with one another, but even that would not be enough. The end of quarrelling ought to open up the space for Christians to work together in order to allow all God's creation to thrive.

Whatever work Christians may do for peace in the world, Paul reminds us that we do this work because we stand in grace through Jesus Christ (5:2). The image of "standing" in grace calls to mind both standing before God in the temple and standing before the emperor in the imperial court.[33] Either situation implies access to exalted personage. Jesus Christ has given us access to the sphere or realm of God's presence, as well as God's peace. In the presence of God, we see God's glory. Like Abraham we cannot boast of glory from our own work; we only hope to share in God's glory. Unlike an audience with an earthly ruler where one needed to have cultivated a reputation for accomplishments or have high social standing in order to be allowed to enter, access through Jesus Christ to God's presence is pure gift.[34] Human glory amounts to nothing in the presence of God's glory, and all those who have access to God through Jesus Christ may hope in God's glory even if they have none of their own.

What does it mean to hope in God's glory? The system of honor and shame in which the Romans lived is important for understanding this hope. Winning glory for oneself or one's family was a primary goal of Roman life, and seeking honor set up serious social competition. In this system, glory was not only a way of raising status but also of being remembered. Winning glory gave a person some measure of immortality because the glory and honor that a person achieved in life would last in others' memory even after one's own death.[35] For Christians, though, sharing in God's glory would give true immortality that would not fade as human memories do.

When Paul says in verse 5 that hope "does not disappoint," the word he uses in Greek could also be rendered "does not put to shame." Some contrast between shame and glory may be at work,

33. Jewett, *Romans*, 350.
34. Ibid.
35. Ibid., 351.

but Paul is adding to the security of God's glory the confidence that our hope is not illusory. We have this confidence because the Holy Spirit has poured God's love into our hearts—into the core of our being. This fullness of love is a reliable witness to our relationship with God, the faithfulness of God, and the hope of God's glory.

In verse 2, the NRSV has added the word "sharing" to try to clarify the meaning of the phrase in Greek, which reads simply "hope of the glory of God." Those who have no glory of their own, or who recognize their own human glory is meaningless, hope to share in the glory that belongs to God. The idea of sharing God's glory has been important for the understanding of salvation as *theosis*, sometimes called divinization or deification, an ancient theology still retained in Orthodox Christianity. In Orthodox thought, when the Bible speaks of God's glory it is speaking of the "manifesting energies of God," or the radiance that manifests the divine Trinity to us.[36] It is through these energies that Christians come to share in the life of God, to the point of living in and through the life of God after death.[37] Because union with God is the Christian's destiny, Christian life now involves preparing oneself for God by following the leading of the Holy Spirit to live a holy life. The Orthodox feel free to use language about human "efforts" and "cooperation" when they talk about the way that the Holy Spirit empowers Christians for sanctification, but they are clear that *theosis* is made possible by grace and is the work of the Holy Spirit.[38] Among Protestants, Methodists have in John Wesley's theology a similar emphasis on holiness with the outcome of glorification in heaven. For both Orthodox and Methodist, hope in the glory of God includes hope for personal transformation in the present to better reflect the glory of God in one's life.

God's glory is not the only thing in which Paul says followers of Jesus may boast. He overturns the usual expectations of honor and shame by saying that we may boast in sufferings (5:3) that would normally be seen to lessen, rather than honor, us. Jewett points out that the specific reference to "our" (or in Greek "the") sufferings indicates

---

36. Vadimir Lossky, "The Procession of the Holy Spirit in Orthodox Trinitarian Theology," in Clendenin, *Eastern Orthodox Theology,* 178.

37. Christoforos Stavropoulos, "Partakers of Divine Nature," in Clendenin, 189.

38. Ibid., 188–89.

that Paul was not talking about suffering in general but may have had in mind specific adversity faced by followers of Jesus in Rome. Even with the cultural emphasis on boasting in glory, the idea of boasting in suffering was not unknown in the ancient world. Enduring affliction was considered to be a virtue because such endurance showed that one had mastered one's emotions. Paul, though, undercuts the idea of boasting in one's own self-control. The process he describes is something from which we benefit but which we do not control. He does not say that our growth is determined by our attitude but rather that suffering "produces" endurance, which in turn produces character, which in turn produces hope.[39] Although we do not control this production, Calvin points out that these virtues are not the "natural effect of tribulation" either. Many people turn against God in suffering. It is when we humbly allow the Spirit to work in us that tribulation may generate the effects Paul describes.[40] The point to see is that we should focus our boasting only on what God is doing in us with these circumstances rather than on our own accomplishment.

Even if Paul intended to refer to specific adversity in the Roman community, his words can shed light on suffering more generally. Having or seeking God's peace does not ensure the absence of suffering, and in fact Luther claims that the justified are more likely to suffer tribulation in the world because they live spiritually (in contrast to the ways of the world), while the unjustified avoid much tribulation because they live according to the ways of the world.[41] Paul's words show that having God's peace, while not preventing suffering, can provide a different perspective on suffering. Standing in grace excludes boasting in one's own accomplishments or social standing, but it makes it possible to boast in suffering. Christians do not boast in the pain

> **Tribulation does not make people impatient, but proves that they are impatient. So everyone may learn from tribulation how his heart is constituted.**
>
> Luther, *Commentary on Romans*, 91.

---

39. Jewett, *Romans*, 353.
40. Calvin, *Commentaries*, 191.
41. Luther, *Commentary on Romans*, 89.

or affliction itself, but rather they boast despite the circumstances that produce the pain and affliction. For Christians who stand in grace, the circumstances that cause suffering do not produce bitterness but rather endurance: that is, they are able to endure the circumstances gracefully. Being in the presence of God enables the person's character to be shaped in a Christlike way, and a character shaped in such a way will not succumb to the potentially damaging effects of suffering but will still be able to hope in sharing the glory of God. Standing in grace makes all the difference to our response, so the positive hope that results is indeed a gift and not our accomplishment. We know we can count on God to fulfill this hope because we already know God's love through the Holy Spirit. Suffering even in situations that seem to be beyond hope may still produce hope of this participation in God's own glorious life. The circumstances may not improve, but even if they persist, they cannot undermine this hope.

5:6–11

Weakness, Shame, and the Cross

We can hope, despite the circumstances that cause suffering, because God has proved that the love that assures us of our hope is trustworthy. Paul points out in 5:8 that even though we were still sinners, Christ died for us. This willingness to die for the low and unworthy when most people would not even die for someone good demonstrates love that cannot be shaken. Several scholars suggest, because of oddly formulated language in Greek, that verses 6–7 are either interpolations (added at a later time by someone else as the manuscript was copied) or a formulaic statement that Paul included because it was familiar to the Romans.[42] Even if these sentences are not Paul's own words, they serve to underscore the remarkable event of Christ's dying for sinners.

The idea of weakness is introduced into the description of this event in 5:6. In an empire where the weak are conquered by the

---

42. Jewett, *Romans*, 357–60.

strong and where boasting in accomplishment is encouraged, weakness was a terrible disadvantage. Weakness clearly had consequences in society. It meant a person could be defeated by someone stronger or bested by someone who could boast in greater achievement. The weak would be disregarded, shamed, and always at the bottom of hierarchical relationships. In the context of this way of thinking about weakness, to say that Christ died for the weak underscores the surprising way that God acts in Jesus Christ. The verse intensifies this point by adding that Christ died for the ungodly. From earlier parts of Paul's letter, we have learned that God is displeased with ungodliness (1:18), that it is related to unrighteousness (1:18), that humans demonstrate unrighteousness by giving glory to a creature instead of to God (1:22–23), and that God's wrath is revealed against this ungodliness (1:16). The ungodly are in a weak and vulnerable position because they deserve God's wrath and they are not in right relationship with God, and yet despite this weakness, Christ died for them.

Although Paul does not explicitly make this point in Romans (he does in Gal. 3:13–14), another thing that makes Christ's dying for us so remarkable is that the method of crucifixion was so shameful that with this death Christ was actually in a position of weakness himself. Paul certainly does make the point in Romans that Jesus Christ took on our condition in order to change it (8:3), so it is appropriate to bear in mind the view of crucifixion he states elsewhere. From the point of view of the law, crucifixion put the one crucified under God's curse. Jesus Christ suffered a death that would place a person outside a right relationship with God, but instead it brings us back into right relationship with God. Perhaps this is why Paul's confidence is so high. Furthermore, from the point of view of the empire, crucifixion was humiliation. If God would resurrect Jesus from this horrible, shameful death, how much more will God justify us (5:9) and save us by this resurrected life (5:10).

We know we cannot expect anyone to act the way that Jesus Christ acted. As Paul points out (5:7) rarely will a person die for another person, not when they are righteous and not often when they are "good" (this adjective may refer to a benefactor, in other words someone to whom we have some kind of obligation),[43] so

---

43. Cranfield, *International Critical Commentary,* 1:264–65.

Christ's death for us clearly defies all reasonable expectation. And yet God's love is demonstrated in this astonishing event. The same God who opposes ungodliness is the one who is shown to love the ungodly.

Paul has already explained in 3:24–25 that Christ's death acted as an atoning sacrifice, putting the ungodly in right relationship with God. Having been justified in this way, we are sure to be saved from wrath. The Greek text for 5:9 does not actually specify that the wrath is God's, although because the only wrath that has been mentioned in this letter is God's, the insertion "of God" in the English translation is appropriate. It is important, though, not to jump too quickly to the conclusion that Paul understood Jesus' death as a means of escaping punishment by an angry God. Sacrifice in Greco-Roman religion often included sacrifice to appease the anger of a god (propitiation), but Jewish sacrifice was more often an act that removed from the people the barrier to their relationship with God (expiation of sin).[44] In chapter 3, Paul used language to describe the atoning significance of Jesus' death that called to mind Jewish sacrifice. The point of the sacrifice was to show God's righteousness, not to appease God's anger. God is righteous when God is faithful to the covenant made with Abraham, so God provides us with a way of responding to God that would replace our ungodly forgetfulness. Our dishonor of God distorts our relationship with God. As ungrateful people giving glory to something other than God, we participate in a kind of treasonous rebellion (similar to dishonoring the emperor) that makes us enemies of God. Imperial protocol would call for conquering one's enemies in order to squelch rebellion, but instead God proves love for those enemies through Christ's death of surprising shame and weakness. The faithfulness of Jesus in sharing our weakness on the cross demonstrates the faithfulness of God to God's covenant. Rather than appeasing anger, this act removes the

> When I was sinking down beneath God's righteous frown, Christ laid aside his crown for my soul.
>
> "What Wondrous Love Is This," author unknown, *The United Methodist Hymnal* (Nashville: Abingdon Press, 1989), #292.

---

44. Frances Young, *Sacrifice and the Death of Christ* (London: SPCK, 1975), 23, 28.

barrier to the relationship, namely, the ungodliness against which God's wrath is revealed (1:18). This act allows for a changed relationship that makes possible a different judgment in the day of wrath.

In a time and culture where enemies were routinely defeated, humiliated, and killed, God acts instead to reconcile enemies. The notion of reconciliation that Paul's word conveys has its meaning in overcoming conflict, which could range from marital quarreling to war.[45] God provides a way for enemies to be in right relationship, and by doing so God is demonstrating God's own righteousness. The death of Jesus Christ makes this reconciliation possible by sharing our situation of weakness, which removes the barrier to the relationship between strong and weak. This reconciliation, though, is not the totality of salvation for Paul. There is a future expectation indicated by the future tense (will be saved, 5:10) not by Christ's death but by his life. Luther took the life that saves to be the resurrection, which brings about "our spiritual resurrection and spiritual life."[46] Wesley takes the life to refer to the ongoing intercession that the resurrected Christ makes for us. He also understands the future tense to indicate the possibility of sanctification that follows justification (reconciliation) in our present life, as well as glorification after death.[47] In other words, future salvation encompasses both how our present life can increasingly be more whole and holy as well as the future that we have with God after this life is over.

Although at every turn Paul has eliminated the possibility of boasting in ourselves, the reconciliation made possible by Jesus Christ is cause for boasting in God (5:11). Because God's righteousness is shown precisely in the weakness that allows for reconciliation, boasting in this God would have been enormously countercultural. Yet this is the God who is to be honored.

45. Jewett, Romans, 365.
46. Luther, Commentary on Romans, 93.
47. Wesley, Explanatory Notes, 537.

FURTHER REFLECTIONS
Atonement

Paul's conviction that in Jesus Christ's death God's love is demonstrated and we are reconciled to God leads directly to questions about atonement. Unlike the doctrine of the incarnation, which was determined by conciliar decision that explicitly rejected some possible understandings of the person of Christ, Christian understanding of atonement has never been formalized into a single official position. Many ways of understanding the significance of the death of Christ have existed side by side for centuries.

Although the Bible itself presents several images to suggest the significance of Jesus Christ's death, and Christian tradition developed several theories, one view predominates in popular understanding in Western Christianity—penal substitution (or penal satisfaction). As just indicated, this predominance is not due to any formal decision that it is the right or proper understanding, but rather to the way it informally matches a particular view of justice in the West.[48] Many Christians take it to be the right way of thinking because it makes sense in light of the way they view guilt. At the same time, many other Christians object to this understanding because of the way they view God.

The penal substitution theory of atonement presents Jesus Christ's death as a substitute for our punishment as sinful human beings. As guilty sinners, human beings deserved to die and be damned. God as (angry) judge must carry out this sentence, but God in mercy sent Jesus Christ to die in our place. By taking on our punishment, Jesus' death, then, removes our guilt and punishment so that we may enjoy salvation. This description fits with the view that guilt deserves punishment and that in order for there to be justice, punishment must be carried out. Although this kind of transaction resonates with a Western sense of justice, it is not without its detractors even in the West. Any God who would require that punishment be carried out through the beloved Son's death strikes

---

48. Joel B. Green and Mark D. Baker, *Recovering the Scandal of the Cross: Atonement in New Testament and Contemporary Contexts* (Downers Grove, IL: Intervarsity Press, 2000), 13.

many as an abusive God. This is not a God who deserves our honor and praise, but rather our outrage.

Whether the response is to accept it or reject it, the penal substitution understanding of atonement has captured imaginations almost to the exclusion of other possibilities. Anselm's satisfaction theory, which talks in terms of debt rather than guilt, also has influence, and sometimes the ideas get mixed together in popular understanding. Penal substitution (or an amalgamated version with Anselm's debt language) becomes the lens through which all Scripture is read so the rich array of images of atonement gets reduced. Paul's description of Jesus Christ's sacrifice often gets forced into this model without recognizing that other interpretations are possible. If the background is God's righteousness as covenant faithfulness rather than satisfying justice through carrying out punishment, then atonement may look very different than the dominant Western model suggests. Dying for a purpose to help the ungodly does not have to mean dying in the place of the ungodly. Paul seems much less concerned to explain a transaction than he is to show that this death demonstrates God's love and faithfulness. If Paul's description of the significance of Jesus' death is read only in light of penal substitution, then we will never explore other possibilities for understanding that significance.

Because no atonement theory has received conciliar dogmatic status, we are free (and perhaps obligated) to continue to reflect on the meaning of Jesus' crucifixion. Rather than always assume penal substitution, we could even consider the possibility that Jesus' death was not desired or needed by God but was rather used by God. Paul's message in the letter to the Romans may lead us to explore how Jesus' faithfulness to God, even when it led to death, disclosed God's faithfulness to us. Seeing his faithfulness opens the possibility for reconciliation with God that leads to our own faithfulness.

In its most basic meaning "atonement" means "at-one-ment." In other words, atonement is about putting a relationship back together again, or reconciliation. So however Jesus Christ's death is understood, it must serve that purpose.

5:12–8:39

The New Dominion

5:12–21

The Second Adam

Although this section begins with "therefore," what Paul goes on to say is not a straightforward conclusion drawn from the previous verses. It does, though, continue to describe how God reconciles us by addressing the deep cause of our ungodliness—living in the dominion of sin. The argument that closes this chapter refers to what Jesus Christ does for sinful humankind, but it does so in a way that does not simply refer to his death. Instead of using the imagery of sacrifice to talk about the significance of Christ, Paul begins to draw a comparison between Jesus Christ and Adam, focusing on the effects that each had on the human situation. Paul has written about the sinfulness of all humans earlier in this letter, but what he has said is more description than explanation. At this point, Paul traces the origins of sin and death to Adam. He does not explain any of the details about how Adam introduced sin, which spread death in the world, or how the problem was transmitted to the whole human race. His focus is not on mechanism but rather on universality: *all* have sinned.

This universality, which in the context of this letter intends to counter the feelings of superiority

> Human beings properly inhabit the realm between the dirt and the divine. Authentic human existence—human life as God intended it—aspires to realize its full potential of godlikeness while consistently acknowledging its creatureliness and limitations. Sin is disequilibrium in this aspiration: humanity failing to reflect its divine calling, humanity forgetting its limitations.
>
> Mark E. Biddle, *Missing the Mark: Sin and Its Consequences in Biblical Theology* (Nashville: Abingdon Press, 2005), xii–xiii.

between Jew and Greek, is made even clearer by showing the presence of sin before God gave the law to Moses. Paul may be reasoning in 5:12, as other theologians have, that because death is introduced by sin, death's presence is a sign that sin is at work. People died between the time of Adam and Moses, so death is clear evidence that sin existed between the time of Adam and Moses. What changed after Moses was that the giving of the law made it possible to regard certain actions as sins by naming the behaviors that displeased God (5:13). Before the law, sin was at work in a general way that may not always have been apparent; with the law, sin can be seen in very specific violations.[1] The absence of specific laws did not mean the absence of sin—as Paul has already argued, our problem lies much deeper than in particular behaviors. The deeper problem of failing to give glory to God was present between Adam and Moses, so death ruled even then, even over those who had not broken specified commandments as Adam had done.

Paul ends by saying Adam was a "type" of the one who was to come (5:14). The basic meaning of the word *typos* that Paul uses is a hollow impression of something that could be used as a mold to produce a shape, and it came to mean a model used for making copies.[2] The interpretive practice called typology draws from this idea that one thing serves as a model for another. It involves seeing in one person or event in history a prefiguring of another person or event in history. Paul is making use of this kind of interpretation. He sees in Adam some important similarity to Jesus Christ, although it becomes clear in his comparison that Jesus Christ is not a simple copy, and in fact Jesus Christ, far from duplicating Adam, overcomes the effects that Adam brought into the world.

> **And Christ did not merely do the same amount of good that Adam did of harm, but far more and greater good.**
>
> John Chrysostom, Homily X, *Homilies of S. John Chrysostom, Archbishop of Constantinople, on the Epistle of S. Paul, the Apostle to the Romans*, 3rd ed., trans. by members of the English church (Oxford: James Parker and Co. and Rivingtons, 1877), 151.

---

1. A. Katherine Grieb, *The Story of Romans: A Narrative Defense of God's Righteousness* (Louisville, KY: Westminster John Knox Press, 2002), 65.
2. Robert Jewett, *Romans: A Commentary*, Hermeneia (Minneapolis: Fortress Press, 2007), 378.

The way that Paul develops this typology is by comparing the effects of one man with the effects of another man. In the Genesis account of the fall, Eve eats the forbidden fruit before Adam does, so some interpreters have felt the need to explain why Adam is the only one who is mentioned here. Origen discusses this situation at length, wondering why Paul would say that sin entered the world in Adam when both the serpent and Eve sinned before he did. Origen concludes that Paul is following the "order of nature" by attributing to Adam the passing on of sin because Adam was the source of Eve, so Adam is the source of all subsequent humanity.[3] Augustine adds more to the description of the situation. In *City of God*, Augustine interprets the roles of the first humans in the fall through 1 Timothy 2:14, which says that Eve, but not Adam, was deceived. Augustine takes this to mean that Eve believed the serpent and so sinned without realizing what she was doing, while Adam sinned knowing that what he did was sinful.[4] This reading reflects the widespread notion that women, for whom Eve is the prototype, are more gullible than men. Like Origen, Augustine also understands that the human nature we all share existed in Adam, so Adam, not Eve, is the type that prefigures Jesus Christ. Although Eve is not specifically mentioned in Romans, interpreters should be aware that how this text is handled with respect to the roles of Adam and Eve can have impact on the way that men and women see themselves and their relationship to one another. The text has the potential to show Adam's own involvement in the fall so that Eve is not blamed alone, but there are negative consequences for women in trying to lessen Eve's culpability by making her (and thus all women) seem less capable of making intelligent, moral choices.

Paul hints in 5:15 that Jesus Christ is not a simple copy of Adam when he states that "the free gift is not like the trespass." If Jesus Christ is not a simple copy, neither does Jesus Christ bring a simple reversal, that is, he is not simply putting things back the way they were. Paul stresses gift and abundance in his language about what

3. Origen, *Commentary on the Epistle to the Romans, Books 1–5,* The Fathers of the Church, vol. 103, trans. Thomas P. Scheck (Washington, DC: The Catholic University of America Press, 2001), 310–11.
4. Augustine, *Concerning the City of God against the Pagans,* Book XIV:12, trans. Henry Bettenson (New York: Penguin Books, 1984), 570.

Jesus Christ accomplishes, which emphasizes how much greater are the effects of Christ than those of Adam. Another factor that keeps simple reversal from being enough is that the world is now governed by forces that were not in power when Adam was created. Sin and death do not simply exist; they have dominion. Jesus Christ breaks their power so that those who receive his free gift of righteousness "exercise dominion in life through the one man, Jesus Christ" (5:17). The exchange of one rule for the other is a clear sign of the fulfillment of the world God had promised, and so by countering the effects of Adam's disobedience, Jesus Christ inaugurates the *shalom* for which Israel hoped, a shalom in which the ungodly are restored to God.

Barth talks about the difference between the effects of Adam and of Jesus Christ as a difference between an "old world" and a "new world." The old world is our whole existence as it has been conditioned by sin. He describes sin as robbery of God because we deny the difference between ourselves and God and set up something of our own creation to receive our devotion. This sin assumes we are independent of God, and so it takes us out of relationship with God. Death has power in this world because it is inevitable; it brings destruction of ourselves and all we hold dear. The inevitability of death exposes the limits of our independence and the falseness of devotion to things of our own creation. Death brings us to crisis because in it we see the judgment of God on our way of living in the world. Jesus Christ answers death with resurrection and so makes it possible for us to turn from the old world to the new. In the new world we have a different relation to God, not denying the difference between us, but rather seeing ourselves properly in light of that difference. Because of the new relation with God, we have a new relation with others, so that instead of being enslaved by things, we reign in freedom.[5]

In 5:18–19, Paul draws out the consequences for humanity of the typological comparison that he has made. Because of Adam's trespass, all of us are condemned; that is, all of us share in the consequences of living in a world ruled by sin and death. Jesus Christ's righteousness,

5. Karl Barth, *The Epistle to the Romans*, trans. Edwyn C. Hoskyns (Oxford: Oxford University Press, 1933), 164–87.

though, leads all to be justified and to live. Because of Adam's disobedience, many are sinners, but because of Jesus Christ's obedience,
many will be made righteous.
Although interpreters have commonly taken the "all" and the "many"
in these two verses to refer to all
humanity when talking about the
consequences after Adam, few have
extended the "all" to the consequences after Jesus Christ because
to do so would be reading Paul to
mean universal salvation. Luther
says that the words "all" and "many"
emphasize not number but rather
the power of sin and grace: namely, the power of one person to affect
so many.[6] This power should not be thought of as linear, external cause
and effect, the way that one billiard ball knocks into another with inevitable results. Rather Paul will go on to describe the effects of Jesus
Christ as participation.[7] Just as we somehow share in the problem that
began with Adam, we have the hope of sharing in the life of Jesus
Christ.

> We are created to serve
> God by loving him and each
> other in freedom and joy,
> but we invariably choose
> bondage and woe instead as
> prices not too high to pay for
> independence.
>
> Frederick Buechner, *Wishful Thinking: A Theological ABC* (New York: Harper & Row, 1973), 55.

Paul again reinforces how much greater is this hope than the
problem by comparing sin and grace (5:20–21). God's law did not
cause sin, but once laws were established, they presented the opportunity for violation. Not only breaking laws but even keeping laws
could be occasion for sin if people sought honor in their religious
accomplishments.[8] So sin increases with the law because sin has
specific manifestations related to the law. But if the law presented
the opportunity for sin to increase, sin presents the opportunity for
grace to abound. The abundance of grace exceeds all increase of sin,
to the point of overthrowing its dominion. Grace exercises dominion by justifying us and making possible eternal life through the resurrected Jesus Christ.

6. Martin Luther, *Commentary on Romans*, trans. J. Theodore Mueller (Grand Rapids: Kregel Classics, 1974), 97–98.
7. Leander E. Keck, *Romans*, Abingdon New Testament Commentaries (Nashville: Abingdon Press, 2005), 145.
8. Jewett, *Romans*, 388.

The Greek word translated in the NRSV as "exercise dominion" (5:21) is *basileuō*, which means to reign or rule. The noun form of this word, *basileia*, is used in the phrase translated into English as the "kingdom of God." Paul is talking about two reigns or jurisdictions that, like ancient kingdoms, require allegiance of those who live in them. There are clusters of ideas connected together in these different jurisdictions, and through the next chapter, Paul uses different words from these clusters without explaining their connection to one another. He groups sin and law together because of the connection he makes in 6:20, but later in chapter 7 he will have to make a careful distinction between sin and law in order to keep their connection from being misunderstood. He also groups together righteousness and grace, both of which belong in the kingdom of God, and they bear a closer, more integral relationship to one another than sin and law do.

To live in the kingdom of sin, under its rule, is to pledge oneself to sin and to follow its ways. When the abundance of grace overthrows the dominion of sin, the justified live instead in its kingdom and under its rule. Paul explains the implications of this change in citizenship from one kingdom to another in the next chapter.

FURTHER REFLECTIONS
Original Sin

Paul's reflections about the effect Adam had on humanity played a significant role in the development of the doctrine of original sin. It has been easy for theologians to take sin to be universal because death is universal. Paul connected sin to Adam; but because he did not attempt to explain the mechanism connecting Adam with the rest of us, later theologians took up the task of answering the questions raised by Paul's ideas. Although Augustine is often credited with having formulated the doctrine of original sin, he was not the first to explore these questions. Several theologians before Augustine had made efforts to explain what Paul had not, and their thinking was also related to other matters, such as salvation, the need for Christ, and the practice of the church.[9]

---

9. Tatha Wiley, *Original Sin: Origins, Developments, Contemporary Meanings* (New York: Paulist Press, 2002), 38.

One of the ways theologians in the early centuries attempted to explain how Adam's sin affects all humankind was that Adam presented all the rest of us with a bad example that has had enduring effect by multiplying. All of us enter into a world that has already been affected by sin, and we are educated by sinners, so sinfulness is formed in each of us.[10] This idea depends on a social explanation for the origin of sin in each of us.

Another possible explanation that also existed in the early centuries was that the source of sin was not socially constructed but was in human nature itself. This view had support in an interpretation of Romans 5:12 that depended heavily on a mistranslation of Greek into Latin. Instead of saying at the end of the verse "because all have sinned," the Vulgate version of Paul's letter said "in whom all have sinned." Ambrosiaster had taken the "in whom" to refer to Adam, an interpretation that Augustine followed, and this understanding provided the basis for the idea that human nature itself was affected by Adam's sin.[11] Although Augustine had worked out this understanding before his controversy with Pelagius, the controversy of the fifth century solidified this view. The Council of Carthage, which supported Augustine over Pelagius, cited Romans 5:12 as evidence that infants are born into a state of sin.[12]

Another way that Augustine influenced the understanding of original sin in the West was his distinction between original sin as "originating" and "originated." In other words, he distinguished between original sin as the first sin (originating) and the condition into which each of us is born (originated by the first sin). The shared condition was connected to our shared nature, so the question arose as to how Adam's action (the first sin) could affect human nature so that later generations of humans were born into this condition. With Augustine, the church accepted the view that sexual intercourse was the mechanism of transmission. But what exactly was transmitted? Although Christian groups have sometimes disagreed about details and emphases, guilt, a wounded nature, and the penalties of suffering and death were all inheritance of that first sin. It is important to remember, though, that this inheritance

10. Ibid., 39, 54.
11. Ibid., 51, 61.
12. Ibid., 72.

was not seen as unjust blaming for something someone else did. Because human nature itself was in Adam and human nature itself is what is transmitted, all humans acted with Adam in that first sin, not as specific individuals but in a solidarity or participation through what makes us human.

Eastern Christianity continued to use Greek instead of Latin, and so it was influenced neither by mistranslation nor by Augustine in the same way. Eastern Christianity has not talked about the effects of Adam's sin on humanity in the same way as Western Christianity. For instance, humans do not share the guilt of Adam but rather bear the guilt of their own actual sins. If they use the phrase "the original sin," Orthodox Christians typically speak of it as meaning the first sin rather than a condition into which all humans are born.

For centuries in the West the doctrine of original sin provided the very basis for how Christians talked about the need for salvation: to remit guilt, to heal a wounded nature, to bring life instead of death. In our time original sin is not such a compelling idea. To understand who we are, we look to genetics. To understand why we do what we do, we have recourse to psychology and sociology. The existence of a first man and first woman, who were the source of all humanity, can no longer be simply assumed. Our modern convictions about individual responsibility rather than human solidarity also obscure the meaning of the doctrine.

At its heart, the doctrine of original sin is trying to express why we fall short of what God intends for us and why we need redemption in order to fulfill that intention. If the answer that our Christian forebears gave does not seem to be adequate, we are still left with the question.

6:1-14

Dead to Sin and Alive to God

After emphasizing the abundance of grace in the face of sin, Paul again uses an imaginary dialogue partner to ask a question to draw out the implications of what he is saying. The imaginary dialogue partner asks a foolish question, taking the way that grace increases in proportion to sin to suggest that we should sin more so that there would be more grace. Paul's answer dismisses this idea as preposterous, but the question allows him to reflect on the kind of relationship that a follower of Jesus Christ has to sin.

We have already seen how for Paul, sin exercises a kind of power. To counter the foolish reasoning of his imaginary dialogue partner, Paul employs reasoning that draws out ideas about power that have their home in the context of empire but are easily understandable in other contexts. He describes sin's power as ruling power; sin has dominion over us, enslaving us to its purposes and exercising influence over us as a kind of lordship. When we are under the lordship of sin, we are bound to submit to its influence. But Paul has just told the reader at the end of chapter 5 that grace also exercises a dominion. To follow Jesus Christ means leaving the dominion of sin and living in the dominion of grace. If that is the case, then the follower of Jesus can no longer do the bidding of sin. By changing dominions, a person has changed lords and loyalties. The suggestion that we should sin more so that grace might increase is preposterous because the person who has left the lordship of sin and stands under the dominion of grace now has a new lord. This person can no longer follow the rule of the old dominion because she or he is bound to the purposes of the new dominion. Exchanging one dominion for another requires a change of allegiances. To continue in sin would show that one has not changed allegiances.

Paul's language of dominions presents an opportunity to reflect on what faithfulness means in our time and place. What are the things that vie for our loyalty and that aim to shape the way we live our lives? What does it mean to live under the control of these things? How would living in the dominion of grace be different?

For Paul, baptism is a clear sign of leaving the dominion of sin and entering the dominion of grace. Whether the followers of Jesus in Rome were Jew or Gentile, they would have been baptized, so this sign provides a way for him to remind his readers in a divided community about the situation that all of them share. Those who are baptized have died to sin because they have been baptized into Jesus' death. By participating in the death of Jesus, the follower of Jesus is dying to the lordship of sin and accepting the lordship of

Christ. In his commentary, Origen explains that "living to" means living in accordance with the desires and will of what one is living to, and conversely, "dying to" means not carrying out the desires and will of what one is dying to.[13] The exchange of allegiance includes an exchange of obedience. This transfer of loyalty is total—as radically different as death is from life—so sin no longer has any claim on the one who has died with Christ. As Barth says, "Grace and sin, then, are incommensurable."[14] To continue to participate in sin, as the imaginary dialogue partner suggests, would be an act of disloyalty. John Wesley held that not even "babes in Christ" will "commit sin"—that is, knowingly violate a command of God—because a Christian leaves sinful behavior behind.[15] To be buried with Jesus indicates the finality of "dying to" the dominion of sin, and Origen reminds us that a person is not buried until she or he is truly dead, so not being fully dead to sin precludes being buried with Christ.[16]

Because a person gives up the lordship of sin by taking on the lordship of Christ, she or he is not simply leaving behind sin but is also gaining what the dominion of Christ has to offer: namely, participation in Christ. Of course, the followers of Jesus knew that the tomb in which Jesus was buried was soon empty. By being buried with Jesus, we are made participants not only in his death but also in his resurrection. To be united with him in death means also being united with him in resurrection (6:5). The Greek word *symphytoi,* translated as "united," is a word taken from ordinary life and means grown together—the way a grafted plant or a healed broken bone grows together.[17] The kind of participation that baptism makes possible is an incorporation into Christ that is a secure joining for a thorough sharing, a kind of bonding. The purpose of this participation is that we might "walk in newness of life" (6:4). Again, the foolishness of the imaginary dialogue partner is displayed. Dying to sin means that a person dies to an old way of life, and participating in the death and resurrection of Jesus means that a person enters a new way

13. Origen, *Commentary,* 349–50.
14. Barth, *Epistle to the Romans,* 191.
15. John Wesley, Sermon 40, "Christian Perfection," II.2 in *The Works of John Wesley,* ed. Frank Baker, vol. 2, Sermons II, ed. Albert C. Outler (Nashville: Abingdon Press, 1984), 105.
16. Origen, *Commentary,* 355.
17. Jewett, *Romans,* 400.

of life. The one who was crucified conquered death, and because we share in his victory, we are no longer enslaved to sin. Walking in newness of life is now possible, and it is also expected (6:6). The proper commitment to the new dominion in which we are privileged to live is to give up sin and live for God.

Although the contrast between death and life indicates a total change, it does not mean that everything about the new life in Christ is completed as soon as we have been baptized in Christ. Luther argued that being dead to sin is not about the absence of sin but about our ability to resist it. Sin's rule has been broken, so even if sin is present, we do not have to obey.[18] Calvin points out that because we still carry "the relics of the flesh" we "cannot do otherwise than walk somewhat lamely."[19] Origen indicated the incompleteness by talking, not about remainder of sin, but about growth in grace. He draws a comparison between how the old keeps aging and how the new must be constantly renewed. For the one who is growing in faith, "there is never a time when his renewing is not increasing."[20] In any case, whether talking about continued struggle with sin or the way we grow spiritually, new life in Christ is not static. It is not simply accomplished as a finished product with baptism. Rather to walk in newness of life means to be on the move, to be ever attentive to what it means to live to God and to exercise our allegiance daily.

> So then let us walk with Christ as new persons and, so to speak, as increasingly more beautiful people, uniting the beauty of our face with Christ, as in a mirror and, beholding the Lord's glory, let us be transformed into the same image by which Christ, rising from the dead, has ascended from earthly lowliness to the glory of the Father's majesty.
>
> Origen, *Commentary*, 360.

Paul ends this section with practical instruction for how to live in this way. The way Paul admonishes not to let sin have dominion over the body to make us obey what the NRSV (6:12) calls "passions"

---

18. Luther, *Commentary on Romans*, 100–101.
19. John Calvin, *Commentaries on the Epistle of Paul the Apostle to the Romans*, trans. and ed. John Owen (Grand Rapids: Wm. B. Eerdmans Publishing Co., 1959), 233.
20. Origen, *Commentary*, 359–0.

(*epithumia*, or desire) suggests that the desires themselves are not the problem. We could hardly stay alive without the body's impulses to do certain things. Sin's dominion over those bodily desires, though, makes us obey them instead of control them. To modern ears, his words about desire (or passion) may sound like a caution about sex. To the ears of the original recipients of the letter, though (and to many theologians of the past), these words probably meant much more. *Epithumia* could include desire for many pleasurable things, including food and comfort. The control of desire was an important topic of reflection in the ancient world that resulted over time in identifying many types of passions that could get out of control. Anger and fear, for instance, could be as powerful as lust. Aristotle's *Nicomachean Ethics* and Cicero's *Tusculan Disputations* both explore the power that emotions have and the power we should have over them. Many philosophers taught that keeping one's desires in check was central to living the good life, and the ancients sought to use reason to control emotions instead of being controlled by them.[21] For instance, anger should be kept from becoming explosive rage. Fear should not become disabling. Intense emotion expresses itself in bodily ways, and obeying passions could lead to physical expressions that could be harmful to the self and to others. If Paul's concern about *epithumia* is limited to sex, we will miss the many ways that sin threatens to take control of our bodies. He reminds us that by being set free from sin, we no longer have to let those desires rule our lives. In fact, we are expected to present ourselves to God, thereby accepting God's dominion of grace and receiving God's grace to resist their controlling power. Paul continues to discuss the power of desire and passions in chapter 7.

> He does not say, let not the flesh live or act, but *let not sin reign*, for he came not to destroy our nature, but to set our free choice aright
>
> John Chrysostom, Homily XI, *Homilies*, 168.

Early interpreters of Paul took the problem of the passions so seriously that theologians in the Antiochene tradition included impassibility as well as immortality

21. Stanley K. Stowers, "Paul and Self-Mastery," in *Paul in the Greco-Roman World: A Handbook*, ed. J. Paul Sampley (Harrisburg, PA: Trinity Press International, 2003), 524–50.

and incorruptibility in the hope for resurrection. Spiritual well-being has to include freedom from the temptations into which the passions lead us. With no passions, sin cannot find a place to enter.[22]

Although this portion of Paul's letter is not really an exposition on baptism, but rather a discussion of sin, Barth uses it as an opportunity to explore some thoughts about baptism as a sacrament. As a liturgical act, baptism belongs to "religion"; that is, it is a human activity, and like other human activities religion stands constantly under God's judgment. Barth even points out that baptism was an act borrowed by Christians from practices belonging to other religions of the time. He also recognizes that baptism is a sign; that is, it points to a reality beyond itself. There are two possibilities. As any human activity does, it has the potential to be "empty and ineffectual" when we mistake the act itself for the truth of God. As a sign it also has the potential to point beyond itself to God's truth. It is not grace itself but a means of grace.[23]

For Barth, the truth to which baptism points is just as overwhelming as the death into which it brings us. Grace exerts shattering power as it makes the old person die so that the new person can live. Barth says, "Your baptism is nothing less than grace clutching you by the throat: a grace-full throttling, by which your sin is submerged in order that ye may remain under grace."[24] This graphic description of what dying to sin is about shows how utterly impossible it would be for anyone who has truly been made new by sharing death in Christ to continue any longer under the dominion of sin. One way of making this sign "empty and ineffectual" is to tame it so that the rawness of the image of death does not remind us of the stark difference between living to God and living to sin.

22. George Kalantzis, "'The Voice So Dear to Me': Themes from Romans in Theodore, Chrysostom, and Theodoret," in *Greek Patristic and Eastern Orthodox Interpretations of Romans*, ed. Daniel Patte and Vasile Mihoc, Romans through History and Culture series, vol. 9 (London: Bloomsbury T. & T. Clark, 2013), 83–102.
23. Barth, *Epistle to the Romans*, 192.
24. Ibid., 194.

FURTHER REFLECTIONS
Baptism

At the time Paul wrote this letter, baptism could be used to appeal across dividing lines of Jewish and Gentile followers of Jesus. In the intervening history that has led to our time, though, baptism itself has become divisive. Matters such as whether the person being baptized must be of an age to declare her or his faith personally, or in what manner water should be used (immersion, pouring, or sprinkling), or the necessity of this rite for salvation have all been points of serious disagreement. Ecumenical dialogue of the past century has brought many churches to better understanding of each other.

Paul's image of being buried with Christ is only one of the images that the Bible offers to help us understand baptism. Others include washing away of sin; new birth; enlightenment by Christ; re-clothing in Christ; renewal by the Holy Spirit; salvation from the flood; exodus from bondage; and liberation into a new humanity that transcends barriers of sex, race, and social status.[25] As a rite with many meanings, baptism points to the richness of the faith into which it initiates us.

Ecumenical dialogue about baptism has helped churches understand this richness in such a way that we can see how different practices of baptism can help us learn from one another rather than divide us. Although most churches consider baptism as a one-time, unrepeatable act, this event must be understood within a lifelong process of nurture and growth.[26] Seen in this way, churches may be able to appreciate different practices regarding the time of life in which a person is baptized.

The rite of baptism makes use of material signs (variously including water, oil, light) that help convey the biblical images associated with baptism and point beyond themselves to God. The use of these elements in baptism affirms the goodness of God's material creation and God's use of created things for God's purposes, but

---

25. World Council of Churches Commission on Faith and Order, "One Baptism: Towards Mutual Recognition," 2006/14, 4.

26. Ibid., 6.

their use in a rite does not restrict God's presence and work to these elements. The few churches that do not practice a rite of baptism are reminders that God's grace is free to work outside ordinarily established channels.

As many of Paul's interpreters have seen, living to Christ takes daily commitment and allows for maturing. For churches that practice baptism, the rite serves as entry into the church, bringing people into the nurturing community where such growth is encouraged to take place. Although focus on the event of baptism has been divisive, focus on "baptismal life," where the event of baptism takes place within a pattern of formation, holds promise for promoting better mutual understanding.[27] Keeping in mind the whole context of what this entry and participation in the community means can help Christians of different traditions recognize their common concerns.

Baptismal life has three dimensions: (1) Formation in faith, which includes not only catechesis for individuals but also the formation of the whole community; (2) the rite of baptism, which may be performed differently in different communities; and (3) participation in the life of the community, which includes sharing in the Eucharist and using individual gifts to serve the church and world.[28] Wherever these three dimensions are found, Christians have good reason to recognize their unity in Christ.

6:15–23

Slaves of Righteousness

Once again, Paul warns against drawing a mistaken conclusion from what he has been saying. Does being under the rule of grace instead of law give us freedom to sin? The answer Paul gives is no, which is clear enough, but his explanation of this clear answer may not be as easily understandable to modern readers. In Paul's time, slavery was embedded in the structure of society. Studies of slavery suggest that between one-third and two-thirds of the population were

27. Ibid., 2.
28. Ibid., 7.

either slaves or former slaves. It was common for a person to sell oneself into slavery for economic reasons or even for eventual social advancement if serving someone of high social importance.[29] This voluntary practice of putting oneself into servitude lies behind Paul's explanation about presenting oneself as an obedient slave (6:16). A person is not any less enslaved because she or he voluntarily took the position. All the restrictions and dangers of being someone else's property apply as equally to the willing slave as to someone enslaved by force. Just so, misusing the freedom that grace provides by voluntarily obeying sin makes one no less a slave to sin.

Paul does not assume the kind of total individual freedom that modern people have learned to hold dear. Rather, he assumes that we must give ourselves in obedience to something, either sin or righteousness. Never our own masters, we must choose whom to serve—sin or righteousness. Although it may seem strange to think of grace as a master, this image does help remind us that grace is not simply a gentle, benign gift. Grace also makes demands of us. To be "under grace" (6:14–15) does not mean living in total freedom without accountability. Being "under grace" means living a life appropriate to the God whose grace has dominion. In 6:17, Paul gives thanks that the recipients of his letter have been emancipated from sin and enslaved to righteousness. Enslavement to righteousness under grace, though, is not an externally compelled obligation. Paul gives thanks that this servitude is "obedient from the heart."

> **The law has been abrogated as far as justification is concerned, but not as far as obedience is concerned. Obedience must be rendered.**
>
> Philipp Melanchthon, *Commentary on Romans*, trans. Fred Kramer (St. Louis: Concordia Publishing House, 1992), 150.

For modern readers, language of enslavement and obedience may confuse or impede our hearing of what Paul wants to say. We like to celebrate our independence and resist acknowledging any "master." Even with our modern freedom, though, we give ourselves to a way of life, that is, we adopt ways of doing things, ways of looking at the

---

29. Jewett, *Romans*, 416.

world, and values. Paul's words serve as an important reminder to consider well what we give ourselves to, because it can come to control us. Giving ourselves to God, in the way Paul describes it, means leading a life marked by Christlike righteousness. Grace sets us free from the law, but we obey nonetheless because our hearts belong to God.

Paul explains that obedience of the heart is to "the form of teaching to which you were entrusted" (6:17). In his *Explanatory Notes*, John Wesley points out that the word (*typos*, as in 5:14) translated in the NRSV as "form" was a mold, so he comments, the word makes "a beautiful allusion, [which] conveys also a very instructive admonition: intimating that our minds, all pliant and ductile, should be conformed to the gospel precepts, as liquid metals take the figure of the mould into which they are cast."[30] In other words, along with the enslavement image is also an image of being molded into the likeness of Christ. Obedience, then, is allowing oneself to be poured into the teaching, and so take the shape of Christ. Modern minds may find it easier to embrace this image than one of slavery.

> **Lord, I want to be like Jesus in my heart, in my heart.**
>
> African American spiritual, "Lord, I Want to Be a Christian" *The United Methodist Hymnal* (Nashville: Abingdon Press, 1989), #402.

After giving thanks that they are obedient from the heart, Paul encourages the followers of Jesus to present the members of their bodies also to their master for sanctification (6:19). The inner life is linked to outward, bodily expression. In other words, a change of heart should lead to a change of behavior. We show outward manifestations of our commitments, so if we obey sin in our hearts, it will show in our actions. Conversely, if we obey righteousness in our hearts, that obedience will also show in our actions. By embodying the commitment that we are making to serve the God of righteousness, we present ourselves to God for sanctification, that is, for being made holy. Paul addressed this letter to "God's beloved in Rome, who are called to be saints" or holy ones. Fulfilling this calling is precisely what Paul is encouraging here.

God calls us to be made holy, to be molded in the form of Christ.

---

30. John Wesley, *Explanatory Notes upon the New Testament* (repr., London: Epworth Press, 2000), 541.

This calling is precisely what is denied when we are enslaved to sin. The only freedom we have in the dominion of sin is freedom from righteousness: that is, freedom from being in right standing with God. If not in right standing, a person cannot be in relationship, and so the person forgoes all the benefits of that relationship. If we obey sin we get what we deserve: our wages are death. If we obey God, we receive God's free gift, grace, which brings us into the relationship with God that means eternal life. The end results of living in these different dominions could not be more different.

> Live virtuously, in order that sin might not rule in you to the destruction of your faith and righteousness.
>
> Luther, *Commentary on Romans*, 106.

Paul notes in verse 21 that they are now ashamed of those things that bring death. It is common to interpret Paul's language in terms of individual behaviors practiced before conversion, things such as sexual activities, misuse of alcohol and drugs, slander, gambling. A convert did those things before following Jesus and is now ashamed of them. It is possible, though, that in a culture of honor and shame, this language has an even broader meaning than the behaviors many people think of in reading this text. If honor and shame are connected to social status, and if faith in Jesus Christ overturns the usual standards for honor and shame, then their participation in the entire social system is something to be ashamed of. A system of exploitation that assigns personal value hierarchically and treats those on the lower end of that scale as worthless is a system of death. This system is what existence is like once Adam has brought death into the world as the result of sin.[31] The followers of Jesus may not fully be extricated from that system, but where once they participated without questioning the system, now they are ashamed of it. Where once these followers of Jesus may have worked to position themselves as high on the scale as they could, perhaps treating those below them poorly in order to get an advantage over them, now they understand how pointless and harmful that behavior is. Living in the dominion of grace obedient

31. Jewett, *Romans*, 423.

to righteousness calls for a completely different way of life. The results of that different way—questioning the system and behaving differently than the expectations of the system—are holiness and eternal life.

The dominion of grace is clearly to be preferred over the dominion of sin, but Barth reminds us that the dominion of grace is not all soft, sweet sentimentality. Just as he did when he described how grace throttles sin out of us, he describes grace in his comments on this text as exerting power. The very power that affirms us also makes claims on us. He says, "As the man under grace, I am created and quickened and awakened. But I am also disturbed, for the demand bids me take up arms against the world of men and against the men of the world. The object which I, as the subject, am bidden to attack is—myself."[32] This demand requires self-examination to recognize the way sin still tries to act as tyrant in one's own life, and it also

> After speaking of the wages of sin, in the case of the blessings, he has not kept to the same order: for he does not say, the wages of good deeds, *but the gift of God*, to shew that it was not of themselves that they were freed, nor was it a due that they received, neither yet a return, nor a recompense of labours, but by grace all these things came about.
>
> Chrysostom, Homily XII, *Homilies*, 185.

requires revolt against that tyrant. Being under grace, then, places us under continuing revolutionary struggle. Because "Grace is knowledge of the will of God, and as such it is the willing of the will of God," what grace provides for us is illumination of the criterion by which we make judgments.[33] We see that our choice is between death and life, with no middle ground. As important as it would be to make good choices with that criterion, no list of what is right and wrong can tell us what those choices should be because the criterion of grace also stands in judgment of any list we could make. Being under grace does not give Christians an easy life. Instead, grace puts us under pressure between its promise and its demand.

---

32. Barth, *Epistle to the Romans*, 208.
33. Ibid., 207.

"To be a Christian," says Barth, "is to be under this pressure."[34] Any
Christian who seriously considers the way that she or he participates
in the exploitative system that supports modern imperial power will
understand the kind of pressure that Barth is talking about.

FURTHER REFLECTIONS
Obedience from the Heart

Paul's description of being obedient from the heart calls attention to
the kind of inner life that is pleasing to God. Because Jesus summed
up the law as love of God and love of neighbor (Matt. 22:36–38),
theologians have devoted a great deal of thought to what kind of
love would fulfill these great commandments. This emphasis on
love has made the heart the locus for explaining both the human
problem and what changes in us when God addresses this problem.

Augustine set the direction for this reflection in the West when
he described the human problem and salvation in terms of how love
and the will are connected. In his understanding, human beings
should love the good, which is God, and this love means having
their wills directed to the good. Before the fall, with wills that were
entirely aligned with God's will, human beings chose only the good
and did only what was right. Before the fall, Adam and Eve lived
in undisturbed love for God and for each other. They were free to
love and serve God, and therein they found their happiness. The fall
began with a turning of the will away from God and toward something else that was pleasing. Instead of loving God above all else,
something of lesser value became attractive and desirable. This
turning of the will from the ultimate good led to disobeying God's
command, but it is important to see that sin began inside before a
sinful act was committed. There was inward sin before there was
outward sin.

In consequence of the first humans' following their own will
instead of God's, human will was enslaved to sin. The will gave up
its freedom to choose what was truly good, and it could not resist
being drawn to lesser goods that attracted it. Because our first
parents were enslaved, we, too, are born into slavery. Any time

34. Ibid., 229.

we know what we ought to do but instead do only what pleases us, we show we are caught in this enslavement. Because the will is directed toward and desires lesser things, it is not free to love God above all else. It may seem to have the power to choose, but it is really in bondage. The result is continual sin at the level of what we love, even if our behavior appears to be without fault. Jesus Christ saves by setting the will free to love God once again above all else.

The idea that our actions follow after what we love—that we act to gain what we desire—has been an important idea in Western theology. To say that our wills are enslaved to sin is to say that we go through life wanting things that God does not want for us. Then we act to gain those things that we want but that God does not want for us. Conversely, to say that we are under grace and enslaved to righteousness is to say that we want what God wants for us. When our wills are conformed to God's will, and we act in accordance with that will, then we are obeying from the heart, loving God above all else and so desiring what God desires. Obedience from the heart rests in relationship with God.

The insistence that we are saved by faith, not by works, is connected to this idea that our actions receive their character from our relationship with God. Actions performed out of trusting gratitude have a different character than those that are performed for personal gain, even if the action looks the same from the outside. To be truly "good," a work must not only benefit others but also have this character of trusting faith. Many Christians tend to focus all their attention on behaviors, but they would do well to remember that a rich heritage of theological insights have called attention to what lies behind the behaviors. God wants us not simply to be obedient but to be obedient *from the heart*. This heritage also reminds us that God sees into the heart as others cannot, so God knows what we are truly giving ourselves to—whether we are enslaved to sin or to righteousness.

> **When people thus focus their attention on their one, true heart's desire, they can discern the joyful work of obedience to which their renewed hearts dispose them.**
>
> Gregory S. Clapper, *The Renewal of the Heart Is the Mission of the Church* (Eugene, OR: Wipf & Stock, 2010), 131.

7:1–6

Drawing an Example from Marriage Law

Paul tries to give an example of the freedom he is talking about by comparing the situation the followers of Jesus are in to the situation of a widow. The example he gives does show how death releases a person to a new situation, but following the example requires some willingness to take the details rather loosely. For instance, in the example of marriage, the wife is released when the husband dies; that is, someone else's death frees her from the obligation. But it is we ourselves who must die to sin, not someone else. Also, Paul has been talking about dying to sin, not dying to the law, so his use of the law in this example leads him later to have to warn against understanding the law as sin.

In using this example, Paul must have in mind the legal requirements for marriage in Hebrew Scripture (perhaps elaborating on Deut. 24:1–4) because his description does not match Roman law. A Roman woman could divorce her husband (thus freeing her to marry another man while the first was still living), and furthermore the husband's death would not immediately release the wife from her marriage obligations because she would lose her inheritance if she did not remain unmarried and mourn his death for a year.[35]

The word that is translated as "married" (7:2) is the Greek *hypandros*, which means "under a man." In other words, the woman is subject to a man, and she is bound to him as his subject legally. Although not considered enslavement, marriage understood in this way exemplifies a binding relationship that requires loyalty and determines one's options, so this example has some of the features needed to bring out insights about the change of dominions Paul has been describing, this time with regard to the law. As long as the man to whom the woman is legally bound is alive, she may not live with another man. If she does so, she is considered an adulteress, having violated her legal obligation to her husband. But if her husband dies, she is no longer legally bound to him, and she may live with another man without being considered to have violated her legal obligation

---

35. Jewett, *Romans*, 431.

to her husband. Upon his death, she is no longer subject to the law that bound her to him.

Notwithstanding the difficulties of the example itself (not only in confusing details, such as who is doing the dying, but also in its assumptions about the relationship between women and men), it is possible to see the way Paul uses this example to show how the death that we share with Jesus Christ through baptism changes the situation that we are in. No longer bound by the law, a new option is available to us. We are no longer restricted to the domain in which we lived (under the dominion of sin), but we may live in a new domain (under the dominion of grace). Dying to sin changes our situation and makes a new life possible.

No longer bound by the law, the follower of Jesus belongs to Christ and may bear fruit for God. Paul now refers to the former way of life as "living in the flesh" (7:5) beginning the distinction between "flesh" and "Spirit" he will continue to develop. As he makes use of this distinction between flesh and spirit, Paul does not use "flesh" to mean the body but rather as an opposition to what is meant by "spirit." He is not talking about simple embodiment but is rather continuing to explain the problem of living under the domain of sin. For this reason, Cobb and Lull suggest thinking of this phrase as "living for the flesh" rather than "living in the flesh."[36] So this mention of flesh in 7:5 does not mean that sin was only in the body, even though there are probably bodily expressions of it.

The law aroused sinful passions. Many people think of passion as primarily sexual desire, and "in the flesh" would then refer to the way our bodies respond to someone who is attractive to us. Keeping in mind the explanation given in the comments for 6:12, passion was understood in the ancient world much more broadly. When John Chrysostom, for instance, comments on how Christians live in this new way, he not only gives an example relating to sex but also to

> **The law affords no power for keeping its standards. It establishes the criterion of righteousness but cannot make one righteous.**
>
> Biddle, *Missing the Mark*, 39.

---

36. John B. Cobb Jr. and David J. Lull, *Romans* (St. Louis, Missouri: Chalice Press, 2005), 105.

martyrdom. Regarding the former, his example is to note how many people in the known world who had become Christians were able to "practice virginity." The latter example shows how many could face death without being overcome by fear. Both are examples of what life in the Spirit could enable Christians to do.[37]

Many different kinds of strong emotions could get out of control, and "living for the flesh" means allowing uncontrolled passions to determine our lives. How might the law arouse sinful passion (7:5)? Perhaps it might do so when we want what is denied to us by the law, or when we feel anger that others do not abide by the rules as we do, or when we fear the consequences of disobedience, or perhaps even when we boast because of taking pride in fulfilling the law's requirements (this last example is in fact what Paul highlights in 2:17–18). In whatever way it arouses them, the law can do nothing to help us control those passions. These out of control passions may demonstrate themselves in or through the body, so our strong emotions lead us to act in accordance with how we feel. As the consequences of those disordered passions are enacted, they bear dangerous fruit (7:5). In contrast, when we are set free from the law, we are no longer under this kind of influence. The compulsion to meet the law's demands (or to make others do so), or to compete with others to show greater compliance, no longer incites us; we are bound instead to the new life of the Spirit.

7:7–13
The Law Is Not Sin

Paul seems to be aware that the way he has linked law and sin could make it seem as though the law is sin, so he raises the question in 7:7 in order to refute it. Because Paul uses the first-person pronoun "I," interpreters have often wondered how much Paul is speaking about himself. Could he be revealing something about his own life before his conversion? Just because he speaks as "I" does not

---

37. Chrysostom, *The Homilies of S. John Chrysostom*, 190–91.

necessarily mean he is speaking about himself. It was common in ancient Greco-Roman rhetoric to use "I" in making an argument, a device called "speech-in-character." This device increased emotional impact by allowing and encouraging hearers to apply the argument to themselves as they identify with the "I."[38] If the character Paul wants to convey is the self as it is affected by Adam's fall, not yet released from the dominion of sin by Christ, then it would resonate not only with his own past but also with that of other converts. It would be no more autobiographical for him than it would be for any of us. It speaks to our personal histories because it recounts a deeply human experience. Regardless of the reference of the pronoun, Paul is clearly trying to explain how the law may be linked to sin without being itself sinful.

Paul has in mind here the explicitly articulated law that was given to Israel. Paul's statement that he would not have known sin if not for the law (7:7) raises the question of natural conscience. Would we really have no way to tell right from wrong without an explicitly stated law? Chrysostom deals with this question by saying the conscience does accuse of sin but not as strongly as the law.[39] Still, Paul's point is not just about clarity of accusation. He is pondering how sin can make use of the law against us. How is it that specific commandments, intended to prevent sin, end up becoming the vehicle for sin?

The example that Paul uses in 7:7 as he discusses this problem is the last of the Ten Commandments, "You shall not covet" (Exod. 20:17; Deut. 5:21). This commandment is not simply about behavior but describes a disposition of the heart. Coveting is more than simple wanting. It is a compelling craving. Paul focuses attention on the disposition itself by leaving off of the commandment the list of things that are not to be coveted.[40] The Greek word that Paul uses in this commandment for the word we translate as "covet" is *epithumeō*, which is related to the word (*epithumia*) translated in the NRSV as passions in 6:12. Coveting is desire that has gotten out of control. Earlier, Paul said that sin exercises dominion by making us obey our passions (desires), and now he is pointing out how the law makes us

38. Jewett, *Romans*, 443.
39. Chrysostom, *Homilies*, 194.
40. Keck, *Romans*, 182.

vulnerable to this kind of dominion. Paul's claim that we would not know what it is to covet if the law had not said, "You shall not covet," can hardly mean there would be no desires if there were no written law. After all, the Gentiles also had desires. Rather, by identifying what sin is, the commandment puts those desires at the disposal of sin. By being the occasion for desire, the law creates an opportunity for sin to exercise its power and thereby gain dominion.

Many have seen in these verses allusions to Genesis 3 even though Paul makes no direct reference to the story of the fall. An exploration of Genesis 3 can show how a commandment of God can be put at the disposal of sin. God had given one command to Adam and Eve: not to eat of the fruit of the tree in the middle of the garden. When the serpent suggests to Eve that the consequences God warned against would not come to pass and that instead she would gain something, Eve looks on the tree as "good for food," "a delight to the eyes," and "to be desired to make one wise" (Gen. 3:6). Desire for the fruit is evident in this description. Many interpreters of the fall story have pointed out that because the disobedient action was rooted in desire, desire produces sin. A few suggest that the problem lies even deeper: namely, in how desire gets produced.[41] A close look at what happens to Eve shows how the deeper problem occurs. Genesis 3 resonates with what Paul is saying not by telling how sin came into the world in the first place, but rather by illuminating our life in a world where sin already exists. The conversation between Eve and the serpent may take place before the fall in the sense that the humans have not been shut out of the garden or cursed, but the serpent already exerts a dangerous influence. In the Genesis account, the serpent's words prompted Eve to look on the tree with desire, so the influence of the serpent brought about the desire. Unlike Eve in the garden before the fall, we live in a world that is already fallen. If Eve was influenced even in the garden by a serpent, how much more so are we troubled because sin is already present all around us. Sin as a powerful reality already at work in the world produces sinful desire that in turn produces sin as act. The presence of sin in the world has

41. Keck, *Romans*, 182–83; Grieb, *Story of Romans*, 72.

an effect on us that is like the effect the presence of the serpent had on Eve, but it is amplified many times over.

Keeping in mind Genesis 3 when reading Paul's words helps to explain how the law became an opportunity for sin. If sin is not just a deed or desire but a power with dominion, this power uses God's commands as an opportunity to create the desire that leads to a sinful act—just as the serpent used God's command to start a conversation with Eve. The command not to covet creates the opportunity for sin to lead us into coveting. In the garden, the serpent drew Eve into a conversation about God's command that led her to question it. For us now, when sin draws us into internal conversation about a command, it is easy to rationalize a way to do what the command prohibits. In doing so, we are beguiled just as Eve was beguiled and look with desire on what has been forbidden. In that way, the law that was intended for our benefit and protection gets misappropriated by sin and weakens our allegiance to God. The commandment gets commandeered for the purpose of leading us into sin's dominion.

Paul's statement that sin lies dead apart from the law (7:8) has led some interpreters to suggest that sin is less active or less recognizable without the law.[42] For instance, some sinful behavior may not even occur to us until we know that it is prohibited. Chrysostom and Origen, though, both point out that if sin were nonexistent or ineffective without the law, there would have been no need for the flood.[43] There was plenty of sin, and it was plenty powerful, before the law was given to Israel. However theologically and psychologically illuminating Paul's discussion of sin and the law may be as an insight about how sin uses the law, this statement in 7:8 should not reduce our recognition of the power and scope of the dominion of sin.

When Paul speaks in 7:9 about having once lived apart from the law, he may be referring to the idea that young Jews take on the obligation of the law at the point of "coming of age," the event that began

---

42. C. E. B. Cranfield, *The International Critical Commentary on the Holy Scriptures of the Old and New Testaments: The Epistle to the Romans*, ed. J. A. Emerton and C. E. B. Cranfield. 2 vols. (Edinburgh: T. & T. Clark, 1973), 1:351; Arland J. Hultgren, "*Pistis Christou*: Faith in or of Christ?" in *Paul's Letter to the Romans: A Commentary* (Grand Rapids: Wm. B. Eerdmans, Publishing Co., 2011), 277–78.

43. Chrysostom, *Homilies*, 194; Origen, *Commentary*, 316.

to be celebrated in bar mitzvah.[44] In taking on the obligation of the law, there is the temptation to become overly zealous about the law. To the extent that Paul may be speaking autobiographically, his own zeal (Gal. 1:13–14) may be informing what he has to say. The problem is not the law, but rather that we are vulnerable to the distorting power of sin. The law is intended to bring life (Deut. 30:15–20), but when sin interferes with its purpose, the result is death.

Paul's concern not to equate the law and sin is important even beyond the law itself. We need to be alert to all the ways that sin can take something good that is intended for our benefit and twist it for harmful purposes. It may do so even if there is no written law but merely unspoken expectations about what is right. Because we are vulnerable to sin's distorting power, even our highest ideals can become vehicles for sinful behavior toward others.

Despite the way sin may distort the law, Paul makes clear that the law is good (7:12). God gave the law to Israel in making covenant with Israel. Israel had the written law for its guide so it could be a light to the nations. The law is holy and just and good. It is intended to bring life and light to all. The law does not bring death. Death comes through the law only when sin twists it for sin's purposes. When it uses the law in this way, sin is exposed for what it is. Such blatant interference with God's commands cannot go unnoticed, and the magnitude of the problem becomes clear (7:13). By showing what God intends, the law makes plain how far we are from those intentions.

> You observe how he every where keeps to sin, and entirely clears the Law of accusation.
>
> Chrysostom, Homily XII, *Homilies*, 195.

7:14–25

The Conflicted Self

Because the law is holy and just and good, it is "spiritual," that is, it is of the Spirit, or of God. If sin is able to use the law to bring death, it

44. Jewett, *Romans*, 451.

is not because there is a problem with the law. Rather the problem is in ourselves. Continuing his speech in character, Paul describes the state of a human being under the effects of the fall. Such a person is "of the flesh" (7:14). Although many have often taken "flesh" to indicate bodiliness or materiality, a better way to understand it in this context is as the alternative to being of the Spirit. "Flesh" conveys what it is like not to be oriented to God but to be oriented to the world without reference to God. This problem surely embodies itself in some way, but the problem is not the body. Being "of the flesh," Paul says, is having been "sold into slavery under sin." Paul is not concerned to explain how or why one gets sold into this slavery; he only describes the condition itself.

Living under the dominion of sin involves a deep and confusing contradiction, namely not doing what one wants but what one hates (7:15). One of the ideas that accompanied the ancient goal that reason should keep the passions in order was that if reason knew what the good was, then reason could direct the self toward the good. Knowing what was truly good, then, should lead to doing what was good. Paul, though, points out that knowing what is good does not always lead to doing what is good. I can agree that the law is good and even want what the law says is good, and still do something else. The explanation for this contradiction is that it is not "I" or the self that is the controlling agent but sin (7:17). As Paul has said, the self has been sold into slavery under sin, so sin is exerting its mastery over the self. Followers of Jesus who were slaves or former slaves would have no trouble understanding that the will of the master took precedence over the will of the slave. They no doubt had direct experience of having to do things that were undesirable or even harmful to them rather than what they truly wanted or what would be beneficial to them.

The statement in 7:17 that sin "dwells within me" along with the English translation of 7:18 as "nothing good dwells within me" could contribute to the idea that human nature is totally depraved—thoroughly sinful. This understanding in turn could lead to the conclusion that humans are bad. Paul's point, though, is something different. Although he is talking about the self, he is not talking about the nature of human beings—what we essentially are. Rather, he is talking about where sin resides, and therefore where it exercises its control. This point is often obscured by the English translation. Paul is not commenting about how much a human can be considered to be good (nothing is good). A better translation of 7:18 would read, "good does not dwell in me."[45] Although a universal power, sin does not rule from a distance or exert its power in some diffused, impersonal way. Sin lives within the self, so its control of the self is near and personal. Because good does not live within the self, it is not in control of the self.

In this situation, sin rather than good resides in the self, so evil rather than the good "lies close at hand" (7:21). Because it is so close, it is much easier to grasp and implement what sin wants instead of what the law directs. So even if one delights in the law (as the righteous do in Psalm 1:2) and studies it regularly with the intention of learning from it and keeping it, the self is in conflict—wanting to enact the goodness of the law but under the control of sin. So even if one knows the good intellectually (with the mind) one may not carry out the good (with the members of the body). What one actually puts into practice is in conflict with what one knows to be right.

> Who then am I? I am he that wills and he that does not perform: I am intolerably both at once. When my will is most steadfast, it does but remind me that the good is—not in me.
>
> Barth, *Epistle to the Romans*, 265.

Trapped in this way, the self is miserable. Furthermore, sin is so strong that it is not possible for the will to resolve itself out of the problem. The self needs to be rescued from it. Jesus Christ is, of course, the deliverer, and Paul thanks God for him (7:24–25). Seeing how powerful sin is when it dwells close to us, this text invites us to consider carefully what we invite to "dwell" in our lives.

In keeping with trying to understand the specific social situation that Paul has in mind, Jewett suggests that the conflict between wanting the good but not achieving it may be related to Paul's

---

45. Keck, *Romans*, 189.

history of zeal for the law. Although he wanted to honor God through keeping the law and defending it against the danger he initially perceived in the followers of Jesus, he ended up doing evil in persecuting those followers. What he discovered in his conver-

sion was that the way he tried to do the good actually opposed the way that God was working in Jesus Christ. His own personal insight about zeal becomes a caution to the Roman followers about their

> **Sin-power is stronger than willpower.**
>
> Keck, *Romans*, 193.

own zeal, which is putting them in competition with each other. Such competition can never lead them to the good they really want, which is to honor God.[46]

Paul's description of the conflicted self became the source for Luther's dictum *"simul iustus et peccator,"* at the same time righteous and sinner. Luther saw that no conflict existed for the carnal-minded, who simply follow their desires rather than follow the law. Believers, though, find themselves pulled in two directions. They know what the good is and want to do it, but they are continually inclined toward the opposite. This conflict might seem like a disadvantage to the believer, but instead it serves as a reminder of grace. For Luther, to know oneself as a sinner because of one's desires makes the imputed righteousness of Christ all the more important. Furthermore, it makes the believer all the more grateful for it. Acknowledgment of sinful desire serves as a check to the arrogant idea that we have it in our own power to live as we ought to live. Instead of thinking of ourselves as healthy and whole, we are, as Luther says, "sick people who are being treated by a physician."[47] To think of ourselves as already recovered puts us in danger of a relapse. Remembering that we are sick keeps us turning to the physician for healing. So *simul iustus et peccator* is not resignation to a hopeless plight but is rather a reminder of our dependence on grace.

The extent and power of sin has recently been explored by theologians in reflection not only about the sinfulness of individuals but also systems. Our participation in systemic injustice may mean

46. Jewett, *Romans*, 467–68.
47. Luther, *Commentary on Romans*, 115.

that seemingly trivial choices may not be trivial at all. What I have
for breakfast or what I wear may have been produced through the
exploitation of others, so even those choices can put us at odds with
the will of God and thereby make us complicit in sin even without
a conscious, willful decision for sin. This problem, too, is bondage
and enslavement to sin. Recognizing this problem helps us see how
deeply conflicted we really are and how thoroughly dependent on
grace we must be.

8:1–17

The Spirit of Life in Jesus Christ

Despite the internal conflict that he describes at the end of chapter 7, Paul is able to affirm the freedom in Christ for which he has
argued earlier in the letter. His "therefore" states this affirmation as
a conclusion that is drawn from all he has said, not simply from the
immediately preceding description of the conflicted self. Adam's
trespass condemned humanity to living in a world ruled by sin and
death (5:16–17). Those who live in Jesus Christ, though, are not
under condemnation (*katakrima*). This Greek word was ordinarily
used in the context of a judgment made in a criminal proceeding. It
included not only the judge's ruling of guilt but also the sentence. If
the sentence was death, then it does not apply to those who live in
Jesus Christ and hope for resurrection.[48] Although the followers of
Jesus live in the same fallen world in which others do, we live in it in
a different way. Not under the rule of sin and with the hope of life
in Christ.

The exchange of dominions brings with it also an exchange of
laws: in Jesus Christ, the law of the Spirit of life replaces the law of
sin and death. If under the law of the previous dominion there was
condemnation, now under the law of the new dominion there is
freedom. The "law of sin and death" (8:2) should not be taken to
refer to the Sinaitic law given to the people of Israel. The Greek word
nomos can mean principle or rule as well as law, and in this context

48. Hultgren, "*Pistis Christou*," 296.

nomos refers to the control that sin exercises—its rule over us. As Paul has already explained (see comments on 7:7–13, pp. 122–26), the written law had been appropriated by sin to serve sin's purpose instead of God's. Because the law had been used in that way, its effect had been weakened, and it could not prevent or overcome sin. In fact, the written law had become the unwilling accomplice to sin as its commands served to increase desire for what was forbidden or as those who kept the written law sought honor in their accomplishments of obedience.

Luther uses Paul's discussion about the weakness of the law to stress human inability to fulfill the law under our own power. Because it is not possible for us on our own to love God above all else, our wills are not truly free to fulfill the law spiritually. When we obey what the law commands, we do so out of self-interest rather than solely out of love for God, so we fail in fulfilling its most important command to love God above all else. Faith alone can set the will free to love God. For Luther, the law was weak because it could not be fulfilled by what humans are able to do, so God acted in Jesus Christ instead.[49]

Paul does not explicitly explain the relationship of the written law to the law of the Spirit of life in Christ Jesus. As we have seen, the Greek word *nomos* is used for the Sinaitic law but can also mean other things. In the case of sin, Paul has been clear to say that the written law and sin must be distinguished from one another. Sin rules in a way that distorts the written law, but the written law cannot be identified with sin. Sin is a principle or power apart from the written law. So should similar reasoning be used to talk about the relationship of the written law to the law of the Spirit of life? Is the law of the Spirit of life a principle or rule that is distinct from the written law? Or is the law of the Spirit of life the written law when it has been restored to its proper function? After all, Paul says in 7:10 that the commandments "promised life." Following Luther's denial that humans have the ability to fulfill what is needed for salvation, some have been hesitant to say that any "law," whether written or of the Spirit, could bring freedom, but Paul does use the word *nomos* as

49. Luther, *Commentary on Romans*, 118.

the subject of the sentence in 8:2. No interpretation has settled this matter and given answers to the questions raised by the use of the word. What does seem to be clear is that Paul is using the word "law" with regard to the Spirit as a mirroring of the phrase "law of sin and of death." The mirrored wording reflects the reversal of dominions that Christ makes possible.[50] Whatever else Paul may have meant by using *nomos*, he surely meant to talk about an exchange of rule.

Another ambiguity in this text is that the word *pneuma* in the Greek text could refer to the divine Spirit or the human spirit. The use of the word in context suggests divine Spirit is meant, as indicated by English translations that capitalize the word, and I will follow the interpretive style of the NRSV. We should be mindful, though, that the Spirit has an effect on the human spirit.

Paul is clear that it is in Christ Jesus that God has acted to reverse the situation of bondage and condemnation. Even though the law promised life, it had been so misappropriated by sin that it could not bring about its promise. In that desperate situation, God sent the Son "in the likeness of sinful flesh" (8:3) to deal with sin as the law was unable to do. This phrase "in the likeness of sinful flesh" might for later Christians evoke reflection about the doctrine of the incarnation, which developed long after

> **The mission of the Son of God is the divine reaction against sin.**
>
> Karl Barth, *Epistle to the Romans*, 278.

Paul wrote to the Romans. Although Paul's words may have important things to say about how we understand that doctrine now that we have it, we should not think that Paul was referring directly to that doctrine.

Instead, let us refer back to what Paul said about the flesh when he talked about the conflicted self. "Flesh" did not simply refer to "body" (see comments on 7:14–25, pp. 126–30). Flesh rather primarily meant being oriented in the world without reference to God—in contrast to Spirit, which meant being oriented to God. It is precisely because of this wrongful orientation (not living in the dominion of God and therefore not giving allegiance to God) that humans are

---

50. Keck, *Romans*, 196–97.

sinful and are in fact enslaved to sin. This is the problem from which we need to be set free and which the law could not address, so God sent the Son "in the likeness" of this condition. One does well to keep in mind here the way that Christ was a "type" of Adam, not a simple, straightforward copy, but made "like" Adam in order to over-come the situation that Adam began. The Son takes on the likeness of sinful flesh by coming to us in our world of sin—a world not ori-ented to God, where strong take advantage of weak—and by taking on weakness (see comments on 5:6–11, pp. 93–98). The Son, who shares the vulnerability of weakness and suffers at the hands of the strong, condemns sin in a world oriented away from God in order to bring it back to God.

The law was given as covenant, to establish relationship with God, and that relationship is its central requirement. Those who walk (live) "according to the Spirit," that is, responding appropriately to God, live in that relationship and thus fulfill the requirement of the law (8:4). To walk (live) "according to the flesh," or without reference to God and therefore responding to the things of the world without tak-ing God's will into account, clearly places one in the dominion of sin and death (8:5). The allegiance that we give to one of these two domin-ions will shape all our values and behaviors. John Wesley describes walking according to the Spirit as being "guided in all our thoughts, words, and actions" by the Spirit.[51]

> That, for Paul, this "walking" is *halakah*, or the ethical pattern of life prescribed by the law, is clear from the contrasting language of the next several verses. The "Spirit" and the "flesh" (like Christ and Adam) are two opposing spheres of action or families of solidarity, so that to be a member of one or the other is to have one's thoughts and actions shaped by that allegiance.
>
> Grieb, *The Story of Romans*, 77.

Paul describes these two ways of living in terms of setting one's mind on something (8:5–6). The word Paul uses for mind is *phronēma*, a noun related to the verb *phronein*, which will be important in what Paul says in later chapters (see comments on 12:3–8, pp. 207–12, and 14:1–12, pp. 229–37).

51. Wesley, *Explanatory Notes*, note to verses 5–11.

"Mind" does not refer only to thinking. "Mind" is more like a mind-set; it refers to a stance, a facing toward what one is living by, so that one's life is directed toward either the flesh (living in the world without reference to God) or Spirit (letting oneself be shaped by relationship to God). One's life is determined by what one is facing.[52] Those very different orientations will lead to different actions and attitudes. For instance, the mindset of the flesh will seek honor in those ways that the world says will bring honor. The mindset of the Spirit, on the other hand, will hope to share God's glory in Jesus Christ (see comments on 5:1–5, pp. 87–93). The ultimate consequence of setting the mind on the flesh, or living in the world without reference to God, is death. The ultimate consequence of setting the mind on the Spirit, or letting oneself be shaped by relationship to God, is life and peace (8:6).

These two mindsets are in stark opposition to one another, so Paul can say that the mindset of the flesh, or living without reference to God, is hostile to God (8:7). One's mindset shows one's allegiance. A mindset that lives without reference to God shows allegiance to sin and to the ways of sin. There is no neutrality. One either lives for God or not, and by not living for God one displays loyalty to another dominion. To live in the kingdom of sin, under its rule, is to pledge oneself to sin and follow its ways. It is not possible to live according to God's purpose with such an allegiance. Living in direct contradiction to the claim that God has on us is a resistance against God. To be "of the flesh," then, is to be against God, an enemy of God, as Paul says in 5:10. One need not be openly and aggressively against God to be in this position. Living in a mindset of the flesh can express itself in subtle forgetfulness of God. John Wesley called people with this kind of forgetfulness "practical atheists, as have not God in all their thoughts."[53] Augustine describes the problem in this way: a person "seeks these lesser, transient goods and fears to lose what must someday be lost."[54] In other words, when we disregard the

---

52. Keck, *Romans*, 202.
53. Wesley, Sermon 130, "On Living without God," ¶7 *The Works of John Wesley*, ed. Frank Baker, vol. 4, Sermons IV, ed. Albert C. Outler (Nashville: Abingdon Press, 1984), 171.
54. Augustine, *Augustine on Romans: Propositions from the Epistle to the Romans, Unfinished Commentary on the Epistle to the Romans*, Society of Biblical Literature Text and Translations, trans. Paula Fredriksen Landes (Chico, CA: Scholar's Press, 1982), 21.

Creator, we then overvalue the creatures. As long as we are fixing our attention on things that will pass away, we are not fixing our attention on God. This forgetfulness is just as effective as open hostility is in showing allegiance to sin rather than to God and preventing us from pleasing God as we should. Even people who acknowledge the existence of God are prone to this problem.

Of course, Paul has explained in 6:12–14 how the dominion of sin has been overthrown so baptized Christians now live in a dominion of grace. He assures the hearers of his letter that they are in the Spirit rather than in the flesh because the Spirit of God dwells in them (8:9). Remember that Paul wrote a letter to be read to an entire community rather than to an individual. He often uses a plural form of "you" (English can only do this with colloquial expressions like "y'all" or "you guys") because he is not talking to a single person. He uses "you" in the plural form in 8:9–11. In our time, English-speaking Western readers (especially those who read the Bible for private study) would probably read this passage understanding "you" as addressing them individually. Indeed, Protestants have a long history of reading Romans as a description of the life of individual believers—examining one's own heart and motives, trusting in one's own justification by faith, seeking to be assured of one's own salvation. This way of reading Paul has had benefit for many, but it also has limits. As theology recognizes the importance of community even in shaping the individual, it may be time to seek another level of understanding to what Paul is saying by looking at what it might mean to think of this passage as addressed to the whole community.

Where is it that the Spirit dwells? Is it in each of the hearers individually or is it in the community? What might be the relationship between the way the Spirit dwells in the community and in the individual? As he talks about the Spirit of God dwelling in them, Paul could have in mind something like God's promise in Exodus 29:45–46 to dwell among the people of Israel.[55] Since Paul is addressing a community trying to learn how to live together again as Jewish and Gentile followers of Jesus, such a reference might remind them to think about how God is with the whole, even across ethnic lines.

55. Jewett, *Romans*, 490.

The use of the plural also calls to mind the discussion in 6:1–14 about baptism as dying and rising with Christ. In 6:11–14, Paul also used the plural "you." Baptism is a rite for an individual that takes place in and through a community. In chapter 6, Paul explains that they were brought into Christ, and now in chapter 8, he states that Christ is in them (8:10). Both passages suggest some kind of life-giving participation in Christ is available in the baptism that takes place in the community. The body may die, but the Spirit who gives life will raise you with Christ. Luther is remembered to have said, "I have been baptized." This knowledge brought him comfort when he struggled, and it is a comfort that is rooted in God's grace through an act of the community. The self-introspection that theology has tended toward over the past few centuries in the West needs to be balanced by this recognition of how God's saving work uses the community.

> Those who have the wisdom of the Spirit delight in God's will and gladly heed it, for they have become like him.
>
> Luther, *Commentary on Romans*, 120.

Paul also warns that anyone who does not have the Spirit does not belong to Christ (8:9). Of course, the warning also implies a corresponding affirmation: if a person has the Spirit that person belongs to Christ. The "anyone" makes reference to an individual, not to the community as a whole, so the individual also matters. Paul, though, returns to speaking in the plural immediately after this warning in (8:10): "But if Christ is in you" (plural). The word translated as "if" does not mean to suggest doubt about whether or not Christ is in you but rather suggests reasoning on the basis of that condition (if, . . . then). In other words, because it is the case that Christ is in you, then the Spirit is life even though the body is dead in sin. The word "but" that begins the phrase implies a contrast to the warning, so the phrase may be offering assurance. You are not and do not have to be an individual without the Spirit because you are in a community where the Spirit dwells.

Paul was not concerned to distinguish Spirit and Christ in the way that the doctrine of the Trinity would later do. It took centuries of theological reflection to show that this distinction was necessary for thinking clearly as Christians about God. Paul's point, instead, is that where Christ is, the Spirit is also.

If Christ is in you, Paul explains, sin and death will not have the last word. The body dies because sin brought death into the world, but belonging to Christ means you will live in him (8:13). The reversal of the two "laws" from 8:2 now becomes especially clear. The "law of the Spirit of life in Christ Jesus" overcomes the "law of sin and death." Life reverses death. What would seem inevitable from the point of view of a world without reference to God is nullified by new possibility that only God can bring about. Belonging to Christ means that the law of the Spirit of life in Christ Jesus will bring you into participation in his resurrection. It is right that if one's allegiance is to the dominion of grace, according to the law of the Spirit, the Spirit of life would give life. It is God who acts in accord with the law of the Spirit of life in Christ Jesus, by faithfully bringing about the life in Christ Jesus that has been promised. In addition to assuring the followers of Jesus of the presence of the Spirit among them, Paul is also affirming God's righteousness.

Because in 8:11 Paul refers to "mortal bodies," that is, bodies that are capable of dying instead of bodies that are already dead, he may have had in mind not only resurrection after physical death but also how we can expect a different quality of life while we are still alive. As Augustine points out, knowing that we are mortal and subject to death troubles us and makes us inclined to satisfy our desires in our temporality instead of remaining fixed on what is eternal.[56] This anxiety leads us into an orientation toward the world without reference to God and deadens our life with God. But because the Spirit dwells in us now, we are enlivened even now. If sin and death do not rule, we will even now know a reversal from deadness to life.

That there are present implications for the change of laws Paul has been talking about comes out in 8:12. By adding the word "body" to "flesh," Paul's words point clearly to the way we enact our sinful orientation. The embodied actions of living "according to the flesh," referenced as "deeds of the body" (8:13), bring up the ethical dimension of this exchange of laws.[57] In saying that we

56. Augustine, *Augustine on Romans*, 21.
57. Hultgren, *"Pistis Christou,"* 312.

are not "debtors" to the flesh, Paul is saying we are not obligated to live according to the mindset of the flesh.[58] This ethical dimension has often been reflected upon primarily in terms of the individual. Theologians of the past have read 8:12–13 as an instruction about bodily desires. For instance, Luther takes the "deeds of the body" as "sinful lusts and passions."[59] Slightly more expansive, Wesley talks about evil actions, desires, tempers, and thoughts, but this list is still highly individualistic.[60] Both Luther and Wesley are thinking about how inner thoughts and feelings lead to outer actions. They interpret Paul's admonition to put those deeds to death not, as some might, to refer to physical asceticism, but rather as a directive for the inner life—to put to death ungodly lusts, passions, and thoughts.[61] Because deeds begin in our thoughts and feelings, this deeper cause is what needs to be addressed by the Spirit, like killing a weed at its root so it will not grow back. The Spirit who enlivens also mortifies, or puts to death. When the Spirit puts an end to the way inner desires lead to sinful deeds, we have the life that the Spirit offers.

This interpretation for our individual inner lives, though, misses the possibility that Paul might have something to say, not only to individuals, but to the community. Keeping in mind that Paul is addressing the Romans collectively (with a plural "you") and calls them brothers and sisters, joined together in Christ not only with Paul but with each other, an interpretation that acknowledges community is worth considering. Jewett takes Paul's reference to obligation in a social direction. Paul explains they are not "debtors" to the flesh, and this word (*opheiletēs*) is the one he used also in 1:14 to refer to his obligations to Greeks and barbarians. The word was used at that time to refer to social obligations that bound people to one another.[62] These obligations were extensive, so they pertained even in family relationships and friendships. Living up to those obligations determined one's honor and reputation.[63] Even now, if some-

---

58. Cranfield, *International Critical Commentary,* 394.
59. Luther, *Commentary on Romans,* 121.
60. Wesley, *Explanatory Notes,* 548.
61. Luther, *Commentary on Romans,* 121; Wesley, *Explanatory Notes,* 548.
62. Jewett, *Romans,* 493.
63. Koeneraad Verboven, "Friendship among the Romans," in *The Oxford Handbook of Social Relations in the Roman World,* ed. Michael Peachin (Oxford: Oxford University Press, 2011), 404–21.

one buys you a meal or a gift or takes care of your children, you may feel "indebted" to do the same thing in return. The hierarchical social system of the Roman Empire established reciprocal duties to hold the system of relationships together. The exchange of services created and maintained social relationships. Against this background, Paul's point could be this: If we are not debtors to the flesh, we are not obligated to serve the flesh, or as he says "live according to the flesh." As we have seen above, the mindset of the flesh seeks honor according to the structure that the world has established, that is, within a system of relationships of superiority and inferiority. This is not the system to which the followers of Jesus are obligated. They do not find their place there. Even though we do not now live in the actual Roman Empire, we should still consider the ways that our own societies implicitly or explicitly determine our obligations to one another, and we should test that system against what the law of the Spirit of life in Christ Jesus would have us do.

Thinking about the debt Paul mentions as social obligation can open up the text to a reading about the community. Although he does not explicitly state the further implication of no longer being debtors to the flesh, it is clear from what he has said previously that we are debtors instead to the Spirit. When we leave the law of sin and death to follow the law of Spirit and life, we exchange one set of obligations for another. Our new obligations are established not by a system of patronage but by being brothers and sisters in Christ, children of God. This relationship is what determines our responsibilities to one another. Reminding a community of house churches that met separately from one another, whose members were both Jew and Gentile, and who came from different social positions, that they were obligated to each other as brothers and sisters rather than as the social system of hierarchy dictates would have been quite a reversal.

To further stress the relationship of being brothers and sisters in Christ, Paul uses the image of adoption, a legal practice in Roman society of designating someone who is not one's physical offspring to be one's heir. It has become common among many Christians to refer to all humans as "children of God" as a way of reminding us that because we have a common Creator who values all that has been created, all humans are of sacred worth. This more recent use of that phrase is not the same as Paul's, because Paul speaks of being children of God by adoption, not by creation. Although it does capture and expand concern about our obligations toward one another, this understanding of all humans as children of God does not help to understand what Paul means in these verses.

As Paul uses the phrase, the children of God are those who (1) are led by the Spirit and (2) cry "Abba! Father!" The words translated as "led" and "cry" both have wider uses in Greek that may point to enthusiastic, ecstatic worship practices in the early house churches.[64] The status of child of God is not given to all humans simply by virtue of being human. It belongs specifically to those who have been led into this relationship by the Spirit. Although this idea may be disturbing to some Christians today who have been accustomed to using that phrase more inclusively, it was an idea that was important for many theologians in the past. Luther points out that the idea of adoption reminds us of grace. None of us is a child of God by nature—simply because we are human—or because of what we have done. Rather we become children of God only by God's gracious action to accept us as such.[65] The idea that "children of God" is a more restricted group than all humans leads to the question about who belongs in that group. Wesley used this text to consider how we can know that we have been adopted. He explored the way in which God's Spirit witnesses to our spirit to assure us of this graciously given relationship.[66] Although grace and assurance are both important ideas to take from this text, it is important to realize that an individualistic interpretation together with the idea that "children" does not include all individuals can lead to self-doubt, obsessive self-examination, or competition with others over who has the Spirit.

Paul is still addressing the whole community ("you" plural and "we"). His intent is not to break down community in competition over who is a child of God and who is not, but rather to underscore the new community we have when we are in Christ. Although Paul

64. Jewett, *Romans*, 496–500.
65. Luther, *Commentary on Romans*, 121.
66. Wesley, Sermons 10 and 11, "The Witness of the Spirit: Discourses I and II" *The Works of John Wesley*, ed. Frank Baker, vol. 1, Sermons I, ed. Albert C. Outler (Nashville: Abingdon Press, 1984), 269–98.

has previously made use of the metaphor of enslavement when he talks about the new dominion the followers of Jesus enter (see 6:18), he now changes this metaphor. The presence of the Spirit in the gathering for worship leads the followers of Jesus to cry out to God as a parent, confirming that they are not slaves but children of God. Their allegiance to the dominion of the Spirit presents them with a new set of obligations—not the obligations of slave to master but rather the obligations of joint heirs because of their common adopted status. English translations of 8:14–15 may obscure some wordplay in Greek. The word translated as "adoption" conveys the idea of "son-making" in Greek (*huiothesias*), so Paul refers to the community members as "sons" (*huioi*) in 8:14. The Greek wordplay between "sons" and "son-making" also calls to mind that in 8:3 Paul says God sent the Son into the world to deal with sin.[67] Through Jesus Christ, God's own Son, we become adopted sons and therefore joint heirs with Christ. The masculine language in Greek has a purpose in connecting all these ideas, but Paul drops the masculine language in 8:16–17 to speak instead of "children" (*tekna*). By shifting to language that is not gender-specific, Paul makes clear that women as well as men are heirs with Christ, thus breaking down one of the traditional hierarchical barriers between people in Roman society and opening the way to think of how other barriers are also overcome in Christ.[68] Adoption makes the followers of Jesus kin to one another, brothers and sisters in Christ, regardless of their place in society.

Crying "Abba! Father!" is an indicator of this adoption. "Abba" is the Aramaic word for "father," so Paul has included both the Aramaic and Greek forms of address to God. The inclusion of both languages makes sense in a community made up of Greek and Jewish followers of Jesus, and since both words indicate the adopted status of the ones who cry out, each group needs to recognize its common inheritance with the other. Because the word "heir" calls to mind Paul's

> We—God's children! In uttering these words we are talking blasphemy or we are singing the song of the redeemed.
>
> Barth, *Epistle to the Romans*, 299.

---

67. Keck, *Romans*, 206–7.
68. Jewett, *Romans*, 502.

discussion of inheritance regarding God's promise to Abraham (4:13–14) the direct address to God in both Aramaic and Greek reinforces the common spiritual ancestry of the followers of Jesus, whether they may be Jew or Gentile. Neither group has a lesser place in the community, and they need to see and treat each other equally as brothers and sisters in Christ.

Of course, the inheritance that joint heirs with Christ receive comes through being baptized into his death. Suffering comes before glory. Just as the Son took on the vulnerability of weakness, which brings social shame, the joint-heirs with Christ must give up the mindset of the flesh that would seek glory in status and power and instead follow the Son's example of accepting the suffering that accompanies weakness in order to gain a more secure glory. The passive "be glorified" indicates that glory is not ours to be won, but rather it is God's to give.

8:18–30

Anticipating the Future Hope

In 8:18, Paul sets up a contrast not only between suffering and glory but also between the present age and the age to come. The idea of the passing of one difficult age into another peaceful one was not only found in Jewish apocalyptic but also in Roman imperial expectations (the emperor returning Rome to its golden age), so Paul's Roman hearers would have no difficulty imagining one age giving way to another. As Paul describes it, the present age is marked by suffering and by the longing of creation itself to be set free from its decay. It is not clear exactly what kind of suffering Paul is talking about. Is it the ordinary suffering that simply accompanies life? Is it the suffering that accompanies the transition between ages? Or is it the specific suffering that the followers of Jesus in Rome may have experienced because of expulsion and harassment? Or is it the indignity of being at the bottom of the social hierarchy? Whatever kind of suffering Paul may have had in mind, it is clear that it cannot compare with the glory that is about to be revealed.

As it was understood in the Roman Empire, human glory meant

the high opinion of others related to status or achievement. Glory was tied to reputation and fame, that is, to being recognized as important or honored by others. In contrast, the Hebrew Scriptures show God's glory (*kavod*) to be God's revealed presence (for instance in Exod. 33:18).[69] God's glory radiates from God's own being. God's own worth shines forth. Others can recognize that glory, but they do not bestow it. As we saw in 8:17, the children of God are glorified with Christ. The passive form indicates that the children's glory is bestowed, not inherent. Because it is bestowed by God and not by other human beings, it will not be temporary and fickle, the way that humanly bestowed honor is. The glory that is to be revealed is God's own glory that will be shared with God's children. In 8:18, the Greek preposition *eis*, which follows the word for "revealed," admits of many possible translations, as a comparison of English translations shows. The glory may be revealed *to* us (NRSV) or *in* us (NIV) or *for* us (REB).

At least some of the varieties of ways to translate *eis* begin to cohere when one notices that in the next verse, what is revealed is the children of God. If the glory is revealed to "us," who are the children of God, and then we the children are revealed to creation, then the glory that is revealed to the children is also revealed in or through the children as they reflect the glory of God.

Barth understands glory not as a compensation for our suffering, but rather as the answer to the question that suffering raises. In suffering, one sees the ambiguity of finitude—the limit, absurdity, and futility of life—and cries out. Is there anything beyond whatever finite and ambiguous reparation we may receive in this world to make this suffering meaningful? Is there any true consolation? There is no consolation in the present world, but the Holy Spirit brings consolation by helping us see that in suffering, God reckons with us. That is, suffering is the door to God because it is precisely where we call out to God and where God enables us to participate in Christ's suffering. God is manifested as the answer to the questioning that arises in suffering.[70] This does not mean that Christians

69. Carey C. Newman, "Glory, glorify," in *New Interpreter's Dictionary of the Bible*, vol. 2, ed. Katharine Doob Sakenfeld, (Nashville: Abingdon Press, 2007).
70. Barth, *Epistle to the Romans*, 305.

should seek to suffer, but rather it is an acknowledgment that Christians are subject to the suffering the world produces. But when it comes, Christians may face suffering confidently because they can find the manifestation of God there. Looking for Christ in suffering allows Christ to help with the bearing of it, and so the glory of God is revealed.

The glory that is revealed is not only for the children. All creation waits and longs for the revealing (8:19). It was not uncommon to personify nature in the ancient world (like Mother Earth), and Paul speaks of creation as having the same kind of expectations that humans have for the new age.[71] Creation, too, suffers in its "bondage to decay" (8:21). It is also fallen and needs to be restored. The cult of the emperor expected that the reign of peace under Caesar Augustus would even transform nature.[72] Paul, though, expects restoration to come, not by military conquest and imperial control, but through the children of God. As the gospel spreads, the children of God become known, and they reflect God's glory, which is not like the glory sought in hierarchical social relationships. Could this possibly make a difference for nature itself?

As later christological reflection began to make use of the rich meanings of *logos* as a way of understanding Jesus, theologians could connect human destiny and the destiny of all creation through the rationality imbued in the whole universe by the *Logos*. This connection is a source of both hope and risk. As humans come to understand the world around us and discover its meaning, we may hope that humans also come to understand more fully our responsibility toward the world. The risk lies in the way human sin affects more than simply human beings: it distorts the entire creation.[73]

> In this powerful symbolization, humans trying to play God ended up ruining not only their relations with each other but also their relation to the natural world.
>
> Jewett, *Romans*, 513.

---

71. Jewett, *Romans*, 511–12.
72. Ibid., 512.
73. Stelian Tofana, "Humankind and Creation as Interdependent in Romans 8:18–23: An Orthodox Exegetical and Hermeneutical Perspective," in *Greek Patristic and Eastern Orthodox Interpretations of Romans*, ed. Daniel Patte and Vasile Mihoc, Romans through History and Culture series, vol. 9 (London: Bloomsbury and T. & T. Clark, 2013), 155–78.

In our time, the idea of creation longing for restoration can easily be connected to ecological issues. We can see the gospel as good news not only for human beings but also for all creation because the hierarchical thinking that leads a person to treat another person as an object—of value only for one's own gain—also leads persons to use and value creation only as it contributes to personal gain. A reversal of those values so that we see creation's worth and goodness as God sees it and act on its behalf is good news. As we stand on the edge of ecological crisis, the idea that the children of God can and should make a difference for creation is both timely and important.

Of course, it must be remembered that humans are creatures, and as created things, the circumstances of humans and the rest of creation are interconnected. Paul knows that creation's need for restoration was not creation's own doing (8:20). The account of the fall in Genesis 3:17–18 lies behind his thinking. Because of Adam and Eve's disobedience, the ground is "cursed." The situation is not simply punitive, though, because just as creation shares in the fall of humans, it can also share in their hope for liberation through Jesus Christ. So creation expects and longs to participate in the freedom of the glory of the children of God. Hope for humans and hope for creation are interdependent. We would do well to remember that our own fulfillment can never be privately achieved because it takes place in a context of cosmic relatedness.

So creation groans in anticipation the way a woman groans in labor (8:22). The suffering is intense, but there is hope for a wonderful gift at the end. Paul's "until now" suggests that this groaning labor has lasted a long time, perhaps since the fall itself—no peaceful gestation period here. The reason for hope does not form and come from within. Creation groans for something to be done for it. Not only creation, but "we ourselves," the followers of Jesus Christ, "groan" (8:23) while we wait for adoption, that is, while we wait to be joint-heirs with Christ in glorification, again something that is not within ourselves but is done for us. Shared painful anticipation shows

> Having the Spirit does not isolate the believer *from* the unredeemed creation; rather, it reinforces the believer's solidarity *with* the creation.
>
> Keck, *Romans*, 212.

the intimate interconnectedness of creation and the followers of Jesus.

Although we have the firstfruits of the Spirit (8:23), there is more to come. The way Paul uses the image of firstfruits comes from practice recounted in Hebrew Scripture, but it also alters that understanding. The firstfruits of a harvest were offered by the people to God, but in this case it is God who gives the firstfruits. The offering of firstfruit acted as a reminder to the people that the land and harvest came as gifts from God (Deut. 26:1–11), but the firstfruit of the Spirit acts rather as a pledge or guarantee that God has started a great work that will be finished. After Paul has said in 8:15 that the hearers "have received" a spirit of adoption, it seems odd to find him now saying that we are waiting for adoption. The reference to waiting does not cast doubt on the adoption that has taken place. Rather, it stresses expectation. The "spirit of adoption" is the firstfruit of the Spirit, but, just as the harvest is not complete when the firstfruits are gathered, more fruits will come. The Orthodox have used this second reference to adoption to stress growth, constant ascent to our communion with God, called *epectasis*.[74] For Paul, we await the "redemption of our bodies" (8:23). Our adoption as joint heirs with Christ includes our bodies, which are still subject to the decay of creation. Paul is here referring to the resurrection of the body, so our groaning expectation is to be raised as Christ was raised.

Paul's expectation for the body is notable for two reasons. First, he does not think of the human being as a soul trapped inside a body from which it needs to be released.[75] Rather, the human is the whole person, soul and body, so God's saving work encompasses the whole of what a human is. This idea does not only imply hope for bodily resurrection but also for the way we treat our own and each other's bodies in this life. Although Christians have sometimes leaned in the direction of denying the importance of bodily welfare in favor of spiritual welfare, Paul's inclusion of the body in the hope for redemption encourages Christians to participate in the Spirit's concern for the body, which can be extended to bodily well-being in this life. Second, to talk about the resurrection of the body

74. Ibid., 169.
75. Keck, *Romans*, 212.

as "redemption" has a distinctly social meaning. In ancient Rome, "redemption" was a word used in the context of captivity or imprisonment in war. One who had been captured by the enemy could be "redeemed" by paying a ransom. Only people of high social standing and wealth could hope to be released in this way.[76] To speak of all the followers of Jesus in Rome as expecting redemption places a value on all of them regardless of social status, and this value extends even to their bodies.

Because we live in expectancy, Paul writes about hope. His first affirmation about hope, though, is somewhat ambiguous, as may be seen from a comparison of translations. Are we saved in hope, by hope, or even for hope? It is unlikely that Paul is suggesting hope is the means of salvation; in other words, he is not saying we are saved by our hoping. Rather, we are able to hope because we are saved. Because of God's saving activity in Jesus Christ, we are able to hope for more than what we see around us. What we actually see when we look at the world is decay, unjust structures, and distorted human relationships. But because we know God's salvation in Jesus Christ, we can hope for more than this.

What we hope for is not seen, but it is not imaginary either. We have reason to hope for transformation because we have already received the "firstfruits" of it. This position of standing between the pledge and the fulfillment is often expressed as being between the "already" and the "not yet." The new age has been initiated, but it is not completely here yet. Living in this tension is not easy, and we groan for resolution, for the fulfillment of the work God has begun. So we wait in hope for what is yet to come. Paul describes waiting "with patience." The word translated as "patience" does not mean simply waiting without irritation or complaint. The word really suggests endurance, steadfastness, and perseverance. Waiting in this tension is difficult, but we express our faithfulness by persevering. Because

> Christian hope produces in us, not only trust and firmness in the faith, but also a different way of living.
>
> Justo L. González and Zaida Maldonado Pérez, *An Introduction to Christian Theology* (Nashville: Abingdon Press, 2002), 151.

---

76. Jewett, *Romans*, 519.

the word means more than just the attitude we adopt while waiting, it opens the possibility for thinking about the time of waiting as a time of activity, not passivity. Even if we cannot bring about the fulfillment of the new age by ourselves (this work is God's), we do not have to wait idly. Creation is groaning for the revelation of the children of God, and knowing ourselves to be adopted, we can and should make ourselves known as those children by the way we live. The time between the "already" and the "not yet" is a time in which the children of God may act, showing the world what God has done for us and giving the world reason to hope for more. We do not have to settle for the brokenness and injustice that we see, but we may reveal through our actions the alternative way of being in the world that God already makes possible.

Existence between the already and the not yet makes followers of Jesus somewhat vulnerable. Hoping for what is not seen could appear to many to be a foolish expectation. Living in and for a new reality and way of doing things puts us at odds with the way things are done now, so we do not rise in social standing or have the usual kinds of influence. Even in such weakness, we are empowered by the Spirit. To persevere in allegiance to God when something else constantly calls for our allegiance takes prayer. Because we stand between times, hoping for things not yet seen, we do not see properly how to pray, so the Spirit works with us to assist us in prayer. The word translated as "sighs" in the NRSV in 8:26 and the word translated as "groan" in 8:23 come from the same Greek word (*stenazō*). So in prayer, the Spirit is groaning with the groaning creation and groaning Christ followers. The Spirit shares in our anticipation of the fulfillment for which we long.

Because the Spirit groans with us and intercedes for us, God knows our longing even when we are unable to articulate it. As Barth points out, whenever we pray, and no matter how good the prayer, we think and speak in the terms we have learned from the world in which we live. So inevitably our prayers are expressed in words and concepts that fall short of divine understanding. But the Spirit sees beyond our articulation to the prayer that lies beneath our utterance, and it makes our thoughts and words into real communion with God.[77]

---

77. Barth, *Epistle to the Romans*, 316–17.

Although we still live only in groaning anticipation, Paul makes a strong affirmation. For those who "love God," all things work together for good. Even though the subject of the sentence is ambiguous (is it God, the Spirit, or the things themselves that are bringing this about?), the affirmation is not in doubt. Because we know and love God, we may be confident that good will come even out of the suffering that is now endured.

Paul further describes those who love God as those who are "called according to his purpose" (8:28). This description sets our love for God in the context of what God is doing, so love for God is neither merely emotional nor does it arise apart from God's own work. Paul addressed the recipients of this letter in 1:7 as "God's beloved in Rome, who are called to be saints." Recalling this opening address shows us that we love God because we are beloved, that is because God first loved us; and because we are loved, we are called to be saints, that is, called to be holy or set apart as God's. Arriving at this point in the letter we can understand more fully the meaning of this salutation. Being set apart for God means living in the dominion of grace—loyal to God rather than to sin. Those who love God are those who live in allegiance to God. When we do so, we are living according to the purpose God has for us as those called to be saints, and all things, even the suffering we undergo because we live out of step with the rest of the world, work together for good.

In 8:29, the idea of calling leads to speaking of foreknowledge and predestination, concepts that have been theologically important in the development of Christian thinking but also have a history before Christian theology. The idea of election, namely, that God chooses some for a purpose, is deeply rooted in Hebrew Scripture. God made covenant with Israel, choosing this people to be the people of God, electing them for the purpose of being a light to the nations. The meaning of that special relationship is a major concern for Paul in this letter. Hebrew Scripture is filled with the idea that God is the Lord of history, not only because of this election but also because of God's foreknowledge of events, as made known to the people through the

> "He first loved us." There, in a nutshell, is what the idea of predestination wants to say and to protect.
>
> Howard G. Hageman, *Predestination* (Philadelphia, PA: Fortress Press, 1963), 73.

prophets. Paul's reference to calling, foreknowledge, and predestination comes out of his Jewish identity and formation. It also may reflect his specific identity as a Pharisee, as Pharisees pondered the relationship between God's action and human action in events.[78]

The emphasis on calling and predestination is a way of affirming God's initiative in salvation. Those who are called, foreknown, and predestined will be conformed to the image of the Son, so the Son Jesus Christ will be the firstborn among a large family of adopted children (8:29). When God decides to save (predestines), God calls. Those who are called are also justified and glorified (8:30). What God begins, God also completes. God initiates salvation as well as carries it out to its fulfillment.

Paul's remarks about predestination are words of encouragement to the recipients of this letter that God would in fact bring the goodness of salvation out of their suffering. Paul is not speaking here of predestination as determinism of all events. Nor is he speaking of any of the theories of predestination that developed much later (such as eternal decrees). The theologically important meaning of predestination in this letter is about God's initiative in our salvation, about God's faithfulness in fulfilling God's purpose for us to be saved, and about how both these affirmations remove all grounds for human boasting in what we have done for ourselves.

FURTHER REFLECTIONS
Predestination

Predestination is certainly a biblical idea, but its implications are not fully worked out in the Bible. Intended as an affirmation about God's sovereignty, this doctrine has raised many questions about how God works and whom God loves, making predestination a contentious idea in theology.

As Christianity spread among Gentiles, and as theologians began to make use of philosophy to articulate Christian ideas, God's transcendence was understood to mean that God is beyond the

---

78. Matthew Levering, *Predestination: Biblical and Theological Paths* (Oxford: Oxford University Press, 2011), 14–15.

conditions of space and time in which the creatures live. For God to be eternal meant that God was outside of time. Being outside of time, God saw all time (past, present, and future) all at once, which explained how God could know things before they happened to us from our point of view.

Beyond matters of knowledge were matters of choice. If God saved whomever God destined to be saved, whom did God so destine? Already in the patristic period, several answers to this question were formulated. Origen made the argument for universal salvation based on God's love for everyone. In other words, because God loves everyone, God chooses to save everyone. Those who freely choose to respond to the gospel are purified in this life, but those who reject it in this life will be purified by fire in the life to come. All will eventually be saved because God's love and desire to save all cannot fail. Augustine, in the context of refuting Pelagius, focuses on avoiding anything that would promote human pride. Not even our response to the gospel is up to us; it is a gift of God. God gives even the faith by which we respond, so we cannot boast in being responsible for our salvation in any way. Salvation is entirely gift, so the ones who are saved are those to whom God has given this gift. Because Scripture suggests that not all respond, it would seem to follow that God does not give this gift to everyone. It is not up to us to explain why God chooses some and not others; it is up to us to trust in God's wisdom and righteousness to know God's choices are good. Like Augustine, John of Damascus believed some will be saved and some will not, but unlike Augustine, he attributed the difference to human freedom, not to God's choice. Although God foreknows who will respond and who will not, God does not choose some for responding and others for not responding.[79] These alternatives arose early in the church's theological reflection, and versions of each alternative have been kept alive, embraced, and developed through subsequent history.

Predestination is not an easy idea to grasp in a culture that promotes individual freedom and choice. To begin to see the

---

79. Ibid., 36–67.

theological point, it may be helpful to think about a very ordinary way that we are not in control of our lives. We do not decide where we are born, and the circumstances of our birth set conditions for many of the decisions we make—ranging from health predispositions to the respect we receive in society and the resources at our disposal. So yes, we make choices, but those choices are made within conditions we did not choose. Theologically, predestination reminds us that Christians make their choice for God within the condition of God's prior love for us, and God's prior action to act salvifically in Jesus Christ. The way that God saves us in Christ is to love us first and evoke our love in return.

Paul's letter to the Romans has been an important resource for all who have thought about predestination, but it is important to remember that he did not himself try to work out answers to the questions that arose later. Paul clearly affirms God's grace and human faithfulness in response to the gospel, but it has historically been less clear how to hold those affirmations together. No option that has been developed has been satisfying and convincing to every Christian. If the full explanation of how and whom God saves is not at our disposal, we can at least understand that in these verses Paul is calling us to thankfulness, to trust, and to hope.

8:31–39
God Is for Us

Paul's words at the end of this portion of the letter have brought comfort not only to the original hearers, but also to countless Christians since. In light of the affirmations Paul has made about God's faithfulness, about God's love, about the presence and activity of the Spirit, and about the freedom given in Christ Jesus, he asks a rhetorical question: "If God is for us, who is against us?" (8:31). The answer to the question ("no one") does not need to be stated because the affirmations in Paul's argument make the answer so clear. Keeping in mind that Paul has already spoken of an impending day of wrath (2:1–16), the question has more than rhetorical significance. Believing that God's wrath is a real and close possibility, knowing that God

Paul proclaims the good news of God's faithfulness: nothing can separate us from the love of God that is in Christ Jesus. He considers and rejects a whole list of things that might seem more powerful than God's love and calls on his hearers to trust the reality of God more than the illusions of the enemy.

Grieb, *The Story of Romans*, 83.

is "for us" is extremely important. The only rightful judge on that day is God; so if God is for us, no one could oppose us.

The questions that follow bring out the implications of having God on your side on that day. This is the God who, although knowing that Jew and Gentile alike are without excuse for their unrighteousness, did not deny the means of overcoming that unrighteousness, God's own Son (8:32). The God who has already acted with such generosity will surely continue to give us everything we need. If God is preparing us so fully for judgment in the courtroom, who could possibly bring charges against us (8:33)? If God acquits us, who could possibly condemn us (8:34)? Jesus Christ himself, who took on weakness and died a shameful death to glorify weak people, who was raised and with whom we also will be raised, and who has a place of honor with God, now intercedes for us. How could anything possibly separate us from such a love?

Paul is realistic enough to know that much might try to separate us from that love. He lists in 8:35 sufferings that often seem to have the power to defeat us, many of which he has by the time he wrote this letter already faced himself. But as he knows personally, not even these things can succeed. Because the love of Christ is sure, we will prevail in Christ. In fact we will more than prevail. We will be "more than conquerors," or "supervictors"[80] (8:37). Neither sufferings in history nor cosmic powers nor anything else will succeed in separating us from the love of God in Christ Jesus our Lord.

80. Jewett, *Romans*, 548–49.

9:1–11:36

God's Faithfulness to Israel

9:1–5

Paul's Concern for Israel

Chapters 9–11 seem to change the topic so abruptly that it has even been suggested that these chapters come from extraneous material worked into Paul's letter.[1] It has been difficult for many to see how Paul's reflections about Israel's place in God's plan fit into his over-all argument. This problem has been particularly acute for the "old perspective" when it looks at the letter as a doctrinal treatise. The excursus on Israel simply does not have a place in standard doctrinal topics.

Another problem for interpreting these chapters is that what Paul says about the Jews seems to be anti-Jewish, and Christians of later centuries have indeed used his words and ideas against the Jews. This portion of his letter has been used to support ideas that range from showing Christian superiority over Judaism to outright con-tempt for Judaism. Theologians have justified supersessionism (the idea that Christians replaced Jews as God's covenant people, whether seeing Israel as lost or treating Israel as obsolete or irrelevant) on the basis of what Paul has been taken to say about Israel in these chapters. Some have even justified persecu-tion of the Jews with Paul's words. For this reason, the major theolo-gians of Christian history say very little that is helpful for

> **Humble acknowledgment by the church that its previous viewpoint was shortsighted is the imperative of the time.**
>
> John T. Pawlikowski, *What Are They Saying about Christian-Jewish Relations?* (New York: Paulist Press, 1980), 65.

---

1. A. Katherine Grieb, *The Story of Romans: A Narrative Defense of God's Righteousness* (Louisville, KY: Westminster John Knox Press, 2002), 86.

understanding what Paul might say to our time. Reading these texts in an anti-Jewish way has been so persistent and pervasive in Christianity that it takes constant, conscious effort to recognize and resist it. Biblical scholarship has done much in recent years to provide a perspective that shows how deeply Jewish Paul's thinking in these chapters really is. Even if what he says about Israel may not be completely satisfying as a way of thinking about Christian-Jewish relations in our time, to use it against the Jews is a gross distortion of his meaning.

Paul is, of course, reflecting on a situation that is very different from the one that we face today. In his time, the followers of Jesus had not yet become thoroughly Gentile and separated completely from Judaism. He did not know, and he could not foresee, that Christianity and Judaism would eventually define themselves in contrast to each other, that Christianity would become the religion of the empire, and that Christians would use that power to persecute the Jews. Since our situation is so different from his, his insights about Judaism have to be considered in light of the history that we now have. The best way to learn from him is not simply to accept his description of the Jewish situation that he knew and hoped for, but to listen carefully to what he has to say about God. Once we understand what he affirms about God in light of the pressing question of his time, we can more faithfully think about the pressing questions of ours.

> Jews and Christians are, historically, more closely linked in beliefs and ethics than any other religions, and for that very reason have greater need for a serious effort towards mutual understanding.
>
> David H. C. Read, "Reflections of an Imported WASP," in *Removing Anti-Judaism from the Pulpit*, eds. Howard Clark Kee and Irvin J. Borowsky (New York: Continuum, 1996), 61.

Although the shift in topics has seemed for many to be abrupt, it does follow from what Paul has been saying. His emphasis on God's faithfulness to those who are called according to God's purpose leads directly into the question of God's faithfulness to Israel, the people who were called according to God's purpose long before Jesus Christ. As a Jew, Paul would certainly have been concerned about this problem, and his hearers may also have shared such concern.

Although he is missionary to the Gentiles, Paul is not forgetting about the election of his people. He has just affirmed that nothing can separate us from the love of God in Christ Jesus our Lord, but what about the Jews who do not follow Jesus? Can their lack of belief in Jesus as Messiah separate them from God's love? The way Paul pursues this question is not to ask why the Jews do not believe. He does not launch into an explanation of why they should accept Jesus as Messiah. Rather, he wrestles with the faithfulness of God to Israel in light of what he has said about God's faithfulness so far. God's faithfulness demonstrates God's righteousness, so his argument is showing the righteousness of God.

As he begins to think through this problem, Paul assures his hearers that he is telling the truth. In other letters, Paul has made similar assurances (2 Cor. 11:31; Gal. 1:20), but this is his most extensive declaration, stating the point in 9:1 both positively ("I am speaking the truth") and negatively ("I am not lying") and claiming it to be Christ's truth confirmed by the Holy Spirit. Classical oratory sometimes used assertions of truthfulness as rhetorical formulas, but even so, Paul seems especially concerned to make this claim. There could be several reasons why Paul needs to stress the truth and importance of what he is saying. Perhaps his mission to the Gentiles has opened him to criticism of not caring about his own people. Perhaps criticism over the very way he presents the gospel in his mission to the Gentiles—that they do not have to take on Jewish obligation to the law in order to follow Jesus—prompts his need to defend the truth of his position. Or it may be that the problem lies not only with criticism of Paul, but also with misunderstanding of the people. A mostly Gentile community that has been without its Jewish brothers and sisters for some time might be leaning toward the idea that the followers of Jesus should all be Gentile.

Following this assurance, Paul expresses "great sorrow and unceasing anguish" (9:2) in his heart. This is not the emotion one would expect to hear after the beautiful affirmation he has made about being more than conquerors through Christ. Those hearing the letter read aloud for the first time would be caught by surprise at this emotional turn. Furthermore, Paul continues in this reversal of mood when he states his willingness to be separated from Christ for the sake of his own people (9:3) right after he has affirmed so eloquently that nothing can separate us from Christ. The whole effect must have been jarring to the original recipients as they heard these statements unfold, and the surprise and intensity of it may have created some sympathy for Paul that might make them more receptive to what he has to say.

Although in Paul's time there were clearly Jewish followers of Jesus Christ, already in his lifetime many Jews were not responding as positively as Gentiles to the gospel. Paul's concern about their situation is genuine, and his willingness to be cut off from Christ on their behalf calls to mind Moses' offer to be blotted out of God's book as he intercedes for Israel after the people made and worshiped a golden calf (Exod. 32:30–32). This expression of solidarity shows that although he follows Jesus, Paul does not consider himself to be no longer a Jew, and by identifying his anguish with Moses, he expresses that solidarity in a deeply Jewish way.

Paul's high regard for his Jewish heritage even as one who follows Jesus is made clear as he goes on. After using adoption imagery in 8:15, in which the followers of Jesus Christ are spiritual brothers and sisters, Paul recognizes that the people of Israel are his brothers and sisters according to the flesh (in the sense used in 4:1). As he talks about the people of Israel in 9:4–5, the use of the definite article "the" in his list of what belongs to Israel shows that Paul is speaking with specificity, not just about general ideas. He is speaking of Israel in terms he has already established previously in the letter. Israel has "the adoption": that is, the people of Israel were chosen by God for personal relationship and have sometimes been referred to as "sons" (Exod. 4:22, Hos. 1:10). Because they have been "made sons" (adopted), they also have "the glory," which Paul said would be revealed to and through the children of God. God has made several covenants through Israel's history, including with Noah (Gen. 9:8), Abraham (Gen. 17:2–8), Josiah (2 Kgs. 23:3), David (2 Sam. 23:5), and of course Moses (Exod. 24:3–8). The announcement of the prophet in Jeremiah 31:31–34 could even suggest that the "new covenant" could be included in "the covenants"; the new covenant is open to Gentiles but does not "belong" to them.[2] With the Mosaic

---

2. Robert Jewett, *Romans: A Commentary*, Hermeneia (Minneapolis: Fortress Press, 2007), 564.

covenant, the law, which is holy and just and good, was given to Israel. The law specified for Israel "the worship," out of which Christian liturgical practices developed. In their covenant relationship, God made many promises to Israel and to specific people in Israel's history. Even though Paul in 4:1–12 shows how Abraham once shared the condition of the Gentiles, the patriarchs, including Abraham, belong to Israel. The promises to Israel include the promise to send a messiah. Jesus, who is recognized as Messiah by his followers, was born to this people. All these things that belong to Israel make Israel a people to be honored, not scorned. Furthermore, by stating they "belong" to Israel, Paul is not suggesting that they have been transferred from Israel to someone else.[3] Rather, as he will go on to argue, Gentiles are given a way to participate in them.

This section ends in 9:5 with a doxology, the translation of which has been debated, depending on how to punctuate the string of phrases that are not punctuated clearly in the Greek manuscripts. Imagine reading those words with no punctuation. Is Christ being blessed as God over all? Or does the reference to Christ end with the reference to the flesh, followed by a separate praise of God over all? The ancient commentators did not typically notice this problem, perhaps because the doctrine of the incarnation made the difference between reference to God or Christ irrelevant. Karl Barth, though, does comment on this verse, using a reading that is different from either of the two abovementioned alternatives. Barth reads God as another item on the list of what "belongs" to Israel. Read in such a way, the verse offers Barth the opportunity to insist on the transcendence of God. Barth reads Israel as a "type" of the church— that is, as representing and having its meaning fulfilled in the church, and it must be recognized that there is supersessionist thinking that informs this kind of typological reading.[4] His reflections about God, though, usefully bring out important self-criticism that the church needs to hear. Barth argues that even though the church "possesses" an idea of "God" and a particular way to worship the "God" we

---

3. James D. G. Dunn, *The New Perspective on Paul*, rev. ed. (Grand Rapids: Wm. B. Eerdmans Publishing Co., 2008), 441.
4. Angus Paddison, "Karl Barth's Theological Exegesis of Romans 9–11 in Light of Jewish-Christian Understanding," *Journal for the Study of the New Testament* 28, no. 4 (2006): 469–88.

conceive, it does not and cannot possess the actual transcendent God who rules all things. Barth is pointing to the difference between a human concept of God and the living God. The transcendence of God remains the main theme of what he has to say about the church throughout his comments on these chapters.

9:6–18

God's Election

Although he sees a problem that brings him great grief, Paul does not and cannot say that God is the source of that problem. Paul has affirmed since his opening statement of his theme (1:16–17) that God has the power to save the Jew first and also the Greek and that God is righteous. He has just praised God as "over all." The righteous and powerful God over all cannot fail those whom God wants to save, but how is God's righteous reliability to be explained in light of the way Israel is responding?

Paul begins to work his way through this problem by ruling out one possibility: the word of God has not failed. God's purpose is not threatened by the very situation that gives Paul pain. Paul's task is to show how God is working despite the apparent resistance by so many of the Jews to God's action in Jesus Christ. He does so by distinguishing between all Israel and a more select group within Israel. There is an Israel within Israel. Because "truly" is not in the Greek text, I will refer to the "select" Israel rather than "true" Israel.

As he works out this distinction, Paul considers the way God acted through Abraham's offspring in the first two generations. Abraham had fathered eight sons—one by Hagar (Gen. 16:15), one by Sarah (Gen. 21:1–2), and, after Sarah died, six by Keturah (Gen. 25:2–4). Only Isaac went on to produce the line later called "Israel." Paul understands from this situation that physical relationship does not secure the promise. Because it is God's promise, God decides to whom the promise is given. Abraham fathered several sons, but God worked through Sarah's son because God had also made a promise to Sarah (Gen. 21:1–3). Paul continues to develop the freedom of God's choice with the example of Isaac's own sons. Rebekah bore twins, Esau and Jacob, but Jacob was to become Israel, and the promise was carried forward through him, not through Esau. God indicated to Rebekah even before the birth of her twins that the expected order of priority according to birth would be reversed. In this case, both sons had not only the same father, but also the same mother and were conceived at the same time. This parity underscores God's freedom to decide the way God would carry out what God will do apart from any external circumstances or even how the sons lived their lives. Neither of them behaved with utmost integrity, but God did what God had promised. Again, it is God's promise, so God decides how that promise will be fulfilled.

The language about loving Jacob and hating Esau (9:13) comes from Malachi 1:2–3. In Malachi, the statement is made in reference to the Israelites (Jacob's descendants) and the Edomites (Esau's descendants). Because the Edomites were actual enemies of Israel, the language of hatred makes sense in Malachi. When Paul uses this reference to Malachi, he is emphasizing that God freely chooses to accept or reject. In light of the problem he is considering, namely that some in Israel respond to the gospel and some do not, it could appear that Jacob represents believers and Esau represents unbelievers. Following this line of thought, many interpreters have used God's choice to love Jacob and hate Esau as the basis to develop a doctrine of predestination—God chooses who has faith and is therefore saved. Although the choice may seem arbitrary and perhaps unfair, theologians have often seen in this example a lesson about God's grace. For Luther, the example of twins shows that salvation is entirely up to God and does not depend on any inheritance or merit or any advantage a person may have in life. Because the choice is completely up to God, Luther says, "This is a hard saying for the proud and prudent. But it is sweet to the lowly and humble who despair of themselves."[5] The arbitrariness of the choice actually becomes important because it shows God's sovereignty and grace as gift, irrespective of our condition.

However much it may emphasize God's sovereignty and grace, many are still troubled by this way of thinking about God's choice.

5. Martin Luther, *Commentary on Romans*, trans. J. Theodore Mueller (Grand Rapids: Kregel Classics, 1974), 138.

Because not being chosen to have faith entails not being chosen to be saved, this idea at least implies the idea of double predestination—that God not only chooses who is saved but also chooses who is damned. John Wesley led Methodism away from a doctrine of predestination precisely because of this problem. Barth talked about the "scandal of predestination" and directed his thinking about the meaning of this text away from questions about who is saved and who is not saved. For Barth, the arbitrariness of God's choice leads us to ask, "Who is this God?" In the face of such freedom and transcendence, God is incomprehensible. The harshness of rejection leads us to ask this question, but one of the ways to come to know this God is "by the transformation of rejection to election."[6] The ones who find God's freedom to elect or reject to be harsh are those who trust in their own righteousness. It seems harsh because we think in terms of what we, or others, "deserve." Those who simply trust in the love of God, though, are not troubled by these words. Rejection is the opportunity for election just as tribulation is the opportunity for help. Knowing oneself to be rejected by God but still holding on firmly to this utterly transcendent God actually puts us in relationship with the living God.

> **How can we comprehend election, save as the transformation of our rejection?**
>
> Karl Barth, *The Epistle to the Romans,* trans. from the 6th ed. by Edwyn C. Hoskyns (London: Oxford University Press, 1968), 352.

Barth not only reflects on predestination. He also takes Paul's distinction between the select Israel and the more comprehensive Israel and applies it to the church. Again, one must recognize the supersessionism in reading Israel as a "type" of the church. If his thoughts about grace can be used without pressing this typology, Barth's reflection on predestination using Esau and Jacob may still have something to say that is worth hearing. He speaks of the church of Jacob—where the miracle of proclamation takes place and the Word of God is truly preached and heard—and the church of Esau—the church in history as a gathering of human beings with all its inadequacies and failures. The

---

6. Barth, *The Epistle to the Romans,* 348.

church of Jacob is an act of grace; God makes the truth known where and when God wills. The church of Esau is all our feeble effort to do what only God can do. Jacob and Esau are also each of us individually: Jacob when we truly rest in and are moved by God, Esau when we simply live out our temporal lives. Thus, Barth turns this text into a text of self-criticism. The distinction he offers in his way of reading this text calls us to discern when the church is truly church and when we truly respond to an encounter with God.

The long tradition of reading this text as the basis for a doctrine of predestination has deflected attention away from the specific question that troubled Paul, namely how to affirm God's righteous reliability in God's covenant relationship with Israel. Not even Barth's redirection to the transcendence of God and the self-criticism of the church helps with this task. Looking more directly at Paul's own concern, Katherine Grieb suggests that the arbitrary choice of Jacob over Esau raised the question of God's justice just as much for Paul and his original hearers as it does for readers today.[7] It does so especially if Paul is thinking of Esau as Israel not responding to the gospel. Does God hate Israel? Although some have seen Paul's thinking here as anti-Jewish, Grieb argues he is engaging in the deeply Jewish practice of lament. It is a cry of the heart that may express the groaning longing for what God will do that Paul talks about in 8:18–25. Paul himself raises the question of whether God may be unjust in 9:14. As he works his way through this problem, Paul raises questions that an interlocutor might ask, as he has done before. He is seeking a way to show how it is wrong to conclude from this arbitrary choice that God is unjust. Having made covenant with Israel, would God simply reject Israel? Paul's citation of Malachi is a step along the way in that argument with God, but it is not the final resolution of it.

Immediately after quoting Malachi, Paul raises a question in 9:14 that takes his thinking a step further. If God chooses whom to hate and love apart from any circumstances that might deserve hate or love, does this imply God's injustice? The form of the question in Greek indicates that Paul expects a negative answer. And Paul gives an emphatic, negative answer: "By no means." He underscores his

7. Grieb, *The Story of Romans*, 92.

negative answer by quoting Scripture. The quotation comes from Exodus 33:19, and the context is God's response to the people of Israel after they have made and worshiped the golden calf. Paul has identified himself with Moses in 9:3 when he is willing to be cut off from Christ for the sake of his people. Now he recalls the words God spoke to Moses when Moses interceded on behalf of the people. God is so displeased with the people that God will not travel with them (because God would be likely to "consume" them). Moses, though, persuades God to accompany them and God also agrees to show Moses the divine goodness. God shows favor to Moses and continues to be in relationship with the people at the precise time when the people have turned to the idolatry against which God's wrath is revealed (see 1:23). After God has passed before Moses, God gives the

> Is God *unrighteous*? No; but He has His own standard!
>
> Barth, *Epistle to the Romans*, 350.

law to Moses again to replace the tablets Moses broke in his anger, and God makes covenant with the people. To answer the question of whether there is injustice in God's free choice of whom to love, Paul recalls God's free decision to be merciful to the people even when they most deserved God's wrath. This account of God's actions shows that God's freedom is the freedom *to be merciful*. Showing mercy to whomever God chooses is fair and just because, as Wesley says, "He has a right to fix the terms on which he will show mercy."[8] Far from thinking that God hates Israel, Paul shows how God remained faithful to the people even when they dishonored God.

Mercy, then, does not depend on any human intention or effort, but only on God. God shows mercy just at the point where God is giving the law to Israel, so their obedience to the law cannot yet be its cause. God is merciful simply because God is a merciful God. By calling to mind this account of God's faithfulness even when Israel deserved wrath and before they could possibly have faithfully obeyed the law, Paul is showing he has good reason to be confident in God's righteous reliability. How could the word of this God possibly fail?

---

8. John Wesley, *Explanatory Notes upon the New Testament* (repr., London: Epworth Press, 2000), 557.

Paul has drawn from Malachi to talk about God's mercy, and now he draws from Exodus to talk about God's purposeful power. In 9:17, he quotes with some changes the LXX account of the words God told Moses to speak to Pharaoh (Exod. 9:16). Even when Pharaoh refuses to free Israel, God's purpose is not thwarted. In fact, the setbacks only serve to make the liberation seem greater. Pharaoh's denial of freedom becomes a means to show God's power all the more clearly. The example of Pharaoh shows that human refusal cannot overcome God's will. God is able to use even disobedience for God's purposes.

> By definition, mercy and compassion do not occur on the basis of fairness or justice.
>
> Leander Keck, *Romans,* Abingdon New Testament Commentaries (Nashville: Abingdon Press, 2005), 233.

Paul indicates in 9:18 that just as God has God's own standard for mercy, God has God's own standard for hardening. The text says only that God hardens, not that God rejects or destroys or damns, but because hard-heartedness is unfaithfulness rather than the faithfulness that saves, many have read this text as referring to election and rejection of individuals for salvation or damnation. To read the text in this way takes us back to the problem of double predestination. But if Paul is still thinking here (as he has been so far in this chapter) of Israel and seeking to understand God's justice in light of their refusal, then the claim in 9:18 is not really about God choosing who is saved and who is not, but rather it is another step in the search for how to understand God's righteousness. Yes, God hardens, but God does so for the purpose of making God's power known and thus bringing more to know and honor God.

9:19-29
The Potter and the Clay

Paul's imaginary dialogue partner asks the question (9:19) that naturally arises from the statement that God chooses whose hearts to harden. Because no one can resist God's will, the ones God has chosen for hardness could not do otherwise than have hard hearts.

How could they be held accountable? This is a question about God's justice or fairness because "finding fault" depends on responsibility. Is it right for God to hold anyone accountable if they could not have responded differently?

Paul does not really answer the question as it is asked. Instead he describes God's right to do as God pleases with what God has made. The image of God as potter was familiar from the prophets. Paul's words especially echo the prophet Isaiah, who presents the clay as having no right to argue with the potter (Isa. 29:16; 45:9). The potter determines what to make from the clay and how the object or vessel will be used. This image again stresses God's freedom to choose. At first, Paul describes the potter's decision about what to do with the clay as making vessels for special use or for ordinary use. The same lump of clay can be used to make different kinds of objects to be used in different ways. As he continues, though, he speaks of "objects of wrath" and "objects of mercy," rather than special and ordinary objects. That the objects of wrath are "made for destruction" and the objects of mercy are "prepared beforehand for glory" has made this another text often used to support a doctrine of double predestination: God not only chooses what to make but also whom to save and to damn. There are reasons not to read this image in that way. The Greek word that the NRSV translates as "made for" (9:22) really indicates a kind of equipping rather than creating, so it could be translated as "prepared for" or "readied for." Normally, a potter would not make something simply for the purpose of destroying it, but a potter may well decide after something is made that it needs to be destroyed and then prepare it for destruction. Destruction is not the reason for making the object, but there may be reasons (such as a flaw, an accident) for destroying the object. Furthermore, as we have seen, Paul is not developing the doctrine of predestination that came later. Rather he

> The vessels of wrath and mercy do not "stand for" specific groups of people so much as the entire image "stands for" the principle of God's impartial and purposeful election.
>
> E. Elizabeth Johnson, *The Function of Apocalyptic and Wisdom Traditions in Romans 9–11* (Atlanta: Scholar's Press, 1989), 149.

is thinking through how to talk about God's righteousness in light of the situation of Israel. Realizing this, it is also important not simply to identify Israel with the objects of wrath. Paul is making a point about what God can do with any of the objects God has made.

It is difficult to recover Paul's precise reasoning in 9:22–23 because the Greek text contains problems for translation (for instance, the Greek sets up a conditional sentence but does not clearly resolve the condition it sets up).[9] A comparison of several English translations reveals different kinds of decisions that translators can make about how to complete Paul's thought. Even if the sentence is difficult to follow, it contains several ideas that can suggest how Paul is thinking through the specific concern he has about Israel.

It seems to be clear that God has a purpose in mind and that this purpose involves showing wrath and power and enduring with patience the objects of wrath. Having these basic ideas in mind, one can recall what Paul said about wrath and power and patience at the beginning of his letter. In chapter 1 we have learned that the gospel is about God's power to save everyone who has faith, the Jew first and then the Greek. We have also learned that God reveals wrath to those who suppress the truth about God, and God shows this wrath by "giving up" those who suppress this truth to the consequences of their misunderstanding. "Giving up" does not mean abandoning but rather allowing the unwillingness to recognize God's truth to run its course. Then we learn in 2:4 that God exercises "kindness and forbearance and patience" (using the same word, *makrothumia*, he uses in 9:22), and this kindness is for the purpose of leading to repentance. Because Paul mentions patience before saying anything about destruction, it would seem that the patience ought to guide thinking about the objects of wrath. They were not made to be destroyed, but something has happened to make them displeasing to the potter. The potter, though, is patient and endures the object in order to show not only wrath but also power.

If we apply the idea Paul is bringing out about God's right to do what God wants to do with the objects God has made to the question about those in Israel who have not believed, then Paul's reasoning

9. Keck, *Romans*, 236–37.

might be like this: Jesus has been declared to be Son of God, Lord, Messiah (1:3–4). Although some in Israel have responded to this good news, many in Israel have not. It must be displeasing to God for God's own covenant people to refuse to acknowledge the power of God that is being revealed in this gospel (1:16). Although God's wrath in this situation is warranted, God is patient and endures their refusal. As with Pharaoh, delaying destruction allows God to show God's power. The delay also allows time for repentance. Paul then completes the picture by asking whether God might be doing all this "in order to make known the riches of his glory" (9:23), a phrase that would call to mind the glory Paul mentioned in 8:18 and 8:30. The ones who are called are justified and also glorified.

It is the "objects of mercy" who are prepared to participate in this glory, and Paul adds that God has called these objects of mercy from the Jews and also from the Gentiles (9:24). By quoting from Hosea, Paul is recalling a time in Israel's history when the people strayed and God called them back to repentance. Paul changes some of the words as he quotes Hosea to fit the situation he is addressing in his own time. "Not my people" and "Not pitied" are the names of children born to Hosea's wife, Gomer, and they represent God's judgment on the people for forsaking the true God. Through the marriage metaphor, Hosea shows that God is faithful despite Israel's straying and will win back the people. Paul changes the quotation slightly so it better serves the purposes for the situation he is writing about. He reverses the order of Hosea's words so that "not my people" comes first. Paul makes it a reference to the Gentiles, who were not the people with whom God made covenant but who have now been called to be God's beloved people. There is generative power in God's spoken word, so for God to call Gentiles "my people" makes it so. They are also called to be children of the living God, bringing to mind all Paul has said about adoption.

Paul quickly shifts from Hosea to Isaiah, and his reference moves from Gentiles to Jews. Paul has already set up a distinction between select Israel and all Israel, and now he makes use of Isaiah's notion of a "remnant" of Israel. Spoken in a situation of conquest, this notion of a remnant was a way of giving hope that all would not be lost. The remnant offers the possibility of restoration. Paul may have associated the words of Hosea and the words of Isaiah because both Hosea 1:10 and Isaiah 10:22 describe the number of Israel as the sands of the sea, but this image is employed differently by each of them. In Isaiah's situation, the numerous Israel will be reduced to a remnant but in Hosea's the full number will be restored as Judah and Israel are gathered together. Although Paul is quoting Isaiah, the resonance with Hosea raises some question about the number to be saved that will arise again in chapter 11. Paul is making use of the Jewish prophetic tradition to work out an understanding of God's righteousness. Both Hosea and Isaiah announced judgment followed by repentance and reconciliation. The idea of a remnant supplied a way for Paul to think about God's faithfulness through a few even if not all responded. The number of Jews who follow Jesus Christ, though small, indicates God's faithfulness to God's plan to save.

If Paul has been working his way through to an idea of God's righteousness, what does God finally look like? First and foremost, God is faithful. When God makes promises, God keeps those promises. Second, God's promises are not bound to the standards and circumstances known by human beings. Yes, God keeps promises, but God also determines how those promises will be kept. God's freedom to choose shows God's transcendence and power. God is in the right to judge, and God is in the right to show mercy. Humans do things to displease God, and God's wrath is surely deserved when that happens. God, though, often bears our rebellion with patience and uses the divine freedom to respond differently than we deserve. God shows power by showing mercy, by freely choosing to accept those whom God could deservedly reject. God's ways are not our ways, but God's faithfulness is not completely unfathomable because we have seen over and over again how God has remained faithful. God does not fail to keep the promises that God has made.

This understanding of God also implies something about how we relate to God. Although God shows us mercy over and over again, even at the point of our greatest fault, we should never presume on that mercy because God is the rightful judge, and God has every right to reject and not only accept. It is just as important to understand God's wrath as it is to understand God's mercy. God shows us a way to live, and when we stray from it, God's wrath shows us what we have done. The patience God shows us in this wrath is so that we will repent—turn back to the way God has shown.

FURTHER REFLECTIONS
Theodicy

Paul's attempt to understand God's justice in the face of a painful situation that does not seem right to him is a form of theological reflection that theologians call "theodicy," (from *theos*—God, and *dikē*—just or right). The question asked by the vessel, Why have you made me like this? is a question that many people ask regarding features of their lives that they may see as limiting: Why have you done (or allowed) this? is a comparable question about circumstances or events. Questions such as these arise because it is hard to hold together the ideas that God is all-powerful and all-just or all-good when things happen that seem to be neither just nor good.

Theodicy is usually a defense of God in the face of the "problem of evil." This problem is a constant challenge to our idea of God, and every person of faith no doubt wrestles at some point with questions about how to understand God when bad things happen. Theologians have tried to address this problem in a variety of ways. Some will stress God's power to do anything and God's control of everything that happens, and so they try to show why God has good reasons to do what God has done. Because God is in control, the painful circumstance or event only seems to be something that should not have happened. God has a reason for it: perhaps God is trying to teach us something (patience or humility) through it. The sovereign God is working for our good even when God causes things that bring about our suffering.

Others argue that God shares power with God's creatures, so not everything that happens is entirely up to God. Humans have free will, and much of the suffering we face in the world is because of poor human choices, not God's will. Other creatures besides humans also have some measure of freedom and power, so even events in nature may not be entirely caused by God. Within this position, it is even possible to acknowledge some element of chance. Whether because of creaturely decisions or chance, God does not determine everything that happens, so there is not always a divine reason for things to be as they are. God still, though, works to bring some good out of things that happen that are not directly caused by God.

Still others point out that we are not in a position to understand what God does and why. This way of addressing the problem reminds us of the huge difference between God and us. We cannot know how God works, and we should simply let God be God. As Job admits after God speaks to him, "I have uttered what I did not understand, things too wonderful for me, which I did not know" (Job 42:3b). God has a purpose, but we do not and cannot know it. God is beyond our understanding.

No single answer has been convincing to all Christians. Different people are comforted in times of trouble by different ideas. Some find comfort in the idea that God is in control. Others find comfort believing that God is not responsible for their trouble. Still others are content to rest in the mystery of God. Theodicy will be an ongoing task, never solving the problem but giving voice to our deepest questions. God is able to bear our cries of the heart, and God helps us bear the circumstances that cause those cries. What we learn from the way Paul works through his own lament is that God is always faithful, even if we do not understand everything that we want to know about how God works.

9:30–33

Israel and Works of the Law

If God is faithful in the way Paul has described, what further conclusion can be drawn about the situation of Israel? Too often Christians, and especially Protestants, have read these verses as a lesson about grace over Jewish legalism, but careful attention to Paul's wording (often obscured by English translation) shows that is not his point. Paul does contrast Israel with Gentiles, but the comparison he draws does not go where readers often expect it to go, and English translations can set up misleading expectations. Paul uses an image of a chase (the word in 9:30 the NRSV translates as "strive" also means "pursue"). Gentiles did not pursue righteousness, but they have nevertheless attained (apprehended) righteousness through faith. In contrast, Israel did pursue something. What was Israel pursuing? It is easy to anticipate a simple parallel: namely, that if the Gentiles attained righteousness (even without pursuing it) Israel must have been pursuing righteousness (and failed to attain it). The NRSV follows this logic and makes righteousness the object of Israel's striving or pursuit. But Paul does not draw such a simple parallel. What Israel pursued was not "righteousness that is based on the law" but simply the "law of righteousness." Paul stresses the law again when he says Israel did not arrive at (attain) the "law," (in 9:31 the NRSV adds the word "fulfilling," which is not in the Greek text).

These NRSV translation decisions reinforce a long-held Christian bias against the law (and the translation decisions may even be partially influenced by this bias). For centuries, Christians have presented a contrast between law and gospel that serves to show the superiority of Christian revelation. Sadly, the widely held idea of Christian superiority has played a role in fueling atrocities against Jews. If the gospel is not only superior to the law but also given as a replacement to the law, then Christians have felt justified in eliminating Judaism. In light of this history, paying closer attention to what Paul says is extremely important.

Paul does not say that the pursuit of the law of righteousness was the wrong kind of goal for Israel to have; the problem is rather that Israel did not apprehend the quarry that it was chasing. So Paul considers why it failed in its pursuit. The reason seems to lie in the way it was pursued, on the basis of works instead of faith (9:32). Israel had been elected by God to be the covenant people, and the law was given as expression of that covenant. As such, the law is God's gracious gift to Israel, a demonstration of God's mercy and faithfulness. Paul calls none of this into question, and in fact he has drawn from these points as he has defended God's righteousness. The right response to such a God is to obey the law that God has given. Paul has already shown, though, that it is not a simple thing to obey the law. The law can be used by sin, the law can lead to boasting, and the law can isolate Israel from the very nations it is supposed to enlighten.

There are many problems that can result from pursuing the law in the wrong way. Especially if there is focus on the "works of the law," understood as those things that mark the Jews off from other nations, relationship with God could be narrowed to special privilege for a few. If that happens, Israel would fail to attain God's intent for giving the law, namely, the intent that the faithfulness to the covenant between God and Israel would make Israel become a light to the nations.

> The gift always preceded the obligation. That is how Israel's covenant theology worked.
>
> N. T. Wright, *Justification: God's Plan and Paul's Vision* (Downers Grove, IL: IVP Academic, 2009), 232.

Israel did not reach its goal because it stumbled (9:32). What caused it to stumble? The Greek text leaves us with more ambiguity than English translation does. The pronoun in 9:33 in the phrase the NRSV translates "believe in him" could mean either "him" or "it." Along with the range of meaning that *pistis* can have, the phrase could just as easily be translated "trust in it." English translations, which must choose between pronouns, often use "him" following the common assumption that the stumbling block is Jesus Christ. The ambiguity in the Greek, though, has led to the suggestion that perhaps the pronoun refers to the law itself. It may be that the reason for the stumbling is the way the law was pursued, namely Israel "trusted in it" by pursuing it on the basis of works.[10] These two possibilities for the pronoun may actually work together. If the problem Paul is talking about is the way Jews trusted in their pursuit of the law, then they would not be receptive to how God would be working apart from the law in Jesus Christ. If this is the case, then Israel does stumble over Jesus Christ, but because of the way they have pursued the law.

The quotation in 9:23 that Paul uses to make his point about stumbling is a composite of several sources (see Isa. 8:14 and 28:16). Paul has put different texts together, and he arranges his compilation to make the point that God puts the stone in the way to cause stumbling. This image implies divine purpose in Israel's stumbling that Paul will go on to explain in 11:11–12.

---

10. Ibid., 245.

It is important not to read this text with a smugness of those who think they see things more clearly than the Jews in Paul's time did, celebrating that we Gentiles attained righteousness without pursuing it while the Jews failed. After all, Christians are often fond of trusting our own ways of pursuing the gospel, even setting and taking pride in "litmus tests" to determine who is really Christian. Do you believe the creeds? Do you speak in tongues? Have you been born again? Matters such as these function as "boundary markers" of who is a real Christian and who is not. It may be just as hard for some Christians in our time to imagine God working in someone who cannot answer yes to questions like these as it may have been for some Jews in Paul's time to imagine God working apart from the boundary markers in the law. These kinds of tests can be divisive of the community. Christians should take care how we pursue the gospel so that we don't fail to attain our own goal.

10:1–4
Zeal for God

The way Paul addresses the members of the Roman house churches draws attention to their spiritual kinship. Although he has expressed willingness to be cut off from Christ for the sake of his physical kindred, he knows that he is still connected through Christ to all of the Roman followers, making them his brothers and sisters. They are his kindred in a spiritual way. To them, he expresses deep feeling for Israel—the Greek *eudokia* (good pleasure, translated in 10:1 by the NRSV as "desire") actually suggests positive delight in them—as well as active supplication for their salvation. By reminding his kindred through Christ of his concern for his kindred in the flesh, he is demonstrating his solidarity with those he will be talking about and inviting his hearers into an attitude of openness to them. Paul is deeply connected to two groups of people: to Israel through his physical descent from Abraham's son Isaac and to the members of the churches through Jesus Christ. His thoughts about Israel's salvation as he writes this portion of his letter are informed by his personal knowledge of both.

Paul knows and can bear witness to Israel's zeal for God (9:2), a common expression to describe the desire to do God's will. In Jew-

> Since Judaism has provided the context for the very development of Christianity, no Christian church anywhere can ignore its attitudes toward the Jewish people.
>
> John T. Pawlikowski, *Christian-Jewish Relations*, 143.

ish literature, "zeal" had been used to describe those who maintained and defended, sometimes by force, purity and holiness according to the law, and it could be especially focused on those laws that marked Israel as distinctive, such as circumcision, food laws, and Sabbath.[11] Zeal to do God's will is a good thing, but it is possible for it to become exaggerated and harmful. In Philippians 3:6, Paul commented on his own zeal with regard to how he persecuted the church before he became a follower of Jesus. Paul, then, knows firsthand how zeal to do the will of God can keep one from seeing what God is doing outside of one's own expectations.

Because Paul bears witness to Israel's zeal, he is affirming Israel's desire to do God's will. He also says, though, that this desire has been uninformed about God's righteousness. Verse 3 is written in Greek with an economy of words, so it has been open to adding extra words to fit interpretation according to the old perspective. Such is the case when the NRSV translates *theou dikaiosynēn* (righteousness of God) as righteousness that *comes from* God. This addition makes Paul appear to be making a point against works righteousness as it has been understood in traditional Protestant theology. This interpretation suggests that Israel tried to become righteous through its own works rather than depending on righteousness that comes from and is imputed by God. A reading alert to the new perspective would instead consider the way that Paul has spoken about God's righteousness as God's faithfulness. Israel has wanted to do God's will to uphold its covenant with God, but it has not understood how God is faithful to the covenant and to all the promises made to Abraham. When Israel obeys the law only to establish its own righteousness in relation to God, Israel misses the

11. Dunn, *New Perspective*, 201.

way that God is working through Jesus Christ. God's righteousness is being faithful to the promise made to Abraham, and this righteousness leads God to work through the faithful Jesus to reach the nations. In this way, Christ is the end (*telos*) of the law. Debates have raged over whether "end" should be understood as goal or as termination. Because Paul continues to affirm in this letter that the law is holy and just and good (7:12), I will take "end" to mean goal. Because Christ fulfills what the law intends, everyone who believes (not just Israel) may be righteous.

> For just as he had to refute the pride of the Jews because they gloried in their works, so also with the Gentiles, lest they wax proud as if they had been preferred over the Jews.
>
> Augustine, *Augustine on Romans: Propositions from the Epistle to the Romans, Unfinished Commentary on the Epistle to the Romans,* text and trans. Paul Fredriksen Landes (Chico, CA: Scholars Press, 1982), 39.

Even theologians who have written comments that have shaped anti-Jewish sentiments among Christians have recognized that Christians need to hear a word of caution for themselves in what Paul says. Christian zeal for God can also be uninformed. Luther speaks of the "arrogant zeal of good intentions" that often blinds us to our mistakes.[12] Such zeal has marked the work of the church too often, and the desire to spread the gospel has served imperialism and colonialism. It has also fueled destructive behaviors against the Jews. A zeal that does not stand willing to be corrected can be dangerous.

10:5–13
The Messiah Saves

When he refers in 10:5 to what Moses writes, Paul is citing the idea expressed in Leviticus 18:5 that the one who keeps the law will live. Leviticus actually attributes the words to God, although they are traditionally presumed to be recorded by Moses. The "but" (*de*) that follows may appear to indicate a contrasting idea to correct the one

12. Luther, *Commentary on Romans*, 146.

Moses wrote, but Paul is not suggesting that Moses got the matter wrong when he recorded these words. The Greek *de* could simply show a change in speakers because Paul is personifying righteousness that comes from faith (this righteousness "says").[13] This new speaker is not issuing a correction to the idea that the law brings life, and in fact the words Paul has the personification speak are also drawn from the Mosaic law. Instead the words of 10:6–7 echo warnings from Deuteronomy about how Israel ought to regard its pursuit of the law. "Do not say in your heart" calls to mind Deuteronomy 8:17 and 9:4. By following the law that God has given, Israel shows its loyalty to God. God shows loyalty to the covenant by fulfilling the promise God made to give land to the people. When this fulfillment happens, the people are not to think (to say to themselves) that it has occurred because of what they have done. Nor are they to think that their prosperity is due to their own actions. The law itself warns against attributing God's gifts to one's own righteousness. Paul's words are not against the law or against obedience to the law, and they are not against works. Rather, they point to the way one ought to do works—gratefully acknowledging God's grace instead of claiming credit for oneself.

Paul does, though, associate Christ with imagery related to the Torah. He employs phrases from Deuteronomy 30:12–13 and Psalm 107:26 (LXX 106) about going to heaven and the abyss (sea)—that is, to the farthest possible locations—to talk about Christ. These images already had a history of use to say that one does not need to ascend so high or descend so low to gain wisdom because wisdom is available near at hand in the

> The Apostle does not here oppose the covenant given by Moses to the covenant given by Christ. If we ever imagined this it is for want of observing that the latter as well as the former of these words were spoken by Moses himself to the people of Israel, and that concerning the covenant which then was.
>
> John Wesley, "The Righteousness of Faith," ¶1, in *The Works of John Wesley*, vol. 1 (Nashville: Abingdon Press, 1984), 202.

---

13. Jewett, *Romans*, 625.

law. For Paul to speak of Christ in this way is to say that wisdom is now near in proclamation of Christ.[14]

As he goes on in verse 8 to quote Deuteronomy 30:14, Paul is linking the "word" spoken of in the law with the "word" that is proclaimed in the gospel. Jesus Christ is the end (goal) of the law. All that the law gave to Israel—the covenantal relationship, the faithfulness of God and the people, the possibility of life—is now proclaimed in Jesus Christ. Confessing Jesus is Lord acknowledges this proclamation. Like taking a loyalty oath to the emperor, this spoken confession of Jesus reveals one's allegiance to him. Spoken acknowledgment is matched with believing in the heart that God has validated Jesus as Messiah by raising him (10:9). A crucified Messiah would need such validation because of the shame attached to his mode of death. Paul uses the word *pisteuō*, which we have seen in the comments on 1:16–17 means not only "believe" but also "trust." Paul asserts that open acknowledgment of Jesus as Messiah, together with belief and trust that God acted to validate Jesus as Messiah, brings salvation. Mouth and heart—the public self and private self—function as one, so there is integrity in one's identity. The external confession displays to whom one belongs because of internal commitment. The integrity of inner and outer life (wholeness) that this allegiance to Jesus Christ brings must surely be included in what Christians expect salvation to be.

N. T. Wright points out that if God's faithfulness is shown in the Messiah's faithfulness (*pistis*), then our faith (*pistis*) is the "badge of God's redeemed people."[15] Christians should learn from what Paul has said about zeal, that it would be just as wrong for Christians today to become overly zealous about a badge of identity as it was for some Jews in Paul's time to be overly zealous about the badges and boundary markers for Israel. Paul's way of linking confession with salvation has often led Christians to insist on conversion from other faiths to Jesus Christ, and all too often that conversion came at great cost to the people. The confidence that we have in our confession of Jesus

---

14. Arland J. Hultgren, "*Pistis Christou*: Faith in or of Christ?" in *Paul's Letter to the Romans: A Commentary* (Grand Rapids: Wm. B. Eerdmans, Publishing Co., 2011), 387.
15. Wright, *Justification*, 209.

as Lord to bring us salvation should not blind us to the possibility of
other ways that God might be working in the world.

In Rome, the confession that Jesus is Lord would have overtones of a "counterconfession to emperor worship" even if it were
not directly aimed against the emperor.[16] The risk of shame in that
situation was real, but Paul knows that the children adopted by God
as joint-heirs with Jesus Christ will be glorified (8:17). Paul's main
point in 10:11–13, though, is less about glory and shame itself than
about who is entitled to hope in such glory. He stresses "all," Jew and
Greek, with no distinction. For the community in Rome, this inclusive statement would have a leveling effect. Neither group stands
above the other, so neither group should be shamed by the other.
All of them are saved by their belief and trust in Jesus Christ; salvation is neither hindered nor made possible by their ethnic identity.
Those who recognize him as Lord will receive his salvation. The leveling effect that Paul describes with regard to Jew and Greek may
be extended to other ways that we distinguish and divide ourselves
from each other: culturally, economically, educationally, racially,
denominationally. God's generosity ignores the way that we try to
organize and group ourselves, and it opposes our attempts to see
any of our brothers and sisters in Christ as lesser. All those who call
on Jesus Christ are saved by Jesus Christ and therefore made one in
Jesus Christ.

10:14–17

Mission

Paul asks a series of questions, each of which has an obvious negative response, and which together work through the conditions for
the points he has just made. Those who call on Jesus Christ will be
saved, but how can they call on him if they do not believe? As we
have seen, verbal confession and belief in the heart go together. The
translation in the NRSV (10:14) of the next question suggests that
the problem is that people cannot believe *in* Jesus Christ if they have

---

16. Hultgren, "*Pistis Christou*," 388.

never heard *of* Jesus Christ. The Greek, though, is open to another interpretation, namely that people cannot believe Jesus Christ because they have not heard him.[17] In other words, because Jesus is not present in the flesh to engage the people the way he once did, the next condition is that he must be proclaimed, which as we will see in the next paragraph, is a way of making him present. It is important to recognize that hearing and proclamation are not restricted to aural and auditory methods. The hearing impaired have just as much need and right to have Jesus Christ proclaimed to them as hearing people do. Paul's use of the word "hear" should not restrict methods of proclamation. People need to be invited to belief in ways that are appropriate to their understanding and reception.

Paul's point about proclamation no doubt is about more than delivering information about Jesus. He said in 1:16 that the gospel (good news) *is* the power of God for salvation, not simply *is about* the power of God for salvation. The proclamation of the gospel has power because it provides an opportunity for God to work. The "word of faith that we proclaim" (10:8) becomes the "word of Christ" (10:17). Proclaiming the gospel is the occasion for God to use human words to reveal the Word, to make present the reality that is being proclaimed.

When Barth began writing his commentary on the Epistle to the Romans, it was the problem of preaching that drove his reflection. When a preacher steps into the pulpit on Sunday morning, she or he stands between two expectations. One is the expectation of the people that they will be assured God is present. The other is God's expectation that there will be people open to God's presence. This situation offers a promise that an event may happen, a promise that can be fulfilled only by God. Proclamation

> The event toward which the expectancy of heaven and of earth is directed is none the less *God's* act. Nothing else can satisfy the waiting people and nothing else can be the will of God than that he himself should be revealed in the event.
>
> Karl Barth, "The Need and Promise of Christian Preaching," in *The Word of God and the Word of Man,* trans. Douglas Horton (London: Hodder and Stoughton, 1928), 124–25.

17. Keck, *Romans,* 257.

> **Evangelism is the outflow of hearts that are filled with the love of God for those who do not yet know him.**
>
> *Together towards Life: Mission and Evangelism in Changing Landscapes,* WCC Affirmation on Mission and Evangelism, https://www.oikoumene.org/en/resources/documents/commissions/mission-and -evangelism/together-towards-life-mission-and-evangelism-in-changing-landscapes.

can and should be this opportunity for a genuine encounter with the living Lord.[18]

How can such proclamation take place unless someone is sent to do it? At this point in the questions, Paul could be speaking about himself, an apostle (one who is sent), and yet the verb he uses (*apostalōsin*) is plural, acknowledging other apostles. All evangelism follows the logic he has outlined. Although the pattern of sending some specific people for mission remains, it is now widely agreed that sharing the good news is not only the task of a few "apostles" but of every Christian. The plural verb Paul uses can help us understand that we are all sent to share good news.

In a time where we have news from many sources and have much control over which sources to use, it may be hard to realize the importance of someone who brought news in the ancient world. Especially when the news was good, the herald would be very welcome. In 10:15, Paul uses, but edits, the words of Isaiah 52:7 to express the joy of the recipients upon receiving this kind of messenger. The way Paul edits Isaiah shows something of what makes for welcome good news about Jesus Christ. His version does not contain reference to a mountain and to peace, a redaction that Jewett suggests would take away possible imperialistic resonances (the mountain calling to mind Mount Zion and peace calling to mind the Pax Romana).[19] If Jewett is right, then we learn something about why this news is good. This Messiah is not furthering human imperial hopes, and so the good news of Jesus Christ is most welcome when it challenges messages from social institutions that act imperialistically by controlling and diminishing human life.

18. Karl Barth, "The Need and Promise of Christian Preaching," 97–135.
19. Jewett, *Romans,* 640.

Paul's use of Isaiah's words about bringing welcome good news, together with insights the editing may bring, may be instructive about a particularly sensitive subject in our time, namely conversion of Jews to Christianity. Paul does not see his Jewishness and his confession of Jesus as Lord to be antithetical. Rather he sees Jesus Christ as the fulfillment of God's faithfulness to the covenant with Israel. The first followers of Jesus were Jewish and Paul had to defend his way of sharing this faith with Gentiles. The situation twenty-one centuries later is quite different. We live with a history of two distinct religions and with a history of Christianity gaining imperialistic power and using that power to persecute Jews. The atrocity of the Shoah during World War II finally caught the attention of Christians and has led to introspection about how Christians should exist in relationship with Jews. Many are realizing that in our time, proclamation to get Jews to confess Jesus as Messiah is not welcome good news to them. Because they have faced genocide, Jews are very concerned about the survival of their community. Conversion to Christianity is considered a threat by assimilation to the survival of that community.

For this reason, a growing number encourage dialogue between Christians and Jews rather than evangelistic mission by Christians to Jews. Dialogue allows Christians to bear witness to faith in Jesus Christ as we explain what we understand to be the significance of Jesus for ourselves and for the world, but such witness is made without a feeling of superiority or attempts to coerce belief. Dialogue also requires listening to Jews express their own convictions and insights. It includes being willing to listen as pain and fear from centuries of persecution or personal discrimination are expressed.

Israel's resistance to absorption by the Church is a refusal to grant that the meanings of Israel are contained and subsumed in the Christian institution, and that refusal is essential for the truthfulness and faithfulness of the Church, tempted as it is to claim a distorted kind of finality.

Rowan Williams, "The Finality of Christ," *in On Christian Theology* (Oxford: Blackwell Publishers, 2000), 102–3.

Although Judaism in this century is different from the Judaism of Jesus' time, dialogue with Jews today can be an important reminder to pay attention to Jesus' own context. We have lost much in understanding our own faith by ignoring Jesus' own Jewish context. In popular understanding, Jesus has been so thoroughly removed from Judaism that many ordinary Christians do not even realize he was Jewish. Without knowledge of this context, Christians become unable to understand the message Jesus wanted to share. Dialogue with Jews now can make us more sensitive to noticing the ways Judaism informed what Jesus said and did.

Understanding Jesus' message better will help Christians proclaim the good news about Jesus better. Christians must be prepared, though, for the disappointment that not everyone will respond in the way they hope. Even in the time of the apostles, Paul understands that although the condition for belief may be met—people hear—they may not accept what they have heard. The language Paul uses in Greek in 10:16 involves a wordplay that is hard to convey fully in English. When he talked about how the good news must be heard, Paul used the verb *akouein*. In verse 16, the word translated as "obeyed" is *hypakouein*. To capture the wordplay and similarity in sound in English, one could say something like not all who hear hearken.[20] Because the Greek *hypakouein* connotes obedience—obeying a command that has been heard—the word sets up what Paul goes on to say about Israel.

Paul quotes Isaiah in 10:16 to show that the prophet also knew that delivering a message from God does not always meet with success. People must hear in order to respond, but hearing does not guarantee the desired response. Although Paul acknowledges the potential for failure, he does not dwell on it. He again states positively that hearing can produce faith and that the hearing that may produce faith is the word of Christ. The real possibility of lack of response should be no disincentive for proclamation. Christ must be proclaimed because this word is what produces faith.

20. Keck, *Romans*, 259.

10:18–21
The Situation of Israel

Having established the importance of hearing proclamation for faith, Paul addresses directly the problem that many of his own people have not responded in faith to the gospel. In doing so, he is working through the double reality that he knows, both that Israel has covenant relationship with God through the law and that so many of his people failed to recognize how God was working through Jesus Christ. The obvious thing to consider, given what he has just said about proclamation, is that perhaps they have not heard the proclamation. The question in 10:18 is phrased to expect a negative answer (as the NASB translates, "Surely they have never heard, have they?") as if not hearing would provide an excuse, but Paul directly refutes this line of thinking. They have heard. How does Paul think they have heard? Paul's quotation from Psalm 19:4 (LXX 18) may suggest that Paul thinks that they have heard because the gospel has already been taken to the ends of the earth, but Paul's intention to go to Spain would indicate he knows that there are places on the earth the gospel has not yet reached. Perhaps Paul's use of this quotation reflects his missionary vision rather than what has been already achieved. Another possibility is that even though the gospel has not yet been proclaimed in every area of the world, it has been proclaimed among both Jews and Gentiles, and in that sense it is comprehensive. Keck points out another possibility the psalm leaves open that lies just beyond the quoted material itself, and Paul may have been relying on his hearers' familiarity with the psalm to make the connection. The psalm from which these words come also includes verses that extol the goodness of the law. Because he believes that Jesus Christ is the end (goal) of the law, perhaps Paul is making a connection between the law and Jesus Christ.[21] Because Israel has the law, Israel has heard its *telos*. And because the *telos* (goal) of the law is Jesus Christ, in a sense they have heard Christ. Whatever reason Paul had in mind, his point is that Israel has indeed heard. This condition for their response has been met.

21. Ibid., 260–61.

So if they have heard him, why have they not believed him? Paul asks another question in 10:19 that expects a negative answer. If they have heard and not believed, it must be because they did not understand. This time he does not refute the implication of the question. Recall that Paul has stated in 10:2 that Israel has "a zeal for God, but it is not enlightened." They are "ignorant" of the righteousness of God. There is something they have misunderstood, but Paul does not try to explain or correct the misunderstanding. Instead he puts the focus on God's response by quoting Deuteronomy 32:21. Moses himself knew how rebellious the people of Israel would be, and he sang about how God would deal with them. The Greek word translated in the NRSV 10:19 as "make jealous" is *parazēlōsō*, which has the same root as the word translated "zeal" (*zēlos*) in 10:2. God will provoke zealous jealousy for "those who are not a nation," a phrase that echoes "not my people," the words used to refer to the Gentiles God has elected in 9:25–26. God will use the very people that Israel has been set apart from to discipline Israel by making Israel angry. Isaiah (65:1) offers support to this idea. The ones outside the covenant with Israel, without the means God provided in the law to seek and ask for God, have nonetheless found God, whose power and righteousness are revealed in the gospel (1:16). Isaiah goes on to speak of Israel. Despite their resistance to the way God is working, God continues to be open to them. "All day long," or continuously, without interruption, God reaches out, offering love and mercy. God does not break the relationship even when they are contrary. The final, and most important, thing Paul has to say about the situation of Israel is that God is faithful.

11:1-10
The Chosen Remnant

Having made the point that God remains ready to accept the people even though they refuse, Paul again asks a question that expects a negative answer, and the negative answer he gives is forceful. This faithful God would certainly not cast them off. Rather than immediately expand on this answer with an explanation, such as "God

By the verb *foreknow* is not to be understood a foresight, I know not what, by which God foresees what sort of being any one will be, but that good pleasure, according to which he has chosen those as sons to himself, who, being not yet born, could not have procured for themselves his favour.

Calvin, *Commentaries on the Epistle of Paul the Apostle to the Romans*, trans. and ed. John Owen (Grand Rapids: Wm. B. Eerdmans Publishing Co., 1959), 410.

would not do that because of the covenant," Paul first gives himself as an example. He belongs to Israel, and he has not been rejected. This point becomes especially important when one remembers that like others in Israel, he had zealously opposed the gospel, but God did not cast him off. Paul's own story shows that God's faithfulness can withstand and overcome human refusal. After giving his personal example, he does go on to give a theological explanation. We have already seen in chapter 8 the link between foreknowledge and election, and Paul reminds us by using the word "foreknew" in 11:2 that Israel was chosen by God. God would not reject the very ones God has chosen, not even when their own prophet Elijah accuses them. Even when human rejection of God becomes violent—killing the prophets, or persecuting those who preach the gospel—God does not abandon the relationship.

Paul uses the example of Elijah to return to the idea of a remnant that he introduced in chapter 9. When Elijah called out to God against Israel, God replied that a remnant of the faithful remained. This remnant is not just the number of survivors who happened to be left after a military conquest. Nor is this remnant to be considered like the scraps left over from the main materials used for some project. God "kept" these persons, who were "chosen by grace." So God is actively involved in their preservation. This group remained faithful, but they did not do so because of "works" but because of "grace." The way that God talked about the remnant with Elijah becomes the way Paul works through the problem of Israel's refusal of the gospel.

Israel failed to attain what it was seeking. We know from what Paul says about zeal in chapter 10 that Israel desired to do God's will, and it attempted to follow God's will by keeping the law. Unfortunately, many had focused so much on keeping the law, perhaps especially pursuing it through particular "works" that maintained communal boundaries, that they missed what God was doing outside their own community. So even though Israel desired to do God's will, it failed to attain God's will in Jesus Christ. Some Israelites did attain this, namely, the "elect" or chosen remnant of Jews who followed Jesus.

As for the rest, they were "hardened." Paul turns to Scripture to describe this hardening. The first quotation Paul uses is from Deuteronomy 29:3, with some language from Isaiah 29:10 mixed in. The hardening takes the form of having eyes but not really seeing and ears but not really hearing (11:8). This language calls to mind the basic problem Paul mentioned in 10:18–19 that Israel has heard but has not understood. When Paul says "down to the present day," he means down to his own time. Even though Israel had the law for centuries, which has as its end (goal) Jesus Christ, most of Israel did not understand the way God was working in Jesus Christ to fulfill the law. The surprising thing about this quotation is that Paul attributes Israel's lack of understanding to God. It is not due to perverse refusal but rather to God's providence. Paul will go into the reasons why God would do such a thing in 11:11–24.

The second quotation Paul uses (in 11:9–10) is from Psalm 69 (LXX 68): 22–23, with some editorial changes by Paul. Reference to "the table" in this quotation is important. The word was used in ancient Greco-Roman religious texts to mean "cultic table," so Paul may be using this quotation to bring to mind the way cultic meals could be divisive, a problem he will have to address with the Roman churches in chapter 14.[22] Although the psalm from which Paul quotes calls on God to punish those who persecuted the psalmist, Paul is not using these lines to ask God to punish Israel. Some Jews (Paul among them) had persecuted the followers of Jesus, but Paul has already made it clear that he prays for the salvation of his people. Furthermore, this chapter will end expressing his hope for the Jews. The word "forever" in 11:10 cannot mean, then, that Paul wishes the Jews to suffer forever.

In his commentary on chapter 11, Barth again turns Paul's argument into self-reflection about the church rather than reflection on

22. Jewett, *Romans*, 664.

the situation of Israel. He takes the language about a remnant to illumine the Reformed understanding of God's election. Even though a specific number is mentioned to Elijah, Barth says the point is not about specific individuals. It is not possible to identify the elect, much less to count them. The whole church is in view, and talk about election of a remnant is a way to identify some characteristic of the whole church, that is, of indicating when the church is open to God and when it is not. God speaks judgment against the church in its human endeavors, but God is also the hope of the church precisely where its endeavors fail and it depends on grace. The one God is both judgment and grace; the one church receives both judgment and grace. Election is a remnant quality rather than a remnant quantity. That is, it is the quality of the church now and again when in its genuine openness to God it somehow reveals God.[23]

The way Barth redirects attention away from Paul's own concern is not unproblematic in that Barth replaces the Jews with the church, but it does raise an issue the church should be thinking about. When is it acting merely as a human institution, and when is it truly open to and responding to God? When is it simply replicating the culture around it, and when is it truly revealing God to the culture around it? Individuals within the church may also consider the way their own lives intersect with the quality Barth has in mind. The question for each to consider, then, is not "Am I in the remnant" but rather "When am I remnant?" When am I open to God so that I become a means for revealing God in the world?

11:11–24
Salvation of the Gentiles

The use of "stumbling block" in the second quotation above (11:9) allows Paul to return to the image of running and stumbling that he used in 9:33. Although the NRSV uses the word "fall" in its translation of 9:33, in Greek the falling is only implied by the role the rock plays in causing stumbling. Now in 11:11, Paul makes clear that even

---

23. Barth, *The Epistle to the Romans*, 391–400.

though God put a stumbling block in the way, it was not to make Israel fall down. Rather, the image one should have in mind is running and tripping so as to have to catch one's balance rather than falling all the way to the ground. Such a stumble would slow down the runner, but it would not prevent the runner from reaching the goal.

This is not to say that the stumbling is not serious. Indeed, Paul uses a word for "sin" or "transgression" (translated in the NRSV as "stumbling" in 11:11b) to express how Israel's response falls short of what it should be. The complexity of divine and human responsibility is evident here. God places the rock in the way of the runner, but the runner is also accountable for not avoiding it. Human responsibility for the problem is described as "sin." Nevertheless, God is using this sin for God's own purpose. Because Israel has stumbled, salvation has come to the Gentiles. In terms of the race image, the stumbling has allowed the other runners to catch up. The analogy with a race brings to mind competition with a winner and losers. Paul accepts this idea to some extent but also changes it. The winner of a race is decided—and so the race is over—when the first participant crosses the finish line. If Jesus had been quickly and readily recognized by all Israel, the mission to the Gentiles would never have had a chance to flourish. By slowing Israel down, God could include more in the saving work of Jesus Christ. So Israel's stumbling means that the world shares in the prize. Israel's defeat means that the Gentiles win, but that is not the whole story. Paul does not think simply in terms of a single winner. Not only are the Gentiles allowed to share in salvation, but also the Gentile "victory" provokes Israel to the zealous jealousy that Paul mentioned in 10:19. It has not been clear to interpreters just exactly how jealousy could have a positive effect, but it does seem that Paul assumes that as in actual competition a defeat may spur a runner to work harder, this provocation will somehow lead Israel to recognize what God is doing in Jesus Christ. As Paul made clear in 10:21, God remains open to receive Israel, and its inclusion in salvation would mean even more for the Gentiles than they already receive. So Israel's losing the race not only allows the Gentiles to gain the prize, but it also provokes Israel in some new way to seek God. The result seems to be an abundance of riches.

Paul directs his next remarks starting in 11:13 specifically to the

Gentile followers of Jesus in Rome. Even though he has emphasized his Jewish identity throughout this portion of the letter and he has not given up that identity, he has been sent to the Gentiles. When Paul talks about glorifying his ministry, he is not talking about boasting in his achievements. When he introduced himself to the Roman churches at the beginning of the letter, he framed his apostleship as a calling by God, a setting apart that is also a servanthood. If he glorifies his ministry, he is glorifying what God is accomplishing through the work that God gave Paul to do. It is not clear exactly what form such "glorifying" took, but in whatever way Paul calls attention to his ministry to the Gentiles, he is doing so to provoke the zealous jealousy he has been talking about among his people in the hope that the result will be that some may be saved.

Verse 15 contains an important and difficult ambiguity. Does "their rejection" mean God's rejection of Israel or Israel's rejection of the gospel? Many interpreters assume God is rejecting Israel, but others argue that Paul means the latter option. In what follows, I will accept the latter option because of Paul's overall argument for the faithfulness of God to Israel (he has just said in 11:1 that God has not rejected Israel) and because I think this reading makes sense within the immediate context of the other images Paul uses.

Paul emphasizes the points mentioned above to the Gentile hearers because they need to understand how their own salvation depends on Israel. Israel's negative response to the gospel opened the possibility of reconciling the world. Not only has Israel's lack of response to the gospel opened the possibility for the Gentiles in Rome to be included in the salvation God offers in Jesus Christ, but it also makes possible and necessary Paul's mission to extend the gospel to Spain so that more of the world may hear the gospel proclaimed. But the current negative response by Israel is not the final word for Paul. Because God remains open to Israel, Paul hopes the original people of God may yet accept the gospel, and doing so would mean "life from the dead." This reference to resurrection is probably making an eschatological point about the end time.[24] Isra-

---

24. Jewett, *Romans,* 681.

el's acceptance would complete the reconciliation, and so the Day of the Lord would come.

Paul moves to two images of part and whole to illumine the effect of something small on a larger whole. There is much disagreement on the exact reference of the terms of these analogies. For the first image, it is common to interpret the "first fruits" to mean believing Israel and the "whole batch" to mean unbelieving Israel. In his first image, Paul is taking for granted the common sacrificial practice among Jews as well as Gentiles of offering a portion of one's goods to the Divine. Numbers 15:20–21 specifies that the first batch of dough made from the grain of the land shall be offered to God. It does not specify that this offering makes any other dough holy, but the logic of the sacrifice may be this: what is given to God becomes holy, and the offering establishes a holy relation between God and the supplicant, so the holy relationship assures blessing on what remains in the supplicant's possession.[25] Although none of this is made explicit, Paul does make the point that the holiness of the portion extends to the whole, and he seems to be able to assume that his hearers will understand it without explanation.

The second part/whole example introduces the idea of roots and branches that Paul expands in verses 17–24. This example is somewhat different from the first because a plant is different from a lump. In the case of a plant, the roots provide nourishment for the branches; they are not simply representative of the whole. The vitality of the plant begins in the roots, and the fruitfulness of the branches depends on them. If, then, the roots are holy, the branches will be holy as well. Whether lump or root, Paul is introducing the idea that the whole is dependent on the part for its holiness.

Despite his other sometimes harsh words against the Jews, when Luther considers the image of the lump in verse 16, he acknowledges that Paul meant the whole of the Jewish people must be honored because of the elect remnant within it. He goes so far as to say "we must respect any community because of the good in it, even when they are in the minority over against the wicked."[26] These words serve as a caution for us against making negative judgments about

25. Ibid., 682.
26. Luther, *Commentary on Romans*, 162.

entire communities based on what we know, or think we know, about individuals. We need to resist the very powerful tendency to embrace stereotypes that lead to scapegoating.

Starting in verse 17, Paul augments the idea of the functioning of a single plant with the idea of pruning and grafting. As he does so, some commentators have pointed out that his description shows Paul was not very familiar with horticultural practices of his day. Even so, he is making a point about how distinct things (whether plants or groups of people) may be brought together to make a whole. Because he began in 11:13 to direct his comments to the Gentiles among the Roman followers of Jesus, the "you" in 11:17 refers to these Gentiles. Some (not all) branches were broken off of an olive tree and then other branches were grafted on. The grafted branches are "wild"; that is, they are taken from outside the sphere of cultivation and brought into that sphere by the cultivator. The tree itself is Israel, a point particularly obvious to the original readers because one of the Jewish synagogues in Rome was known as the "Synagogue of the Olive."[27] Paul is explaining that the outsider Gentiles have been brought into the relationship that God had established and maintained with Israel. Once they have been made part of the plant, they are nourished by its roots. From what Paul has already said, this means they are made holy by its roots. Although branches are the visible, fruit-bearing part of the plant, they cannot boast in superiority or achievement (11:18). The roots support them, and they remain dependent on those roots. Paul's suggestion turns the normally competitive cultural expectation on its head. Rather than seeking personal glory, they should boast of the roots that support them.

> However different Christianity as a predominantly Gentile religious movement becomes from living Judaism, it can understand itself only through its own interpretation of ancient Jewish traditions.
>
> John B. Cobb Jr. and David J. Lull, *Romans* (St. Louis: Chalice Press, 2005), 150.

How easy it is to go through life without acknowledging all the support we get from others, many of whom may not be visible to us.

27. Jewett, *Romans*, 685.

The image that Paul uses invites reflection on ways we depend on others for the fruit we bear. It calls for us to be mindful of relationships we may otherwise take for granted and to acknowledge what those relationships add to our lives.

To eliminate grounds for boasting even further, Paul reminds the Gentiles of what it means to be grafted. The broken branches (the Jews who did not respond in faithfulness to Jesus) may indeed have been pruned, but the grafted branches (the Gentiles) are part of the plant only by their faithfulness to Jesus (11:20). They do not belong to the plant for any reason inherent to them. The proper response to their inclusion is not pride (*hupsēla phronei*) but rather is standing in awe of God's kindness and severity. They should gratefully and humbly recognize that they have been joined to something they had no right to. Since they are included because they are faithful, they should realize that ceasing to be faithful could make them vulnerable to pruning (11:22). God will not treat them differently than God's own original people. If God would be willing to break off those who were born into the covenant, how much more would God be willing to break off those who are merely grafted onto it? In previous arguments, Paul has been clear that the Jewish followers of Jesus have no reason to boast in their chosen status, and now Paul is equally clear with the Gentile followers that they have no reason to boast in their status either. Competition among the members of the church is completely ruled out.

These words not only serve as a warning about pride, which could be the first step to losing faithfulness, but also as a reminder about God. Because God may be either pleased with our faithfulness or displeased with our lack of faithfulness, God may act kindly or severely. Because God is the only legitimate ruler of the world, God is the ultimate judge of our allegiance. God is merciful, yes, but God cannot be fooled. God sees clearly how things are and responds accordingly. We have no claim on God's mercy, so when we receive God's kindness, it comes to us as grace.

> **Paul could hardly have emphasized more strongly the importance of the believer's continued reliance on God's kindness.**
>
> Keck, *Romans*, 276.

Nor can we take refuge in our past status; we must instead continue to stand in faithfulness. Our allegiance must be shown every day. This means the possibility of falling is constantly present, but it also means the possibility of being reconciled is also always open. If they do not persist in negative response to Jesus Christ, the branches that were broken off may be grafted back in. If God can take something that does not belong to the tree and make it part of the tree, how much more can God take what belongs to the tree and restore it (11:24).

It is interesting how Paul uses the competitive culture of the ancient world in different images, using competition positively to make his point when he speaks of a race but undercutting competition when he speaks of a plant. Perhaps he is trying to convey different points to the different audiences among the Roman hearers. Paul is not speaking directly to Jews who have rejected Jesus but rather to the Jewish followers of Jesus who still understand themselves to be Jews. Like Paul, they may be very concerned for their own people. Especially if the Jewish followers in Rome keenly feel their difference from the Gentile followers, perhaps outnumbered and marginalized by them, then the way the race image provokes jealousy may encourage them to stay the course and to continue to share the gospel with their Jewish brothers and sisters. When speaking directly to Gentiles, Paul needs to say something quite different. If the Gentile followers are the dominant group, then they need to be reminded their majority status does not make them better. Anything that encourages competition for this group in effect encourages exerting their power over others. Instead, they need to be reminded that even though they may fit more easily into the empire than the Jewish followers do, they are not to take on its values. They have been grafted to another plant and receive their life from it.

FURTHER REFLECTIONS
Jews, Christians, and Covenant

Paul's image of Gentiles being grafted onto the tree of Israel lost its imaginative power as Christianity became increasingly Gentile;

and it was rather quickly replaced in Christian thinking by supersessionism, that is, by regarding God's covenant with Israel as old,
legalistic, and needing to be supplanted with a new and improved
covenant of grace through Jesus Christ. This way of thinking has
been so damaging to Judaism that Christians in recent decades
have been looking for other ways to think about Jewish-Christian
relations. Reflection on covenant, which is important to both Jewish and Christian traditions, has led to two possibilities that have
dominated conversation on this matter so far.

The first follows something of Paul's thought, that is, taking the
covenant with Israel as primary and exploring how Christians share
in that covenant. This approach is known as the "single covenant"
theory. It does not suggest that Christians are really Jewish or should
become Jews, but it sees Jesus as opening a way for people who are
not Jewish to participate in the covenant that God established with
Israel. The single covenant theory makes a decisive attempt to undo
supersessionist thinking, and it clearly recognizes the importance
of Judaism for Christianity.

The second possibility is the "double covenant" theory, which
understands God to have made two covenants, one with Israel and
one with Gentile Christians. The second covenant does not replace
the first, rather they are parallel and complementary. This approach
allows each religion its own distinctiveness, but even though Christianity is clearly "new" it is not superior. Because each faith has equal
and complementary value, each has its own integrity. This approach
supports dialogue between Christians and Jews, but there is no
suggestion of the need for conversion.

Theologians have only begun to work toward a new understanding of Jewish-Christian relations. There is much work still to be
done, but it has already become evident that "single" and "double"
may not be adequate ways of describing both the overlap and distinctiveness that characterize the relationship between these two
faiths. Furthermore, the importance of recognizing the presence of
religions other than these two is pressing.

Irving Greenberg has pointed out that when we speak of Jewish-
Christian relations in terms of covenant, we should remember that
before Moses, and even before Abraham, God first made covenant

with Noah. The purpose of that covenant was the repair of the world (*tikun olam*). The covenant with Noah suggests not only a basis for Jewish-Christian relations but also for relations with other faiths.[28] God's partnership with humanity that this covenant represents may lead us to a better understanding of our need for each other, for the work we need to do together, and for affirmation of the different ways that God shows love and care for all people and for all creation. This understanding of the Noahic covenant invites us to consider that God can work with all of us, and we can work with each other, to mend the world.

11:25–36

Salvation of Israel

Paul's hope was for a church of Jews and Gentiles together, so his reflection about the salvation of Israel must be seen in that light. Paul addresses the recipients of the letter as brothers and sisters, members of a common family that Paul has argued for in two ways. Not only are Jewish and Gentile followers of Jesus adopted as children of God (8:12–17), but they also can all claim Abraham as their spiritual father (4:16). Although they belong to a common family, they have suffered from misunderstanding, and Paul does not want them to continue in ignorance that leads to misunderstanding. So he will explain to them a mystery.

> Paul intends to stress not uniformity, but unity in diversity. The pluralistic diversity of peoples in their ethnic and cultural variety is maintained, although in Christ this pluralism becomes nevertheless a unity.
>
> J. C. Beker, "The Faithfulness of God and the Priority of Israel in Paul's Letter to the Romans," *The Harvard Theological Review* 79, nos. 1–3 (1986): 13.

The word "mystery" was known in apocalyptic literature to refer to knowledge disclosed by God.[29] Paul has knowledge that the recipients of his letter lack, and he wants to share it with them so they

28. Irving Greenberg, "To Repair the World: Judaism and Christianity in Partnership," *Review and Expositor*, 103 (Winter 2006): 159–78.
29. Hultgren, "*Pistis Christou*," 416.

will not be ignorant. The Greek of 11:25 uses a double negative, "I do not want you not to know." All of them, whether Jew or Gentile, share this ignorance; and he will enlighten all of them. He also wants to share this knowledge because they need to realize they are not as wise as they think they are. Their own self-constructed ideas of who is favored by God have been built on lack of understanding of what God is doing. Paul has been explaining what they need to know in the previous verses, but now he supplies a summary statement to make sure they will get the point. Part of Israel is stubbornly refusing to respond to the gospel, but as Paul has explained, this stubbornness serves the purpose of allowing the Gentiles to come in to the saving relationship with God that Jesus Christ makes possible. This knowledge corrects two misunderstandings. On the one hand, by thinking they are favored, Gentile followers have missed their dependence on Israel, and even on Israel's hardness, for their salvation. Paul seems to imagine a limit to Israel's stubbornness, though. It will last until the full number (literally "fullness") of Gentiles has come in (11:25). Paul is able to conclude, then, that at the end of the need for their stubbornness, all Israel will be saved. On the other hand, by thinking they are favored, Jewish followers have missed the crucial role Gentiles play in the salvation of Israel. As Paul has explained, the Gentile acceptance of Jesus Christ serves the purpose of increasing Israel's zeal for God. The same delay that allows for Gentile inclusion also allows time for the Jews to be goaded to faithfulness, so Paul expresses the hope that all Israel will be saved (11:26). The mystery that Paul reveals to the church in Rome corrects the "wisdom" each group thought it had about its superiority over the other.

Because Paul has used language that suggests quantity ("fullness" and "all") in expressing this mystery, these verses have led to speculation about how many will be saved of either group. With regard to Gentiles, the translation "full number" might suggest a quota, and some have taken it to be the number of the elect. But many understand "fullness" to indicate a large but unspecified quantity. Wesley spoke of a "vast harvest."[30] Calvin explains that it is "to be taken for a great number: for it was not to be, as before, when a few proselytes

30. Wesley, *Explanatory Notes*, 567.

connected themselves with the Jews; but such was to be the change, that the Gentiles would form almost the entire body of the Church."[31]

With regard to Israel, interpreters have had even more difficulty knowing what to think about "all." Related to the question of number is what Paul meant by "Israel" at this point in the letter. Could he be talking about the remnant of 11:5 as the select Israel, so "all" refers to the whole remnant? Or could "all Israel" like "fullness of Gentiles" refer to all the elect, Jew and Gentile alike? Or does he mean the whole of ethnic Israel? There has been no consensus among Christian interpreters about the complex issues raised by Paul's words. Some do suggest that indeed all Israel (meaning every Jew) will be saved. Others acknowledge that not all Jews will finally be saved because some are permanently blinded to the truth.[32] Interpreters who understand Paul to mean all or many Jews will be saved usually expect this to take place eschatologically, in God's time rather than in our history. Still others do not understand Paul to be talking about the Jews at all, but rather about the church.[33]

Although Paul understands himself to be sharing a "mystery" or divine knowledge, his expectation for Israel had to be shaped by his own historical context. In his time, he could still imagine that Israel as a whole would come to Christ, but history played out in a very different way. Israel was indeed provoked by Gentile Christianity to zeal for God, but within its own distinct religious expression, often defined over against Christianity. Paul did not anticipate this development, so if the divine knowledge of the mystery he shares is to have meaning for us now, we now have to look to what God would want us to know in the current situation. Paul's clear conviction throughout this letter has been that God is faithful. God will not reject Israel precisely because God is faithful to the covenant that God makes. Paul has also maintained throughout this letter (and it is apparent in others) that even in Christ Gentiles do not cease being Gentiles and Jews do not cease being Jews. God is able to work with the specific identities that we bring to relationship with God.

---

31. Calvin, *Commentaries*, 436.
32. Jeremy Cohen, "The Mystery of Israel's Salvation: Romans 11:25–26 in Patristic and Medieval Exegesis," in *The Harvard Theological Review* 98, no. 3 (July 2005): 247–81.
33. Calvin, *Commentaries*, 437.

In 11:25–26, Paul affirms God's saving work for Gentiles and for Israel. At the very end of this chapter, Paul admits that God's ways are inscrutable. Even when relating a "mystery," Paul cannot know how God does what God does. Similarly, we should not think ourselves wiser than we are regarding what we think we know God will do, and we should certainly never use what we think we know to support Christian superiority. In our time, sharing Paul's conviction about God's faithfulness to us in our own social locations ought to include openness to how God may work in ways we do not expect and that may not be identical across all groups in order to bring all to fullness of life.

Paul's understanding of the "mystery" he relates comes through in the way he quotes Scripture. Paul turns again to Isaiah, starting with 59:20–21. Where Isaiah says he will come *for* Zion, Paul says the Deliverer came *from* Zion. Paul's concern for Gentiles affects the way he understands the prophecy. Isaiah's prophecy originally intended for Israel is quoted to speak to a predominantly Gentile church at the heart of the Roman Empire. He also, though, shows concern for the Jews when he adds words from Isaiah 27:9, which suggest that God keeps covenant with Israel (Jacob) by removing sin, and perhaps he is thinking of the sin of stubbornness that God has used for God's purpose with the Gentiles.[34] The mystery that Paul delivers is actually his interpretation of Scripture in light of the situation he is addressing to the recipients of his letter in Rome.

The combined reference to sin and covenant in 11:27 may explain how in 11:28 Paul can talk about Israel as "enemies" and "beloved" at the same time. By refusing to acknowledge the way God is working in Jesus Christ, Israel does not give proper honor to God, and so they are "enemies" of God. But we have already seen in 5:6–11 how God treats enemies. Instead of defeating them the way an emperor would, God acts in love to change the relationship. Because God's gift and calling are "irrevocable" (11:29) God honors the covenant made with the patriarchs. The chosen people have always been and always will be beloved. Although God used their refusal for the sake of the Gentiles, God will not forsake Israel.

34. Jewett, *Romans*, 703–4.

Reference to the covenant may be all that is needed to convince the Jewish followers of Jesus in the Roman church of God's mercy to the Jews who have not followed Jesus, but the Gentile followers may need more. So Paul reminds them (11:30) that they were themselves disobedient rebels (enemies), as Paul has already described in this letter (1:18–23, 5:10). They have received mercy because of Israel's stubborn, disobedient refusal. They should remember, then, that just as God showed mercy to them, God will show mercy to Israel (11:31). Those who understand their own need for mercy and are grateful to have received it ought not to begrudge it to others. Paul has already explained about the universality and power of sin in chapter 3, and here he makes the point that because all are imprisoned in disobedience, all may receive mercy (11:32). At a time when few actual prisoners could expect any kind of mercy, the extent of God's mercy to all demonstrated power in stark contrast to human exercise of power. God does not treat mercy sparingly the way that human beings do.

For many of us, God's generosity to others is troubling. It violates our sensibilities to imagine that God could treat as mercifully as God treats us those who have caused us harm or inconvenienced us. Part of growing into the mind of Christ entails increasing recognition that God's love is larger than ours is, and then asking for grace for our love to become a larger reflection of God's.

In fact, God's ways are so different from the ways to which we are accustomed that Paul ends this portion of his letter with a hymn that celebrates the vast difference (11:33–36). It is not clear whether this is Paul's own hymn or whether he uses a hymn already in existence and perhaps known by the Roman church. The grandness of God

---

He shows that it is very far from being the case, that we can glory in any good thing of our own against God, since we have been created by him from nothing, and now exist through him. He hence infers, that our being should be employed for his glory: for how unreasonable would it be for creatures, whom he has formed and whom he sustains, to live for any other purpose than for making his glory known?

Calvin, *Commentaries*, 448.

exceeds anything that we may know, and we are not in a position to understand the mind of God or the ways God achieves God's purposes. The richness of God is the genuine mystery.

The inscrutability of God serves to remind us not to mistake our own ideas of what God does for God's own understanding. This point serves as a reminder to the Roman church that their "wisdom" falls short of God's true wisdom. They need humility to be instructed. The hymn makes a further affirmation that supports the instruction Paul is trying to provide. God is the source, the sustainer, and the end of all things, so all things are in God's care. We will never understand everything about God, but we know this: God is the reality that embraces *all*. This is the ground for arguing as Paul does that God's mercy extends to all. We may not understand how God manages to extend that mercy so comprehensively, but the reality of it calls for praise and thanksgiving. The only proper response to the majesty and generosity of God is to give God glory.

In Romans, Paul leaves us with a tension about salvation that has never been, and may never be, fully resolved in Christian theology. The image of a Day of Wrath where God's judgment holds all accountable is very strong at the beginning of this letter, but in the context of talking about the Jews, Paul's vision is one of expansive grace that will finally prevail over sin and unbelief. We cannot know what these two views mean exactly for the ultimate destiny for everyone beyond death, and we should be reluctant to make judgments about whether or not others will be "saved." Ultimately, only God saves, so only God knows. What we can affirm about God is that God knows us better than we know ourselves, and we will be judged according to God's assessment of our lives. Salvation does not eliminate accountability or distort the truth about us. God's mercy is shown despite what God knows about our disobedience. This is the very meaning of grace.

12:1–15:13

Living in the New Dominion

12:1–2

Acceptable Worship

With these verses, Paul begins to draw practical conclusions from all he has said. In this letter directed to a specific audience, Paul is exhorting a specific group of people about specific problems, not setting out general counsels for all Christians in all times. To recognize this point does not detract from the meaning these exhortations may have for us now. His letter was preserved and read by the churches for centuries precisely because it has helped Christians since Paul's time understand their lives before God and their obligations to each other. In order to make the connection between what Paul had to say then and what we might learn from Paul now, we must be careful to make sure we understand what he said and why he said it to the community he originally addressed. Only then can we engage in prayerful adaptation for our time of the wisdom he shared then. Reading these exhortations as timeless, general counsels actually makes them less valuable to us because we bypass the specific reasoning Paul used to understand how life before God should be lived.

The word that Paul uses to begin this portion of his letter is *parakalō* (12:1), a common formula in letters of Paul's time for diplomatic correspondence.[1] Less than a command, it is a strong urging that reminds the hearers of their loyalty to the sovereign and encourages fulfilling the obligations that go with that loyalty. Paul is not giving the Roman followers of Jesus a command or rule, but neither is he simply making a request. He is urging them to demonstrate

---

1. Robert Jewett, *Romans: A Commentary*, Hermeneia (Minneapolis: Fortress Press, 2007), 726.

in their lives their loyalty to the God he has been describing throughout the letter. Being baptized into Jesus Christ brings us into life with
this faithful and righteous God, so we must consider well how that
life should be lived. Paul's use of "therefore" in this sentence is not
merely a word to show a change of subject; rather, it indicates that
he is drawing conclusions from all that he has said previously. To
understand his reasons for drawing these conclusions, the reader
must keep the scope of his previous argument about the faithfulness
and righteousness of God in view.

Paul addresses all the members of the Roman churches (using
"you" in the plural), so he is urging Jew and Gentile alike, not simply as individuals but as people who are in community together. As
before, addressing them as "brothers and sisters" (NRSV) reminds
them of their familial connection through Jesus Christ and through
Abraham. Because they are loyal to this faithful and righteous God,
they have obligations to one another. For so long, Paul's letter has
been read as a message primarily about individual salvation that we
would do well to think carefully about what it means to hear Paul's
message as a community. Do we genuinely accept each other as
brothers and sisters? Do we understand and fulfill our obligations to
one another? Do we let our life together be defined by our relationship with God or instead by our connection to things outside this
community (work, status, economics)? Are we able to recognize
our relationship with Christians outside our own congregation/
denomination/region?

To reinforce the connection between all that has been said before
and the counsel that is to follow, Paul beseeches them "by the mer-
cies of God." Paul has shown God's mercy at work throughout his
description of God's faithfulness, but especially in 9:15–23 and
11:30–32. If the followers of Jesus have obligations on the basis of
their allegiance to God, it is on the basis of a faithful and merciful
God, and it is only through that mercy that they may fulfill their obligations. The counsels that Paul will commend to them are not new
laws, but rather they are his idea of the appropriate response to the
mercy God has already shown.

In the ancient world, and especially in Rome, where offering actual
sacrifices in temples was a regular occurrence, Paul's instruction to

present a sacrifice to God would have immediate relevance. Sacrifice was common to the religious life of the ancient world, and Paul uses the ordinary religious language of his time. What Paul tells them to present is unusual according to the ordinary sacrificial practice of the day. The basic idea of a sacrifice is making an offering to the divine, and it was common for that offering to be a life given through the slaying of an animal. Other kinds of ritualized offerings could be made: for instance, the firstfruits offering mentioned in 11:16. Although Paul uses common religious language, he suggests something different, though, than offering something representative (an animal or some other gift to stand in our place): Paul tells them to present their own bodies. That is, they must give their whole selves to God. As Calvin says, Paul does not mean merely "our bones and skin," but rather is designating "all that we are: for the members of the body are the instruments by which we execute our purposes."[2] Although Paul addresses them as a community, this reference to offering one's own body highlights the responsibility of each individual to participate as fully as possible.

It was not unknown in the ancient world to recognize that personal righteousness and service to the deity was preferable to a ritual offering. Certainly, Isaiah (1:11–17) and Amos (5:12–21) make this point, but also some Gentiles (such as Isocrates) recognized it.[3] Paul's instruction for the Roman followers to present their bodies as

sacrifices means that they themselves are the offering to God. The sacrifice of animals required the offering of a life through death, but this sacrifice of oneself is to be "living." This offering is not made to God through death but rather through the way that the life is lived. To say that we should present our very selves to God as a living sacrifice is to say that our daily life

> By calling it living, he intimates, that we are sacrificed to the Lord for this end,—that our former life being destroyed in us, we may be raised up to a new life.
>
> John Calvin, *Commentaries on the Epistle of Paul the Apostle to the Romans*, trans. and ed. John Owen (Grand Rapids: Wm. B. Eerdmans Publishing Co., 1959), 451.

2. Calvin, *Commentaries*, 452.
3. Jewett, *Romans*, 727–28.

ought to be a form of worship, an ongoing offering. Everything we do should not only be guided by God but also offered to God.

This ongoing offering of daily life is also described as "holy" and "acceptable." The basic meaning of "holy" is to be "set apart," that is dedicated to God, and so set off from the profane world. The offering of ourselves, though, is made within our everyday life, not apart from it. To be "holy" then means that by offering to God our ongoing daily living, we should be offering a life that is not simply defined by our ordinary surroundings. While not physically removed from "the world" we are set apart by being defined by our relationship to God, and so we may resist certain values and practices that are common around us. This is what makes our lives "acceptable" to God, not in the sense that we are earning acceptance but rather that God finds our lives to be well-pleasing.

The NRSV 12:1 translates Paul's description of this living, holy, acceptable sacrifice as "spiritual worship." The Greek word (*latreia*), translated as "worship," is used in the Septuagint to refer to cultic activity in the Jewish temple, understood as duty in service to God.[4] The Greek adjective used to describe this worship is *logikos*, which is related to the word *logos* (word or reason). The NRSV footnote shows that the adjective could be translated as "reasonable." Greek philosophers used the word *logikos* to describe the rational faculty of the human, the intellect; and for philosophers, the intellect was higher and closer to God than the body. This assumption led to a highly intellectual, and very individual, form of devotion to God. This orientation carried into Christian theology as concern for the interior life of individuals, for instance, in Melanchthon's comment "When Paul here demands rational worship, he demands a good motive in the user, namely, true impulses of fear and faith toward God."[5] Paul has made it clear that it is precisely the body that is presented for this worship. As we have seen Calvin note above, the body carries out the intent of the mind, so mind and body together, the whole self, worships. But even as he is modifying philosophical

4. Leander E. Keck, *Romans,* Abingdon New Testament Commentaries (Nashville: Abingdon Press, 2005), 292.
5. Philipp Melanchthon, *Commentary on Romans,* trans. Fred Kramer (St. Louis: Concordia Publishing House, 1992), 211.

understanding about rational worship, he is also modifying ordinary understanding of worship itself. This worship is not carried out in a temple as one performs cultic duties, but rather it is carried out every day in one's living. Both Jewish and Gentile followers of Jesus would be challenged by this image to think in a new way about how best to honor God.

Paul's words about presenting your bodies as a living sacrifice hearken back to the way he spoke of presenting your "members" in 6:13 and 6:19. In the previous portion of the letter, Paul has explained that we have to give ourselves to something, we must live either in the dominion of sin or the dominion of grace. We show our allegiance to the dominion to which we belong through the way we carry out our lives, in all our daily actions. Because the followers of Jesus have left the dominion of sin and accepted the free gift of the dominion of grace, they are obliged to demonstrate their new allegiance daily. Keeping this background in mind, we may be able to connect Paul's ideas with theology that developed after him to get an idea of what his words might mean for our time. A *logikos* worship could be understood as a worship that conforms to the *logos* incarnated in Jesus the Christ. This worship is embodied and enacted daily as we seek to be more and more Christlike. Each of us participates as individuals in this process, but this worship is not simply individualistic. The community as a whole aids our formation as it gathers all the individuals for sharing together in the body of Christ. It also acts together to do God's work in the world. This, not merely private piety, is the kind of worship best suited to a community that has been baptized into Jesus Christ.

If conformity to Christ is the substance of living, holy, acceptable sacrifice, then Paul's next admonition in 12:2 is especially pointed: "Do not be conformed to this world" (literally to this aeon, or present age). Paul is thinking eschatologically, that the present age will soon pass away; so taking on its values and practices means not

> Paul presents the bodily service of a community for the sake of world transformation and unification as the fulfillment of the vision of worship that would be truly reasonable.
>
> Jewett, *Romans*, 730–31.

only adopting the ways of the dominion of sin, which has everything in its power, but also adopting ways that are soon to be gone. For Paul, the present age will soon be displaced by the age to come, and while it is now only breaking in, not fully established, the age to come already exerts its power and demands allegiance. It makes no sense for a community that has committed itself to the dominion of grace to continue to live in loyalty to the dominion it has set aside. Such conformity is not *logikos*, neither reasonable nor Christlike. Even though the urgency of thinking about the end of the age has faded after two thousand years, the point is still important. Whenever the church models itself after the social order that prevails in the present age, it betrays the dominion to which it claims to belong.

Because Paul knows that we have to give ourselves to something, he does not simply tell his hearers what to leave behind; he also tells them to be transformed by renewing their minds. Because *logikos* was used to talk about mental faculties, it makes sense for Paul to speak of how the mind is affected. In doing so he is not playing body and mind against each other. Instead, he is pointing to the intimate connection between them. *Logikos* worship must include the mind as well as the body. When our minds are renewed after the mind of Christ, we more clearly discern the will of God. Understanding the will of God is the first, necessary step toward enacting it with our bodies.

> He knew people cannot transform themselves. However, people can place themselves in situations and relationships in which transformation is more likely to happen.
>
> John B. Cobb Jr. and David J. Lull, *Romans* (St. Louis: Chalice Press, 2005), 162.

Keeping in mind that Paul is addressing the whole community, this transformation is not restricted to individuals. The community as a whole needs to discern and to enact together the will of God. For the churches in Rome, this transformation will call them to think and behave differently about the specific problems that Paul has heard about and will comment on in chapter 14. For the churches now, such transformation is a constant requirement. In the absence of urgent expectation of the imminent coming of the new age, the pressure to conform to this age is always with us, so it must be steadily resisted. The task of the community to be transformed by the renewing of its mind is every bit as necessary and ongoing as the task of any individual. Discerning the will of God includes as a first step identifying those ways that our values and practices mirror the world around us instead of expressing our allegiance to the dominion of grace. Then discernment must consider how to enact instead what is good, acceptable (well-pleasing), and perfect to God. The word "perfect" translates the Greek *teleios* (full, mature). Related to *telos* (end, goal), this fullness does not require that we enact God's will without any mistake or flaw, but it does require that we pursue the goal that God wills and not one determined by the present age or our own selfish desires. Discernment of that will is key.

12:3–8

A Renewed Mind

Paul interrupts this flow of thought to address the recipients of his letter again in a way similar to verse 1. Although the second address interrupts the flow of the exhortation, it reinforces that the exhortation is made to everyone together on the grounds of what God has given. What Paul has to say is for everyone to hear and to respond to because God has shown grace and mercy to all of them. Having established in verse 2 that a transformed mind to discern the will of God is what is expected of the followers of Jesus, Paul returns to the mindset that is appropriate to such a transformation.

Paul has already talked about mindset in 8:5–8, where he was concerned to show that we live according to the dominion toward which we are oriented. Now he adds another concern about the mental outlook that should be adopted by a follower of Jesus. The language he uses to express this concern reflects language used by philosophers, poets, and orators to express the importance of restrained moderation in the life well lived.[6] The wordplay (based on *phronein*,

---

6. Jewett, *Romans*, 739–40.

to think or have in mind) of the Greek is lost in the English NRSV translation of 12:3. Paul uses a form of *phronein* four times in verse 3, twice to form adjectives that mean something like "high-minded" (or "arrogantly-minded") and "sensibly-minded." The classical background of this terminology (such as Homer's use in the *Odyssey*) warned against overreaching one's limits and encouraged the virtue of prudence.[7] Roman hearers would no doubt have caught the references to these classical ideas. As they listened to the letter read, they may also have realized that Paul used *phronein* in 11:20 when he warned the Gentiles not to become proud (*hupsēla phronei*), thinking they are more secure than the Jews. It is easy to think too highly of ourselves when we forget that we depend on God's grace and trust instead in our own abilities or status. To think "with sober judgment" or to be sensibly minded requires us to see ourselves as we really are, recognizing our dependence on God and our connection to each other.

We see ourselves in a fair and sensible light when we judge ourselves according to the faith that God has given. Because Paul uses the word "measure" it may appear that he means God measures out different amounts of faith to each of us, and our thinking is affected by how much we receive. It is more likely that Paul means "measure" not as amount but as criterion. In other words, we should measure our thinking against faith.[8] We are sensibly minded when we consider ourselves and those around us according to the criterion of faith that God has given us. The full meaning of *pistis*—not only belief but also faithfulness and trust—is the measure we must use. For instance we avoid high-mindedness when we trust in God rather than in our own place in the world. Do we think about ourselves and about others according to faithfulness in God rather than according to the measures for judgment given by society and culture? How does our faithfulness compare to God's faithfulness?

If we allow faith to form our judgments, then we can see more clearly how we belong together in one body. Paul uses this metaphor of the body also in 1 Corinthians 12. It is an image that can be understood by everyone; it requires no particular experience or education

7. Ibid., 739–40.
8. Keck, *Romans*, 297.

to understand (the way an example from history or literature would), so in using it, Paul is speaking in a way that every member of the community, regardless of status or ethnicity, could follow. At the same time, the metaphor of being one body had been used widely in classical writings, especially to talk about civic relationships, so those who had education would be able to recognize the common idea that held their society together. The body Paul is talking about is not united in citizenship but rather united in Christ. The oneness that this body shares comes from common baptism, which makes them not only members with distinct functions but also members of one another. Superficial distinctions that have been assigned to individuals in society according to class, ethnicity, or education are overcome so that in Christ we all belong to and with each other. The only distinctions that matter are the ones based on gifts given to us by grace. We have been given different gifts so that we can contribute different things to the whole community.

> By applying this similitude, he proves how necessary it is for each to consider what is suitable to his own nature, capacity, and vocation . . . for no member possesses all powers, nor does it appropriate to itself the offices of others.
>
> Calvin, *Commentaries*, 458.

The gifts that Paul names are not exactly the same as the ones he lists in 1 Corinthians 12:7–10 or 28–30. Paul is not trying to provide an exhaustive account of all the gifts God has to give. Nor is he ranking them as if some were better than others (to do so would contribute to "high-mindedness"). Instead, he is giving examples of gifts that enrich the community. Because he has not yet visited Rome, he may not know exactly which gifts have been given to that community, but he can show how members of the body may contribute to one another. Paul writes his list with such economy of words that some translations (such as NIV) supply verbs that are not in the original in order to make the English read well. Paul's concern seems to be simply to list a variety of gifts that may be in the members to be used for the sake of the body.

The first gift he names (12:6), prophecy, should not be understood as merely predicting the future. Calvin and Wesley both connected this gift to interpreting Scripture.[9] Prophets speak on behalf of God to the community for the benefit of the community. Paul adds to the gift a phrase translated as "in proportion to faith." The word translated as "proportion" in Greek is *analogia*, a word used in math and logic to indicate a right ratio or proportion when comparing things to one another. The Greek word gives us our English word "analogy." The phrase is somewhat unclear, but like "measure" it suggests a kind of criterion rather than an amount. Because prophets speak for God, they must speak in accord with the faith God gives, not speak for themselves individually or subjectively. As Paul has said in 1 Corinthians 14:29, when prophets speak, others should weigh what the prophets have said to consider how well they express the faith. The phrase Paul uses here (analogy of faith) has been borrowed by theologians of later centuries to express the need for coherence of ideas in doctrine and in biblical interpretation. In other words, specific theological ideas have to be understood in connection with the whole of Christian faith and more obscure passages of Scripture may be clarified by interpreting them in light of other passages that are easier to understand. Wesley, for instance, in his note on this phrase speaks of the "general tenor" of the oracles of God, and even of the "grand scheme of doctrine."[10] Systematizing into a grand scheme is not what Paul has in mind. He is concerned that there be some exercise of discernment about prophecy in order to guard against individual misappropriation of the gift.

The word translated in the NRSV 12:7 as "ministry" is *diakonia*, which means "service." He is not talking about a specific office of ministry, but rather is using a term that appears in the New Testament to refer to a wide range of service done for the community. Because no specific form of service is named, Paul's point seems to be that if one has been given the gift of serving, then one exercises that gift in service. The same point is made about teachers. Paul is not saying what they teach or should teach, only that if one has the gift of teaching, one employs it in teaching. If the members are

9. Calvin, *Commentaries*, 460; John Wesley, *Explanatory Notes upon the New Testament* (repr., London: Epworth Press, 2000), 569.
10. Wesley, *Explanatory Notes*, 569–70.

distinguished by their gifts, and if they are given those gifts for the sake of the body, then every member has something important to share, and every member has a responsibility to use his or her gift.

Similarly, exhorters must exhort (12:8). The word Paul uses is *parakalōn*, which also suggests comforting. A person with this gift must be able to discern the psychological and social needs of another person and respond appropriately, sometimes with consolation and sometimes with admonition. This kind of spiritual care would be essential for a community that Paul was telling throughout the letter to resist participation in the values of the world around it. The members could not hope to stand in contrast to what was going on around them without such encouragement.

> **The teacher lays the foundation, while the exhorter builds upon the foundation.**
>
> Martin Luther, *Commentary on Romans*, trans. J. Theodore Mueller (Grand Rapids: Kregel Classics, 1976), 172.

The last three gifts that Paul names in 12:8 follow a different pattern than the previous three in that the description does not simply repeat the word for the gift. His words suggest not only that the gifts must be used but also something about how they should be exercised. The giver (or contributor or sharer) should give with generosity. The Greek *haplotēs* that means generosity also indicates simplicity or single-mindedness. The kind of generosity Paul has in mind is that one who has the gift of giving should give with integrity, not calculating what might be gained from the gift but only motivated by how one's own giving reflects God's giving. The gift that most brings glory to God and serves the body best is one given without mixed motives.

Although all the named gifts suggest leadership of some sort, Paul mentions "leader" specifically. This could suggest he means someone with administrative responsibility, although no particular role or office is suggested. The leader should perform necessary tasks with diligence (or eagerness or earnestness). Whatever the duties of the leader Paul had in mind, communities need conscientious and efficient guidance in their daily life, neither aggressive for personal power nor negligent and ineffective.

Paul ends his list with "the compassionate" (*eleōn*) perhaps

For who that is receiving
a kingdom, is of sad
countenance? Who that is
receiving pardon for his sins
continueth of dejected look?

John Chrysostom, Homily XXI, *Homilies of S. John Chrysostom on the Epistle of St. Paul the Apostle to the Romans*, 3rd ed., trans. members of the English church (Oxford: James Parker & Co., 1877), 373.

meaning those who perform acts of mercy for those in need, such as caring for the sick and dying. Those who give care to people in distress know how draining such work can be. Nevertheless, Paul instructs them to exercise this gift "in cheerfulness." A dour or stressed demeanor in the caregiver can only add to the burden of the one cared for. Even though many outside the church also held the ideal of doing acts of mercy cheerfully, the followers of Jesus had a special motivation. Because they knew the mercy of God in Jesus Christ, they showed mercy with a glad and grateful heart. Not only this one, but all the gifts have God's mercy as their source, so they should all be exercised with this spirit.

12:9–21

Genuine Love

Although the NRSV translates verse 9 with imperative language, Paul is not explicitly telling his hearers what to do. Paul simply describes love, and he does not even use a verb to do so. In keeping with the approach he has established of urging rather than commanding, he describes and lets the hearers draw their conclusion from what he has said. The description makes clear what they should do, but it does so indirectly and gently. He only says "The love genuine," to which we can supply the verb "is." Because he says "the" love, it is likely he is not speaking about love in general, but rather about the love that a sensibly minded follower of Jesus who knows the mercy of God will have. This love hates evil and holds on to the good. He goes on to describe this love with regard to how it is expressed in community. It is shown to one another as "brotherly love" (*philadelphia*), with the kind of fondness and cherishing one has for family members. The NRSV translation of *proēgoumenoi* in

12:10b as "outdo" could suggest the kind of competition Paul is surely trying to eliminate in the community. Paul's point is better put as "taking the lead in honoring one another."[11] Paul is encouraging giving honor to others, not seeking it for oneself. By encouraging them to "take the lead," Paul may be prompting them, in a situation of rivalry between Jews and Gentiles, to take the first step to find a way to honor the other group. Wesley points out that honoring others comes naturally if you really look for the good in others and if you are honest about your own sins and shortcomings.[12] In addition, genuine love is eager to serve the Lord with diligence. It is also joyfully hopeful, endures suffering patiently, and prays continually. It expresses itself in sharing (*koinōneō*) (12:13, NRSV "contribute") among the saints within the community and in showing hospitality to strangers. All this is simply a statement of what the love is like for one who follows Jesus, who gives oneself daily to Jesus, and who has a renewed mind. Although there is no explicit imperative, there is certainly an implied expectation. This is the way a faithful follower of Jesus enacts her or his trust and loyalty. If you claim to follow Jesus, and your life is not like this, you need to undergo some serious self-examination.

> And if you love your neighbor as yourself, you will not be able to prefer yourself before him.
>
> John Wesley, "On Love," II.8, in *The Works of Wesley*, vol. 3, ed. Albert C. Outler (Nashville: Abingdon Press, 1987), 385.

More explicit instruction on the basis of what this love is like starts in 12:14. A genuine love that holds fast to the good blesses instead of curses persecutors. The dating I have accepted for this letter is mid- to late fifties. If that dating is correct, Nero would not yet have begun his persecution. However, the followers of Jesus have already known some persecution. Some Jews, such as Paul himself, had targeted the followers of Jesus for persecution. A more direct problem for the community to which Paul writes concerned the deportation of Jews, including Jewish followers of Jesus in these churches, from Rome (see "Why Romans, Why Now?"). Paul does not identify any particular persecution, nor does he name a particular persecuted

11. Jewett, *Romans*, 755.
12. Wesley, *Explanatory Notes*, 570.

group among them. He speaks to all the Roman followers, which suggests they should be in solidarity with each other, regardless of the persecution that may be faced. Genuine love does not react to mistreatment with hatred but rather wishes for the well-being of the persecutors, speaks of them well, and prays for them. This behavior shows the transformed mind of the follower of Jesus. Because this kind of transformation is extremely difficult, the solidarity of the whole community is important for encouraging one another to truly adopt this outlook.

Paul continues to show what the solidarity of genuine love calls for. It is empathetic, rejoicing in another's happiness and weeping in another's sadness. To be "members of one another" (12:5) means experiencing each other's lives in all their ups and downs. The body knows no isolated celebrations or crises. The depth with which we share in each other's experiences is possible because of the way we have been joined together in Christ. The more we gain the mind of Christ, the more we will be attuned to the other members of the body. This

> For many weep with them that weep, but still do not rejoice with them that rejoice, but are in tears when others rejoice: now this comes from grudging and envy. The good deed then of rejoicing when our brother rejoices is no small one.
>
> John Chrysostom, Homily VII, *Homilies*, 99.

empathetic love also rules out envy of another's success or taking pleasure in another's misfortune. If love is genuine, we will want only the best for the other members of the body, and our response to what happens to them will correspond to their own response.

In 12:16, Paul returns to his concern about "mindedness," using again the Greek *phronein* or a related word three times in one verse. He begins with a shared mindset, that is, they should share with one another the mental outlook of faithful followers of Jesus, which does not mean they must agree on every detail of opinion or practice. It is not uniformity that makes a community one, but rather common values and commitments. This mindset will not be directed to high things but rather to the lowly. Paul is clearly cautioning against superiority. Communities can be destroyed by many kinds of imagined superiorities: superior talent or intelligence over more common abilities; superior status in society or even in the church over more ordinary members; or superior spiritual achievements that have not been gained by all. A mindset that looks to identify advantage over others rather than sharing with others in the humble faithfulness of being grateful to God for salvation leads to destruction of relationships. Genuine love expresses the shared outlook of gratitude and faithfulness even if there are other kinds of differences. Finally, do not come to think of yourself as wiser than you are. This admonition is a caution against thinking you have achieved an especially high spiritual status or that you have all the answers.

Although a certain kind of solidarity is called for within the community, Paul's remarks in 12:17–18, using the language of "all," seems to expand thinking to relationships outside the church. Counsel about nonretaliation is, of course, present in the Jewish tradition (see Prov. 20:22) and is in conformity with Jesus Christ's words (Matt. 5:38–42) and actions, but the idea also existed in the larger culture.[13] In light of the treatment the Jewish followers have received from Rome, Paul's caution against reprisal has relevance for how they get along with others now that they have returned from deportation, but his words may be more than pragmatic. When Paul recommends that they "take thought for what is noble in the sight of all" (12:17), he is acknowledging that some views in the larger culture deserve respect. Although the followers of Jesus must always stand over against values in the culture that are in conflict with the gospel, they must also be alert to where some values may be shared.

Paul goes a step further in 12:18, not merely warning against retaliation, but urging peaceful relationships with all those around them. He recognizes that peace does not depend entirely on how the followers of Jesus behave. Other parties, with different motives and habits, also contribute to what happens and may cause conflict. Still, the followers of Jesus should make every effort to live in such a way as will keep the peace. Even when they resist cultural values, they should not do so in a way that seeks to deliberately disrupt the peace of their social world. Paul's concern made good sense in a world that was hostile to the followers of Jesus and where they had little power.

---

13. Jewett, *Romans*, 771.

In the United States in our time, protests, strikes, and civil disobedience are accepted ways of attempting to make a change. Paul's warning does not need to eliminate the possibility of making use of such avenues for speaking out, but we would do well also to remember his caution that we should act nobly in the sight of all even when participating in these methods for change. All behavior done in the name of Christ shapes the way that the world views Christians, so we should be conscious not to misrepresent the faith we hold.

> If we desire to attain this, we must not only be endued with perfect uprightness, but also with very courteous and kind manners, which may not only conciliate the just and the good, but produce also a favourable impression on the hearts of the ungodly.
>
> Calvin, *Commentaries*, 472.

Because it was so common then as now to seek peace by defeating and destroying enemies, Paul adds a clarification that they should not seek vengeance (12:19). By addressing his hearers in this verse as "beloved," he makes this instruction personal. If the main event for which revenge might be sought is the deportation of the Jews, and if there were hard feelings in the Roman churches because the Gentile followers were slow to accept the Jewish followers back into the community, then this matter would be quite personal. Paul tells his hearers to leave room for the wrath of God to do its work. Keeping in mind what we have learned about the wrath of God (see comments for 1:18–32, pp. 27–37), that it is not angry destruction but revelation intended for correction, Paul's words serve as a reminder that God can make a deeper peace than any we can attempt, especially with our vengeful motives or means. It is God's place to make things right, with complete knowledge of the situation and fair consideration of what should be done. Paul has already established in 2:1–16 that the only rightful and impartial judge is God. Because God's perspective is so much broader than ours, God's way of judging our enemies may be far beyond what we could imagine. Rather than extract vengeance ourselves, we need to leave room for God to work.

Paul offers a different model for behavior than revenge (12:20). If our enemies are in need, we relieve that need rather than leave them in their suffering. Calvin points out, "it is a kind of indirect retaliation when we turn aside our kindness from those by whom we have been injured."[14] One can certainly draw from Paul's words the need for humane treatment for enemies such as prisoners of war and criminals. But suppose Paul had something more personal in mind. If he is addressing the enmity within the community between Jewish and Gentile followers, he may be giving instruction about how they are to show hospitality to each other. When they have common meals in their house churches, they should invite those who are hungry and thirsty even if they are outside the group expected to come. This would be a way of "taking the lead" in honoring the other. No one knows exactly what Paul means when he says this action will "heap burning coals on their heads," but it could refer to the shame they may feel at being treated with love when they have not been loving. The point, though, of acting in this way is not to cause shame. The point is rather about the behavior of those who follow Christ. We need to reflect genuine love in our lives, not cursing but blessing, as a response to the great love we have received from God.

Leaving room for God's wrath not only requires forgoing our own revenge but also not closing off relationship with those who have wronged us in some way. We cannot treat our enemies in the way Paul describes without interacting with them. This is hard work that requires struggle. Underscoring the struggle is Paul's use in 12:21 of the word *nikaō* (conquer) that was used in the Roman Empire for military victory. Although it is extremely difficult to act generously toward those with whom one has enmity, Paul is clear that we must not be overcome (conquered) by evil but rather we must overcome (conquer) evil with good. Although Paul's imperative gives no direct instruction about how exactly one goes about that—and his words do not require us to endanger ourselves or others (for instance, in cases of domestic violence) to remain in relationship—we are counseled to act differently than we may want or than others may expect. We are to enact genuine love, even toward our enemies, as a response to the love we have received, leaving room for God to do the actual conquering of evil as only God can do. We play our part, but the victory belongs to God.

---

14. Calvin, *Commentaries*, 475.

13:1-7
God's Authority and Government's Authority

The change in subjects from 12:21 to 13:1 is so abrupt that it has been suggested that this material is not original to Paul but was added by a later scribe. This suggestion has not been convincing to most scholars because no existing manuscript is without this section.[15] Theologians of the tradition tried to explain the inclusion of these reflections about government in several ways. Melanchthon suggests that Paul is acknowledging the work of God in this area as well as informing us that the godly may participate in it. Calvin wonders whether some special circumstance in Paul's time required him to say something, but he also sees the matter has relevance for every time, especially when there are those who think the kingdom of God cannot be established unless human governments are abolished. Wesley simply recognizes that Paul is writing to believers who live at the seat of imperial power. Chrysostom says Paul wants to show that Christ is not subverting human governance but is trying to make it better.[16]

However abrupt a transition this may seem to be, this passage does continue some lines of thought that Paul started in the previous chapter. Paul began to speak in the previous section of his letter about living peaceably with all. By reminding the recipients of this letter in 12:19 that they are to leave room for the wrath of God, he is reminding them of God's ultimate authority. These ideas come together in this section regarding how to live peaceably with the imperial government when living at the center of its power. Living peaceably may have been especially important for the Jewish followers who had already been deported once from Rome. As he begins this portion of the letter, Paul leaves behind the gentle urging of the previous section and uses an imperative. He is openly instructing his hearers to be subject to the governing authorities. Paul is not writing a treatise on political government, nor is he giving a command

15. Keck, *Romans*, 311
16. Melanchthon, *Commentary on Romans*, 216; Calvin, *Commentaries*, 477; Wesley, *Explanatory Notes*, 571; Chrysostom, *Homilies*, 392.

for all times and all places. He certainly could not have anticipated forms of government that were to arise in later centuries, especially because he expected the eschatological fulfillment of God's reign to happen very soon. He is writing to followers of Jesus in Rome about how they ought to live in Rome in the early years of Nero's reign. This matter was of enough concern to him to give direct instruction about it. The question that readers who live in very different circumstances must ask is what they can learn theologically from what Paul says that can inform their own reflection on how to live faithfully in their own circumstances.

Jewett points out that the reasoning behind Paul's imperative to be subject to the governing authority is more subversive than it may seem at first glance. In whatever way the Roman Empire justified the authority of its government, it surely did not do so by appealing to the God who is made known in the Jewish Scriptures read by the followers of Jesus. Nor would it have recognized the authority of this God. To say that all authority is from God, against the background that the Roman imperial government crucified Jesus and deported many of his followers, is to unveil the way the ruling powers have not themselves submitted to the authority of God.[17] If every person is to be subject to the authority of the government because it is under the authority of God, and if any who resist will stand under judgment, then the empire itself stands under God's judgment.

On the other hand, the followers of Jesus may live peaceably in the empire knowing that by submitting to its authority they are really submitting to the authority of God. They may participate in the system, especially in those ways Paul names in verse 7, such as paying taxes and showing respect, knowing that they are not dishonoring God. They may do so knowing, even if the Roman authorities themselves do not, that they are obeying the authority of God. For

> For though tyrannies and unjust exercise of power, as they are full of disorder, are not an ordained government; yet the right of government is ordained by God for the wellbeing of mankind.
>
> Calvin, *Commentaries*, 479.

17. Jewett, *Romans*, 789–90.

So then earthly authority has been established by God for the benefit of
the nations. It has not been established by the devil, who is never at peace
himself and has no wish to see the nations living in peace. God's purpose is
that men should fear this authority and so not consume one another as fish
do; his intention is that the imposition of laws should hold in check the great
wickedness to be found among the nations.

Irenaeus, *Against the Heresies* V, 24:2, in *Documents in Early Christian Thought*, eds. Maurice Wiles and
Mark Santer (1975; repr., Cambridge: Cambridge University Press, 1998), 226.

any followers of Jesus in Rome who had some kind of position
within the governmental structure or who were slaves of people who
had such positions, the reassurance that they could continue to do
their work was important.

Following Jesus, then, did not require resisting the authority of
the empire. Because of the empire's enormous power, such resistance was futile anyway and would certainly lead to harsh treatment.
Paul himself had experienced harsh treatment, such as imprisonment, at the hands of government officials. Paul does not recommend that the followers of Jesus in Rome provoke the government
to punish them. He seems to understand that the government keeps
the order of society, and it is good for the followers of Jesus to live
peaceably in that order. At the beginning of his reign, Nero's admin-
istration of the empire was praised by the Senate for restoring some
of its autonomy.[18] This positive start to Nero's rule may account for
why Paul could recommend cooperation on the part of the followers
of Jesus. Later, of course, Nero would turn on the followers of Jesus,
and their fear of government would be far more justified than Paul
imagined it would be at the time he wrote this letter.

In ancient Rome, not only punishment but also commendation
of good works could be a public matter. Civic officials could recognize good works that had been done on behalf of the community, for
instance, building public baths or roads; so the idea that the government could give approval to good behavior (13:3) was not unheard
of. One reason Paul may have felt the need to speak about the public
reaction of civic officials to the conduct of the followers of Jesus is

18. Ibid., 47–48.

because of his own history of public disturbance and imprisonment. Because he planned to visit Rome and get support for his mission to Spain, he needed to assure the community it had no cause for concern about what might happen on his arrival. His words about the importance of public approval could signal that they need not worry about him or his work. He would thus be more likely to gain cooperation from Roman followers of Jesus for his mission to Spain.[19]

In keeping with the idea that God's authority lies behind governmental authority, Paul uses the word *diakonos*, the same word used for leaders in the church, to talk about governmental authorities in 13:4. These governmental servants have deadly power to carry out wrath. Although Paul has just warned the Roman followers not to seek vengeance, he now acknowledges that the government has the power and authority to oppose evildoers. This acknowledgment serves as a warning about their conduct, not only because of the potentially deadly consequences they face with those who have such power and authority but also because their own consciences will trouble them. So they should conduct themselves as good citizens should, paying taxes and respecting those in positions of respect— in other words, participating in the system financially as well as socially without giving reason for offense or attack.

Many think Paul's attitude toward government suggests a passive acceptance of the status quo, and so Paul's thinking has been objectionable to those who recognize that government does not always serve the will of God and can use its deadly force to gain power and assets unjustly. In his commentary, Barth contemplates what he understood to be the alternative to accepting the status quo: namely, revolution (perhaps his thinking was influenced by the Russian Revolution of 1917). He reminds us of the futility of revolution because any human endeavor, no matter how well-intentioned as a corrective, will still stand under the judgment of God. The utter transcendence of God means that God will always stand as a negative contradiction to anything in the realm of human history. Revolution can never take us outside of the realm of human history, so it will always fall short of realizing God's will and will always stand under

19. Ibid., 793–94.

God's judgment. For Barth being subject to authority (God's authority through the governing authorities) means leaving the judgment of the governing authorities to God.[20] Barth's commentary was written and revised (the sixth edition appeared in English translation in 1932) before Hitler became chancellor of Germany. In the context of the Third Reich, Barth was largely responsible for writing the Barmen Declaration, which resisted the theological claims of the state and called the church to follow its true Lord. Without denying that the state has responsibility for order, and without attempting a revolution, Barth resisted the injustice of the state and the church's collaboration with it. Leaving judgment to God did not mean for him passive acceptance of whatever the state did, and his criticism of the state and of the church was intended to call attention to the transcendence of God and God's judgment of history.

> Judgments as to when injustice is sufficiently serious to call for civil disobedience, or even rebellion, are extremely difficult to make. All governments act unjustly in some respects, while still maintaining crucially important order. Nevertheless, the Christian must put some limit on passive support of egregious injustices.
>
> Cobb and Lull, *Romans*, 171.

Of course Paul could not know or anticipate that no amount of cooperation by the followers of Jesus would save them from Nero's persecution. Nor could he anticipate the number of ways that Christians would have to negotiate how to exist with various forms of government through time and across the world. What it takes to live peaceably with all differs depending on a number of factors, such as whether the government is hostile to or supportive of Christianity, how much power Christians have in their setting, how much freedom is given to religion, and more. Before Christianity and the empire became intertwined, Christian leaders had to defend their peculiar practices that did not allow them to participate in society in the same way that other citizens did. Tertullian, for instance, argued that although Christians did not worship the emperor, they revered

---

20. Karl Barth, *The Epistle to the Romans*, trans. from the 6th ed. by Edwyn C. Hoskyns (London: Oxford University Press, 1968), 483–85.

him as second only to God. And so they prayed for the emperor's safety, but they did so to the one true God. Similarly, Origen made the case that although Christians did not serve in the military or accept public office, they were doing something equally important by praying against the demons of war and leading churches.[21] After Constantine, Christians no longer claimed exemption from participation in social order and government. This new situation allowed Christians to be more mainstream, but it also led to an ongoing struggle between the power of the church and the power of the state, which has been resolved in various ways at different times in history and in different places.

It must be noted that where Christians have had power in government, that power has not always been used with an awareness of being under God's authority. The difference between claiming God's authority as justification for one's own ideology and putting one's position at the disposal of God's authority is enormous. Christian history has exhibited too much the former and not enough of the latter. Paul's reflections on authority can be just as subversive to a government run by Christians as to one run by ancient Romans. To fail to consider the humility and obedience to which Paul's reflections call us is to completely fail in our obligation to God.

Today, Christians have to work out their existence with government under very different circumstances. In some locations, Christianity remains a minority religion; in others, church and state still function together closely; in yet others church and state have been formally separated. No single model of interaction works for all Christians around the world. To consider how to negotiate existence and responsibility to government in light of what Paul says, we must consider what enables us to live peaceably with others, what kind of participation is in accord with our faithfulness to God, and we must always be mindful that the ultimate authority belongs to God.

---

21. Maurice Wiles and Mark Santer, *Documents in Early Christian Thought* (1975; repr., Cambridge: Cambridge University Press, 1998), 226–30.

13:8–10

Responsibility to One Another

From the concern about one's obligations to external authorities, Paul moves to a discussion about obligations within the community of followers. When Paul tells them not to owe anything to anyone, he could have in mind both financial and social debts. The patronage system of ancient Rome set up social obligations and relations of dependency. To tell the followers of Rome not to owe anything may have partly meant to make sure they paid what was due (financially and socially), but it may also have discouraged participation in patronage that would saddle them with obligations outside the community of followers.[22]

Instead of taking on obligations outside the community, the one obligation to which they should commit themselves is to love one another (13:8). Paul speaks of love as fulfilling the law. We are under obligation to others, and we do need to obey the law, but the obligation and obedience are both carried out by loving one another. This is what God's authority requires of us and how we are subject to it. Protestant commentators have pondered how to explain a requirement for fulfilling the law without jeopardizing the commitment to being saved by grace with the imputed righteousness of Christ. To do so, Calvin and Melanchthon both remind us that the kind of love Paul is talking about is never fully achieved by sinful humans and so we never love enough to make ourselves righteous. We must still depend on grace.[23]

In 13:9, Paul names four of the Ten Commandments as representative of the other commandments. Jewett suggests that Paul chose these four because they had particular relevance for the followers of Jesus in Rome, many of whom lived in the slums and tenements of the city, where theft, murder, and coveting possessions were part of life. The commandment against adultery would have relevance for a community with close relationships between men and women from different families.[24] All these are summed up in another

---

22. Jewett, *Romans*, 805–6.
23. Calvin, *Commentaries*, 485; Melanchthon, *Commentary on Romans*, 223.
24. Jewett, *Romans*, 810.

> By the words "as thyself" all hypocritical love is ruled out. Hence whoever loves his neighbor on account of his money, honor, learning, favor, power and comfort, and would not love him if he would be poor, lowly, ignorant, hateful, submissive, and boorish, would manifestly have a hypocritical love. He does not love the neighbor as such, but on account of what he has, and this is his own interest and so not "as thyself."
>
> Luther, *Commentary on Romans*, 185.

commandment found in Leviticus 19:18, "you shall love your neighbor as yourself." The more specific laws intend to show us what is required by following this one.

In finding a way to summarize the law in a single point, Paul is doing what some of the ancient Jewish sages also did. Hillel is said to have stated, "That which you hate do not do to your fellows; this is the whole law, the rest is commentary."[25] The question asked of Jesus by the lawyer in Matthew 22:36 challenged him to give a similar answer. The summary commandment that Paul cites is the second commandment that Jesus named. Why does Paul not mention the first commandment? Paul has already made it clear in chapter 1 that every human should honor God (1:21), the one, true God, not an idol. He can here focus on the commandment about loving neighbor because his concern in this section of the letter is about human relationships, and he is preparing to address specific human problems in the Roman house churches. It also may be said that one of the ways we honor God is by treating well the ones that God has created, so the two commandments that Jesus named are not unrelated, and Paul understood that.

In Paul's summary, four negative commands are summed up in one positive command. As Paul explains, love cannot do wrong to another. Although it may be true that the command to love implies avoiding harm to others, does the converse also hold? That is, does avoiding harm to another person adequately express loving your neighbor as yourself? Theological commentators on Paul's words have not been content to speak of love only in terms of what we should avoid doing. Chrysostom ties this command to Jesus'

---

25. Babylonian Talmud, *Shabbat* 31a, quoted in Keck, *Romans*, 327.

conversation with Peter after the resurrection, where Jesus makes clear that if we love him, we must feed his sheep (John 21:15–17). Luther also takes this command in a positive direction as he criticizes the rich—because they use their money to erect buildings and acquire holy items—for not helping the poor.[26] Many have seen, then, that the kind of love that fulfills the law is not simply a sentimental emotion, nor is it even simply not doing harm; a proper understanding of this commandment calls us to active caring toward those around us. If we understand the scope of what it takes to love in this way, then, the Protestant interpreters have an important point to make when they say we can never on our own love enough to fulfill the law. Could we ever say that we have done enough good for others?

> Even in the world of shadows love must come into active prominence, for it does not stand under the law of evil. Love of *one another* ought to be undertaken as the protest against the course of this world, and it ought to continue without interruption.
>
> Barth, *Epistle to the Romans*, 492.

13:11–14

Be Ready for Hope's Fulfillment

The final verses of this chapter bring an eschatological horizon into view. For Paul, knowing the time (*kairos*) underscores the importance of what he has been saying. Paul has already appealed to the day of judgment to talk about behavior, and now he stresses the urgency of paying attention to what is coming. Paul is telling the followers of Jesus in Rome that the time in which they are living is a critical time, so they should be alert. The metaphor of sleeping and waking up conveys that now is not a time to be inattentive, but rather those who have been baptized in Christ should focus on what the life into which they have been baptized means. The morning they have been waiting for is drawing closer, the day

---

26. Chrysostom, *Homilies*, 400; Luther, *Commentary on Romans*, 185–86.

when the salvation they began to hope for when they came to faith will be fulfilled. The one who is faithful to the faithfulness of Jesus has no reason to fear the Day of the Lord. Instead it is a time of joy for the time of salvation. They must be ready for that for which they hope.

The usual way to prepare for a new day is to dress after waking up. The dressing that Paul says is needed in this critical time is to put off works of darkness and put on armor (or weapons) of light. When Paul says in 13:12 that we should lay aside works of darkness, he may have been thinking of the way many people engage in behavior at night that they would not engage in during the day when they live more conventionally decent lives. For people in Rome, excessive behavior at evening feasts was common practice, and excessive behavior often leads to quarrels and strife.[27] Such behavior was common in the order of the empire, as it is in other times and places, but this order is passing away. The night will soon give way to the day. How many of us allow ourselves to behave differently when we know our behavior is hidden to others than we do when we think our behavior is exposed? The passing of the old order means that we no longer have the cover of darkness and secrecy, so we should live at all times with the honor and integrity that can bear the scrutiny of day.

The idea that what one needs to wear for the coming day is weaponry suggests that the dawning of a new day with a new order will bring struggle. In the critical time when the night is leaving but the day is not yet fully here, those who belong to the day will have to struggle against the things that belong to the night, that is, the ways of the old order. Even in the twilight, they must live as if the day were fully light.

In 13:14, Paul talks about getting ready for the new day in a slightly different way, this time by putting on the Lord Jesus Christ. Using the title "Lord" reminds the followers of their allegiance to the one who reigns in the new day. The one who reigns is Jesus Christ, the very one who died a shameful death by crucifixion. Unlike the shameful things that must be hidden by darkness in the

27. Jewett, *Romans*, 825.

old order, the shame that he took on for the sake of others is not shameful in the day that is coming. For the ones who give allegiance to the Lord that rules the coming day, the flesh no longer rules. Both Chrysostom and Calvin make a point of saying that as long as we still live in this body, we must take care of it. We must, then, satisfy the desires that keep us alive and healthy. Paul's point is not about hurtful self-denial. Rather, they say it is about excess and letting the desires rule us so that our aim in life is to gratify

> For He would have our soul to be a dwelling for Himself, and Himself to be laid round about us as a garment, that He may be unto us all things both from within and from without.
>
> John Chrysostom, Homily XXIV, Homilies, 409.

them.[28] The desires of the former way of life—and they include more than physical desires (for instance, desiring honor)—should not rule us. This Lord overturns the expectations and gratifications of the old order.

By reminding his hearers of the Day that is coming, Paul brings a sense of urgency to the instructions he will be giving throughout the rest of his letter. He calls them to a way of living that will not be easy, but which is the way of life to which they committed themselves in their baptism. They need to be prepared to "go against the grain" of the accepted way of the world in which they currently live. They do so with the help of the one to whom they have given their allegiance.

Although Paul seems to be thinking quite temporally, so that the Day of Judgment will come soon in time, Barth interprets his words without such a temporal expectation. He understood the Day of which Paul speaks to be in constant tension with our history, qualifying all we say and do. Knowing the time, then, does not mean having in mind a date of a future occurrence but rather becoming aware of how our history is relativized by the eternal God. In every moment, we must be mindful of the Day. We do indeed await the Parousia, but not as if it will arrive in temporality. Rather to await it continually means to "accept our present condition in its full seriousness; we

28. Chrysostom, Homilies, 408–9; Calvin, Commentaries, 490–91.

should apprehend Jesus Christ as the Author and Finisher; and then we should not hesitate to repent, to be converted, to think the thought of eternity—and therefore to love."[29] The constancy of this demand requires us to ask in every moment where our allegiance lies, and whether or not we are displaying our allegiance to Jesus Christ in our thoughts and actions.

> But rather, knowing that the eternal 'Moment' does not, has not, and will not, enter in, we should then become aware of the dignity and importance of each single concrete temporal moment, and apprehend its qualification and its ethical demand.
>
> Barth, *Epistle to the Romans*, 501.

14:1–12

Problems in the Community

After reminding his hearers of the eschatological horizon of their faith—of their twilight struggle as night becomes day, and of their allegiance to Jesus Christ—Paul turns to addressing particular behaviors that have disrupted the ability of the Roman followers of Jesus to be in community together. The urgency of struggling to live for a new day becomes focused on their particularly difficult and concrete situation. All that he has said up to this point prepares them to hear this specific instruction for their community. Paul does not describe much about the situation he is addressing, presumably because his hearers knew what he was talking about. Nor does he state how he came to know about this situation. Later readers are left having to infer an understanding of unexplained conflict from what he does say in chapters 14 and 15.

Paul speaks of two groups: the weak and the strong. These labels may not be Paul's own designation of the situation because the labels do not really arise from the ideas he is trying to convey to the Romans. Furthermore, he uses the labels very sparingly, only in 14:1–2 and 15:1. He may be adopting labels already in use in the community. If so, it would be unlikely that the persons in the group designated as

---

29. Barth, *Epistle to the Romans*, 501.

"weak" would have called themselves weak. The group that considered itself to be strong, then, is probably the source of these epithets. By adopting these terms, Paul leaves off the reference to Jew and Greek that he had been developing previously. This change in terms minimizes attention to ethnic differences and allows him to focus on behavior and status. In what follows, although I cannot completely avoid using the terms "weak" and "strong," I will often identify the groups as the ones who eat and the ones who abstain in order to focus on the behavior and allow the meaning of "weak" and "strong" to emerge from how Paul uses those words.

Because these labels "weak" and "strong" probably originate with the group that considers itself to be strong, by using these terms, Paul may also be emphasizing what he has to say to this group, namely, to welcome (show hospitality to) those they considered to be weak. In the ancient world, the term "weak" could refer to many ways of being inferior or powerless, such as economic, physical, political or social. In English, 14:1 is often translated as naming a specific weakness, "weak in faith." Grieb points out that "in faith" in Greek could instead modify the verb, so Paul might be saying "In faith, welcome the weak."[30] Even if Paul does adopt "weak in faith" as an epithet, he does not necessarily share the judgment that the behavior that the "strong" consider to be weak is fundamentally a problem with faith. Rather, the problem in the community may arise because of different understandings of what faithfulness to God means.

Because "weak" is connected to eating or abstaining from eating meat, many have taken the matter involved in this conflict to be one of religious scruples, perhaps regarding keeping kosher, or perhaps because they could not be sure the meat sold in the market had not been offered first to an idol. The ones who abstained from eating meat are often thought to be Jews, but some Gentiles also kept a vegetarian diet as an expression of asceticism. The divide between the ones who abstain and the ones who eat did not necessarily fall strictly between Jewish and Gentile followers of Jesus (Paul includes himself as a Jew among the "strong" in 15:1). Even if the groups may not divide cleanly between Jews and Gentiles, it is easy to imagine

---

30. A. Katherine Grieb, *The Story of Romans: A Narrative Defense of God's Righteousness* (Louisville, KY: Westminster John Knox Press, 2002), 129.

that many Jewish followers, who are only recently returned to Rome (see "Why Romans, Why Now?"), may be considered by many Gentile followers to be "weak." The two problems that Paul will take up in this section could relate to boundary-marking, which Dunn shows was of particular interest to many Jews at this time. So the two groups to which Paul refers may well have been Jewish (or mostly Jewish) and Gentile (or mostly Gentile). Still, as stated above, Paul does not highlight ethnic differences in this portion of his letter. Calling attention to ethnicity would be counterproductive to his task of trying to help them see each other as brothers and sisters in Jesus Christ.

The question of who are the ones who abstain and the ones who eat is less instructive to us than is the question about their attitude regarding the practice each adopted and the attitude held toward the ones who behaved differently. Those who abstained from eating meat surely did not think they did so because of lack of faith, rather, they were trying to keep faithful to their God by being careful about what they ate. Whereas the ones who eat saw weakness, the abstainers understood themselves to be obedient.

The ones who eat were "strong" in part because they were a group that had the power to name and to exclude. They used a term of honor for themselves and a term of shame for the others. We have already seen how Paul's understanding of the gospel is that Jesus Christ upsets the sociocultural understanding of honor and shame (see especially comments on 5:6–11, pp. 93–98), and Paul's instruction to the ones who eat to welcome the ones who abstain upsets the incursion of honor/shame hierarchy into the body of Christ. Even when sociocultural hierarchy is not as closely tied to honor and shame as it was in the ancient world, the inclination to measure and divide others into superior and inferior groups is a constant pressure on any community. The tendency

> **Paul argues that Christians are just as accountable to God for their *attitudes* towards their brothers and sisters with whom they disagree as they are accountable for the *decisions* they have made that divide them from one another.**
>
> A. Katherine Grieb, *The Story of Romans* (Louisville, KY: Westminster John Knox Press, 2002), 128.

to want to be in the superior group is so prevalent that theological commentators have consistently identified with the "strong" as they interpret this passage. It is common to see comments about how "we," the "strong," should treat "them," the "weak." Chrysostom goes so far in his elevation of the "strong" as to say that Paul is merely addressing the "strong" as a gentle way of rebuking the "weak."[31] In the face of such a pervasive tendency to establish hierarchy in the community and claim superiority for our own group, Paul's instruction has lasting and compelling significance.

Paul's specific command (14:1) to the ones who eat is to welcome the "weak." The Greek *proslambanomai* has been shown to have some overtones that are important for understanding Paul's meaning. To be welcomed or accepted into a group implies sharing a cause or purpose with others in the group. To welcome someone socially means to extend hospitality to that person, often sharing food at the table.[32] In a situation where lines of demarcation have been drawn to indicate who is superior and who is inferior, Paul instructs welcoming those whom you consider to be inferior as those who share your cause as equals.

Because bringing groups together with different values and behaviors could be very uncomfortable, Paul goes on to specify that the purpose of welcoming them not be for disputation. Jewett points out that the kind of quarreling that Paul rules out is not spirited debate that can lead to greater clarity and understanding for all, but rather what he rules out is a kind of intellectual competition aimed at bringing about conformity to the dominant position.[33] Welcoming should not bring others into coercive situations but rather create space for exchange in the context of mutual respect.

Commentators who have identified with the "strong" have also often missed the idea of equality in welcoming, so they have read Paul's instruction as a condescending concession. In other words, the reason to avoid quarreling is so as not to shake the faith of the weak, as if their faith would crumble if their scruples were questioned. Paul does not say, though, that faith is at risk. His explicit

31. Chrysostom, *Homilies*, 417.
32. Jewett, *Romans*, 835.
33. Ibid., 836.

message (14:3–4) is mutual acceptance of each other—no despising, no passing judgment. God has welcomed all of them. God has accepted all of them, so they should act appropriately toward each other as acceptable to God. It takes a strong faith on both sides to be able to do what Paul calls for.

Although Paul's initial command is for the ones who eat to welcome the ones who abstain, he is not just correcting the ones who eat. The two sides in the conflict each have their own way of contributing to it. The ones who eat feel superior to and so "despise" the ones who abstain, but the ones who abstain also act improperly in this situation. They pass judgment on the ones who eat. The ones who abstain, with their specific understanding of what obedience to God looks like, need to be reminded that God also accepts the ones who eat, even though they adopt different behavior. The ones who eat, with their more expansive diet, also serve God. When Paul reminds the ones who abstain that they have no right to pass judgment on another person's servants (14:4), he is making two points that would be obvious in the original context. First, given the authority that a master had over a servant, Paul is reminding them of a point he has already made in this letter: the only one with authority to judge is God, who is the master they all serve. Second, the word translated as "servant" is *oiketēn*, which was the term used particularly for a house servant. The emphasis, then, is not simply on being a servant but on being a member of the household (*oikos*).[34] This choice of words reminds them they are members of the same household.

Paul expands the point that God alone can judge them. In Paul's words about not passing judgment, one should keep in mind his reflection on judgment in 2:1–16, namely, that in passing judgment on others, you condemn yourself. Furthermore, Paul is confident that when God judges the ones who eat, they will be upheld. As we learned from the example of Abraham in 4:1–12, God may regard as righteous whomever God wants. God's welcome is entirely up to God, and we are not in a position to change or question that.

When the disagreement at hand is about what to eat, welcoming

34. Ibid., 841–42.

and accepting one another at table is not a simple matter, especially when house church gatherings included table fellowship. The problem arises not because of what a person eats in private but rather in the context of eating together. The way these followers of Jesus figure out how to share food will reveal how well they really regard each other as brothers and sisters. Coming right after Paul's reference to the command to love your neighbor as yourself in 13:9 and his reminder that the new day is dawning, the difficulty of eating together serves as a test of obedience and readiness. Will they be able to put on Christ in this trying situation? Will the ones who eat treat the ones who abstain as equals? Will the ones who abstain refrain from passing judgment on the expansive choices of the ones who eat? Will each recognize the other's behavior as an expression of faithfulness to Jesus Christ?

Although we may no longer feel the urgency of a new day dawning that Paul did, the way we treat each other as Christians when we face deep disagreement is still a test of our obedience to the command to love one another and of our readiness to put on Christ. Too often Christians live out competition that breaks the body of Christ instead of living out the faithfulness to one another that our faithfulness to our Lord requires. As important as it is for each of us to come to an understanding of how best to honor God, we must always be ready to welcome those whom God has already welcomed.

In addition to the problem of eating is the problem of observing sacred days. Paul does not clarify which days were the cause for disagreement, but many have suggested the particular point at issue might be regarding which day to treat as the Sabbath (Saturday or Sunday) and whether or not to continue observing Jewish festival and fast days. The word translated in the NRSV as "observe" in 14:6 is a form of *phronein*, and the original hearers would realize he had just used this word (in 12:3) when he spoke about being "sensibly minded" instead of "high-minded."[35] In their concern to honor a day to the Lord, they should hear this echo of the importance of mindset. They should not be proud but should rather remember their dependence on God's grace. Once again, the question of the precise days is

35. Ibid., 846.

less instructive than what Paul has to say about attitudes toward the observance and toward each other.

Although the instruction to welcome one another remains in the background, Paul directs his attention here to personal conviction (14:5). It is important, he says, to be convinced in one's own mind, but Paul does not regard such conviction as coming from personal, self-serving reasons. The conviction he is talking about lies rather in one's understanding of what honors God (14:6), and it is expressed in giving thanks to God. Such honor and gratitude are not the property of any particular conviction; they may be present regardless of which day is observed and whether one eats or abstains.

When Paul's thoughts on the two problems of eating and observing sacred days are taken together, it seems Paul is trying to affirm openness to others without falling into an "anything goes" consequence. Openness and conviction go together. Even as he affirms their personal conviction, he also reminds his hearers that others have conviction too. As Barth saw, this chapter puts a question mark against our conviction so that we do not mistake it for the ultimate truth of God.[36] A certain generosity of spirit is required to recognize that others are also trying to honor God in what they do, even if what they do is different (and perhaps unacceptable from one's own point of view). In the face of painful disagreement with other Christians, Paul calls us to look beyond the problem itself to the God we all serve.

As he says in 14:7–9, we do not belong to ourselves, but to God. Paul has already made the point in 12:1 that we should present ourselves as living sacrifices. Whether our sacrifice comes in our living

---

But although a difference of opinions or modes of worship may prevent an entire external union, yet need it prevent our union in affection? Though we can't think alike, may we not love alike? May we not be of one heart, though we are not of one opinion? Without all doubt, we may. Herein all the children of God may unite, notwithstanding these smaller differences. These remaining as they are, they may forward one another in love and in good works.

John Wesley, "Catholic Spirit," ¶4 in *The Works of John Wesley,* vol. 2, 82.

---

36. Barth, *Epistle to the Romans,* 504.

or in our dying, it is offered to God. Neither the specific matter of what to eat or what day to worship are matters of life and death, and Paul is not suggesting that these specific problems have such dramatic stakes. He is calling us to see that our sacrifice is in the totality of who we are, so even how we address problems with relatively low stakes matters for what kind of offering we make to God. To take seriously that we have died to sin and entered into a new dominion means that the Lordship of Christ extends to everything that we are and do.

Paul connects our living and dying with the death and resurrection of Jesus Christ. Paul has already made the point that being baptized into Christ's death brings us into his resurrection (6:5–11), so we are to live to God just as Jesus Christ does (6:10). Because through Christ we are connected to each other, our living and dying to God is done together in community. Disruption of our life together tarnishes our living sacrifice to God.

In 14:10, Paul returns to the particular disruption that threatens the Roman churches. One group passes judgment and the other group despises. Neither attitude is fitting for those who live and die for God. These attitudes to one another make no sense at all in light of what the followers of Jesus Christ know, namely that on the coming day of judgment, all will stand before God to be judged. On this Day, we will each be accountable for our own behavior.

> This conclusion invites us to humility and lowliness of mind: and hence he immediately draws this inference,—that *we are not to judge one another*; for it is not lawful for us to usurp the office of judging, who must ourselves submit to be judged and to give an account.
>
> Calvin, *Commentaries*, 503.

Not only does our concern about what another group does deflect our attention from considering how we ourselves ought to honor God, but passing judgment and despising are both attitudes that manifest that we have put ourselves in God's place, usurping what only God has the right and authority to do—to judge and to regard as worthy. The behavior in the churches of these groups toward one another is poor preparation for standing before God in accountability.

Matters of worship still divide Christians, whether across denominations, or within denominations across cultures, or even within individual congregations. Passing judgment and despising others are just as effective in drawing boundaries as "works of the law" were in the ancient world, although the former create boundaries within the community rather than around the community. They pose a threat to the faith and faithfulness of the community. Notice that in the face of this serious threat, Paul has so far not offered a solution. What he has done instead is to call both groups to consider what it really means to be a follower of Jesus. The theological insights he has presented in the earlier parts of his letter ground his hearers in what it means to honor God, to be faithful, to leave the dominion of sin and belong to the dominion of grace, to be brothers and sisters to one another—all things they will need to consider as they work out these problems among themselves. As churches today face the many problems that disrupt our life together, these insights should also inform the way we attempt to work through our differences with one another.

14:13–23

Pursue What Makes for Peace and Mutual Upbuilding

Eating together at a communal meal is important enough that Paul does have some words to say about how to approach the problem of eating together. Paul begins with a wordplay using the Greek *krinein* (14:13): no longer pass judgment (*krinein*) on one another but judge/decide (*krinein*) not to place a stumbling block or obstacle for another. As his second use of *krinein* shows, his encouragement to stop passing judgment does not eliminate thinking about the problem and drawing a conclusion. Rather he directs the effort of making a judgment toward avoiding

> When we permit ourselves to judge others, we are caught up in condemnation: the result is that we merely succeed in erecting the wrath of God as an idol.
>
> Barth, *Epistle to the Romans*, 516.

harm to a brother or sister in Christ. Although "passing judgment" has been named previously as the problem of the ones who abstain, Paul's inclusive language—"let us" and "one another"—indicates the instruction is for both groups. Perhaps this is a tacit recognition that "despising" is also a way of passing judgment on others. Much of the actual instruction that follows is directed to the ones who eat. Although the two groups need to consider the effect they have on each other, the ones who eat have more power as a group and so must act with great care.

Paul leads into his discussion about eating with thoughts about what is "unclean." In 14:14, the verb form of the word "unclean" (*koinon*) is recorded in the words of Jesus in Mark 7:15 (defile, make unclean). Because Mark's Gospel was written after Paul wrote this letter, Paul would not be referring directly to this verse. But Paul does not need direct reference to the words of Jesus to be persuaded in Jesus Christ that nothing is unclean in itself. The designation of food as "clean" and "unclean" had been a way of showing through food laws the distinction between Israel as the people of God and the Gentile population.[37] The meaning of Jesus Christ for Paul, as he has already made clear in this letter, is that in him, God has acted to expand the way salvation comes to the world, so the distinction breaks down. For Paul, the very meaning of the gospel is to make nothing "unclean." Paul shows how deeply convinced he is of this meaning through the double affirmation that he knows and is persuaded.

Paul understands, though, that not everyone shares his conviction. As he has already shown in 14:5–6, it is not only possible but also permissible for the followers of Jesus Christ to have different convictions. Each may honor God according to how they are convinced to do so. For this reason, he follows the statement of his own conviction with "but" because he knows there is an alternative view. The thing itself may not be unclean, but if someone thinks it is unclean, for that person, it is unclean. Acknowledging this alternative does not simply mean that this thing is unclean only for that person. It also calls us to consider that if the person believes her- or

---

37. Jewett, *Romans,* 859.

himself to be honoring God by distinguishing between clean and unclean, then this way of honoring God is to be respected as appropriate devotion.

As we have seen, the particular pressure of this problem arises in the common meal that the followers of Jesus share when they come together as house churches. The question they face is how to honor the different convictions of the people who eat together in community. What is at stake is the integrity of holding conviction, of respecting the way that God is acting persuasively in one's own life as well as in the life of another person. If most of the ones who eat were Gentiles, then they would also constitute the majority of the community in Rome. Although Paul eventually uses the label "strong," he never says "strong in faith." It is possible, then, to recognize in the term "strong" the kind of power that the majority often has. The majority often finds it easy to impose its beliefs and practices on those in the minority, and in doing so, the majority does not show respect for the beliefs and practices of the others. Those in the minority are not allowed to have the integrity of their convictions. They may even be expected to change their convictions to suit the majority position. The power that the "strong" exercise in this situation needs to be kept in check.

This understanding of the responsibility of the ones who eat to the ones who abstain may help clarify how their actions may be a "stumbling block" or "hindrance" that may injure the weak (14:15). If the ones who eat do not respect the convictions of the ones who abstain about how they ought to honor God, then the ones who eat call into question the faithfulness of the other group. The pressure that the majority puts on the minority to conform can make the minority members cease to trust in their own knowledge of God and instead adopt beliefs and practices of which they are not convinced. When they act counter to their convictions, their trust in God is not made manifest, so their faithfulness is not enacted

> Today everyone regards only what is his and what he may do according to his "right"; but he does not consider what he owes to others and what edifies both himself and his neighbor.
>
> Luther, *Commentary on Romans*, 203.

and is therefore compromised. Damaging the faithfulness of one for whom Christ died should be a horrifying consequence to any who care about their brothers and sisters in Christ. It is not merely "offensive" to them, but actually hurts their relationship to God.

So Paul says (14:16) do not let "your good," your own faithfulness in embracing the freedom to eat anything, be "spoken of as evil" (Paul says *blasphēmeisthō* using the word that gives us the English word "blaspheme"). The ones who abstain, who are put in this position by the ones who eat, no doubt express their understanding of being wronged. This way of speaking, of course, exacerbates the problem for the ones who abstain of "passing judgment" on another group. Gaining the conformity of the minority by denying their convictions, then, does nothing to unite the community.

Paul turns his attention to what would unite the community. He begins by directing attention to what really matters. The kingdom of God does not consist in decisions about what to eat or drink, rather it consists in "righteousness and peace and joy in the Holy Spirit" (14:17). The followers of Jesus in Rome may have felt that they were showing their righteousness in what they ate or did not eat, but Paul is calling them to remember the different way he has been talking about righteousness throughout this letter. Paul rarely uses the phrase "kingdom of God" (*basileia tou theou*) but his use of it here is a reminder of how he has been talking about righteousness. He has used *basileia* language in 5:21 to talk about how sin and grace each exercise a different kind of rule or dominion. As he unpacks the meaning of living in the dominion of grace in chapter 6, he speaks of being obedient from the heart rather than from external obligation (see comments on 6:1–14, pp. 106–13). Grace sets them free from the external obligations of the law, but this freedom is not opposed to obedience. The focus in the dominion of grace is not on the laws (about eating), whether in keeping them or in being free from them. Rather the rule of grace opens them to the possibility of a different righteousness—being molded into the likeness of Jesus Christ. Serving Christ, then, is the mark of this new obedience of the heart, and they are all servants in this household. Living under this new rule means not looking to the laws to see who follows them or who does not follow them. Rather life in this dominion is shown in serving and honoring the one who rules in this dominion of grace. Furthermore, Paul has already made it clear that one fulfills the law by loving one's neighbor (13:8–10). Obedient service under the rule of grace, then, means carrying out this command. If the one who serves Christ is pleasing or acceptable to God (and Paul has just reminded his hearers that they have all been welcomed), then human approval should follow. The servants should not reject the one the master has welcomed.

The kingdom of God consists not only in righteousness but also in peace and joy, so Paul urges them to pursue the things that will serve peace and the upbuilding of one another (14:19). In the salutation, Paul has wished them peace from God, which is not like the peace the empire can secure (see comments on 1:1–7, pp. 15–18). Followers living in Rome would know all about peace gained through military victory, but Paul is not encouraging the end of conflict because one group has won the argument and the other has lost. Instead, they must pursue peace that cannot be separated from securing the welfare of each other. Peace and joy in the Holy Spirit that belongs to the kingdom of God is found in their common life together. They must pursue it together and gain it together.

Paul's positive encouragement toward uniting the community does not give specific directions for how the Roman followers should build one another up. Perhaps he feels no need to repeat his reflection on communal life in chapter 12. He does offer specific instruction about what they should not do. Paul addresses himself to the ones who eat, likely because of the way their strength can be misused. If the kingdom of God is not food and drink, how wrong it would be to tear down the work of God because of food! The ones who eat are correct that they are free, but they misuse their freedom if they cause another in the community to stumble (14:20). Paul is here making a point similar

> *Being right is not the most important thing.* Where being right prevails, we "live to ourselves" (v. 7). Where self-actualization is the paramount good, one must prevail. And then the good ends up "being spoken of as evil" (v. 16). The well-being of the fellow believer—even "the weak with regard to faith"—is more important than being right.
>
> Keck, *Romans*, 348–49.

to what he has said to the Corinthians (1 Cor. 6:12), but he is doing so by showing the consequence to another. Freedom in the dominion of grace means freedom to be obedient from the heart, and obedience to the command to love your neighbor as yourself is the summation of what this freedom should look like. So if eating and drinking unclean things at the communal meal lead your brother or sister in Christ into mistrusting their convictions about how to honor God, then it is wrong to eat and drink.

Because Paul spoke in 14:13 in an inclusive way to both groups, it is possible that the ones who abstain could also put a stumbling block in the way of the ones who eat. With less power, it is less likely that the ones who abstain are in danger of doing so, but it is possible to imagine that the ones who abstain could attempt to use their own conviction to veto the conviction of the ones who eat. Such an action would also have a negative consequence for some members of the community in not allowing them to honor God according to their own conviction. Working through this problem in a way that does justice to both groups requires commitment to care about the other's conviction as much as one cares about one's own.

Although it has been in the background of what he has been saying, Paul finally uses *pistis* in 14:22. We have our own faith before God, our own trust in God and our own way of enacting that trust in faithfulness. The ones who do not "condemn" or judge (*krinein*) themselves for what has been approved by testing and discernment are blessed. The word Paul uses for "approve" (*dokimazein*) is the same one he used in 12:2 to speak about discerning the will of God. So approval is not a matter of finding personal or private reasons, much less is it simply about what one likes, but rather it comes after careful consideration of what would honor God. If one has worked to discern the will of God to decide how to enact one's trust in God, then one has no reason to judge that enactment negatively. Such a person is blessed or happy, knowing the joy in the Holy Spirit that belongs to the kingdom of God.

Without such confidence in the way they enact their trust in God, persons will be haunted by questioning judgment. The reason for preserving the integrity of conviction becomes clear. They cannot be truly faithful if they are not enacting their trust in God. If they do something for any other reason (such as conformity to someone else's understanding of faithfulness) than because they have discerned it is the will of God, then they are not truly enacting their trust in God and therefore are not truly honoring God. When measured by what faith/faithfulness ought to be, this action falls short and is thus sinful. The problem Paul is identifying is not just a matter of preserving the integrity of conscience or conviction. Rather disturbing the path to faithfulness that we all should follow puts us in

> Paul urges the "strong" Christians to protect the less-confident brothers and sisters for whom Christ died so that the others might enjoy that same blessing and escape the condemnation that comes from doublemindedness.
>
> Grieb, *The Story of Romans*, 129.

the situation that Paul describes in 1:21, that is, of not being able to truly honor and give thanks to God. A member of the body of Christ who is obedient to the command to love simply cannot do that to a brother or sister for whom Christ died. Even if working out a concrete solution to the problem is extraordinarily difficult, the alternative consequence is unthinkable.

15:1–6

Obligation to One Another

Paul conveys to his hearers that there is an obligation that follows from all he has said in response to the attitudes that factions in Rome hold toward one another. The Roman world was filled with social duties from one person to another. Paul has already used the language (*ophelein* and *opheiletēs*) of owed obligation occasionally in his letter (see 1:14, 8:12, and 13:8). Here he uses the same language to show that his exhortation about how to act toward one another is more than good advice. Followers of Jesus Christ have a duty to other followers of Jesus Christ. Although social duty is something his Roman hearers would readily understand, Paul's description of this duty is not exactly what a Roman would expect. Duties in Rome were reciprocal to some degree, but the obligations generally worked in favor of the powerful.[38] The powerful received services and honor from the weak persons who submitted to them. Paul reverses this usual pattern of social duty. The strong are obligated to the ones they consider to be weak.

As mentioned earlier, Paul uses the labels "strong" and "weak" very rarely, and 15:1 is the first time he refers to the "strong" (*dynatoi*). Also, he does not in this verse refer to the weak as a group, that is, to weak people, but rather to "weaknesses" (*asthenēmata*). This shift in terminology opens the possibility that Paul may intend the lesson of obligation to extend beyond the specific situation of abstaining from meat. Many kinds of weaknesses can exist in a community, and there are many ways of having and exercising power over people with those weaknesses. So the obligation of the "strong" that Paul has in mind may extend beyond eating to many ways of being powerful in relation to others. The NRSV translation "failings of the weak" (15:1) unfortunately calls to mind insufficiencies of faith or moral choice, when in the ancient world "weaknesses" could more readily suggest inferior economic or social status. There are many ways that factions can arise in the community. We can learn from the specific problem Paul addresses between the ones who eat and the ones who abstain that we must find a way to negotiate any differences for the good of the whole community, not just one faction in it. It is just as easy for factions to fall into passing judgment and despising each other over differences of economic and social status as it is over food. Even when differences arise concerning another kind of "weakness," those attitudes are no less damaging to our brothers and sisters in Christ. The obligation that Paul names is binding for all followers of Jesus even when new times and places present us with different challenges.

Paul includes himself among the "strong," and he could do so not only because he accepts the freedom to eat anything but also because as an apostle, he is a leader among the followers of Jesus. In other words he has power. Acknowledging he is among the strong does not mean he claims superiority. Rather, in this context, it shows

---

38. Ibid., 877.

he is willing to take on the same obligation that he explains the powerful must take on in the Roman churches.

This obligation has two components to it: bearing the weaknesses and not pleasing oneself (15:1). Bearing weakness does not mean grudgingly putting up with the annoyance of the weak. It should be understood according to what Paul says in Gal 6:2: "Bear one another's burdens, and in this way you will fulfill the law of Christ."[39] In the specific context of eating together, this obligation probably means the "strong" should place themselves under the scruples of the ones who abstain and therefore restrict themselves to eating acceptable food. In other ways that weaknesses might be understood, it could mean giving assistance to those who are economically disadvantaged, or it could mean treating as equals those of a lower social status.

> The bearing of infirmity is a wholly existential occurrence; it is a genuine being weak with the weak.
>
> Barth, *Epistle to the Romans,* 524.

The positive obligation to bear weaknesses is amplified by the negative obligation not to please oneself. The verb translated as "please" implies accommodation, and it would be very unusual to expect the powerful to accommodate to someone else. It was, of course, the job of servants to please their masters, but in the larger culture, masters do not act like servants. Paul's words are intended to instruct the powerful.[40] With them, he clearly reverses the social expectation. It is the powerful who should accommodate themselves to the weak, not the weak to the powerful.

The obligation of followers of Jesus to one another does not stop here, though. In the next sentence (15:2), Paul speaks more inclusively about "each of us" pleasing the "neighbor." The weak also have "neighbors" to please. Each person, no matter how weak, can contribute something to the upbuilding of the community. In a society that allowed the powerful to show their power by being benefactors, the idea that the weak also had something to give was important for showing that they were not merely weak but also had some measure of power to act on behalf of someone else. The recognition of the

---

39. Ibid.; Keck, *Romans,* 349.
40. Jewett, *Romans,* 877.

We are directed to please them 'for their good'; not barely for the sake of pleasing them, or pleasing ourselves; much less of pleasing them to their hurt, which is so frequently done, by those who do not love their neighbor as themselves. Nor is it only their temporal good which we are to aim at in pleasing our neighbour; but what is of infinitely greater consequence; we are to do it for 'their edification'—in such a manner as may conduce to their spiritual and eternal good. We are so to please them that the pleasure may not perish in the using, but may redound to their lasting advantage; may make them wiser and better, holier and happier, both in time and in eternity.

John Wesley, "On Pleasing All Men," ¶2 in *The Works of John Wesley*, vol. 3, 416.

agency of the weak was just as much a reversal of social expectation as the accommodation of the powerful was.

Although as the letter unfolds, Paul arrived at this statement of obligation through a consideration of a problem in the community, the real foundation for this obligation is not just a pragmatic solution but rather is found in Jesus Christ. Jesus did not act self-servingly but rather put himself in service to others (15:3). Furthermore, although "pleasing oneself" is the usual behavior of the powerful, Christ identified with the weak by not pleasing himself. The quotation from Psalm 69:9 (LXX 68:10) read with reference to Jesus shows him in a position of weakness—humiliated by insults—rather than getting what he wants. If Paul means this quotation to bring to mind the taunting at Jesus' crucifixion, then he is connecting our obligation to one another with a number of things he has already said about how we follow the Christ who was crucified. By being baptized into his humiliating death, we cannot seek glory in the way others do. We have died to the dominion of sin and cannot hold the values of that dominion. Just as Jesus took on weakness and suffered shameful death, we should bear the weaknesses of the ones for whom Christ died. If the followers in Rome are to "put on" *this* Jesus Christ, then they must act in the way Paul has described.

Although he has quoted Scripture already in this letter, Paul feels the need here to provide some rationale for using this particular psalm in the way that he has. The apparent need for a rationale has puzzled commentators. Could it be needed because the Scripture is so directly connected to Jesus? Could it have been a comment added to later manuscripts by a copyist? Jewett suggests that the rationale is needed because the psalm is addressed to God, but Paul uses it to address the Romans. In other words, he has changed the "you" to whom the text is speaking.[41] Paul is reinterpreting the text so that it serves the current context. He may feel such adaptation is allowable because the purpose of all Scripture is to instruct us. The purpose of the instruction is to give us hope through steadfastness and encouragement (15:4). Perhaps Paul means that by encouraging us to be steadfast in bearing the weaknesses of our neighbors, the reinterpreted instruction of this Scripture gives us hope for a community that lives faithfully in the new dominion of grace. Being a part of such a community would also encourage us to be steadfast in the mission that God has given us and allow us to hope for all to live in the dominion of grace.

> What is written of Christ is written for us, in order that we may learn to imitate him. Hence we must understand this as something which is presented to us of Christ, not merely in a speculative way, but by way of example for us to follow.
>
> Luther, *Commentary on Romans*, 210.

If with his rationale, Paul has shifted the subject of address in the psalm from God to his hearers, in 15:5 he regards God as the one who may bless the hope that comes from the instruction. Paul prays that the God who is the model and source of steadfastness and encouragement may give you the same mind (*phronein*, which the NRSV translates "harmony") among one another. Throughout this letter, Paul has used the word *phronein* to refer to the mindset that belongs to the life of the Spirit in the dominion of grace (see comments on 8:1–17, pp. 130–42). Such a mindset is not proud but "sensibly minded," remembering dependence on God's grace. So when Paul asks God to bless the Romans with the same mind, he is not asking for uniform agreement in what they think about eating or observing sacred days. Instead, he is asking that they all have the mindset of living in allegiance to the dominion of grace, which will turn

41. Ibid., 881.

> We pray that we may be given zeal for both peace and concord.
>
> Philipp Melanchthon, *Commentary on Romans,* trans. Fred Kramer (St. Louis: Concordia Publishing House, 1992), 288.

them away from the pride of perceived superiority and enable them to bear one another's weaknesses. This kind of life together would indeed be "in accordance with Jesus Christ." It would also enable them to glorify God together, not only in voice, but also in practice.

15:7–13

A Wide Welcome

Previously in 14:1, Paul had instructed the "strong" to welcome the "weak," but now in 15:7 he tells all of his hearers to welcome each other. With these words, Paul goes beyond the attitudes he talked about in 14:3. Not only should they stop despising and passing judgment, but they also should actively receive each other just as Christ has welcomed each of them. In the context of the problem that Paul has been commenting on, this instruction to welcome each other had a very concrete meaning. That is, Paul is telling them to welcome each other at the common meal when followers of Jesus Christ gather together. Because the followers met where one of them lived, this instruction meant actually welcoming each other into their homes.[42] So if the problem in Rome is that people have had trouble eating together, Paul's solution is to tell them to eat together. They must not avoid the problem, but rather they must work through it in the presence of each other, keeping in mind his counsel in 14:13–23 about how to do so. They must learn how to show actual hospitality to each other.

What would it be like if Christians could face their problems with one another as squarely as Paul called the Roman followers of Jesus to do? A Christian response to disagreement should be neither denial nor open conflict, but rather acknowledging that different convictions may lead Christians in different directions and working

---

42. Ibid., 888.

together to see how each may respect the conviction of the other. If Christians could actually live out the obligation to one another that Paul names, then our life together would be a powerful witness indeed to what God can do.

The followers of Jesus Christ live in a dominion ruled by grace. The God who gives this grace is the one who has acted in Jesus Christ to overcome the fundamental human sin of not giving thanks and honor to God (1:18–23). By doing so, this God has accepted treasonous enemies (5:10) and made them friends. The ones who worship this God do not bring honor to God by fighting with each other and shutting each other out. Rather, they bring glory to God when they imitate the model of Jesus Christ. It is in welcoming that we become like the one we follow.

Although he has avoided using ethnic distinctions as he has talked about the problems among the Romans, Paul returns now to connect his reasoning to the matter of the distinction between Jews and Gentiles. Jesus Christ identified with the weak, and this identification includes the Jews, who were not powerful people in the empire. He has become a servant of the circumcised (15:8). This servanthood is not for the purpose of raising the circumcised above the uncircumcised but rather for the truth of God, confirming the promises to the patriarchs and enabling the Gentiles to glorify God. Jesus came to the Jews, among the Jews, and he shows that the promises made to the Jewish patriarchs are reliable. The promise made to Abraham is shown to be reliable as God's mercy displayed through Jesus brings Gentiles to glorify the true God instead of idols (15:9). Jesus Christ is simultaneously for the Jews and the Gentiles. Whereas the Roman followers of Jesus have tended to focus on "us" and "them," the very meaning of what God is doing in Jesus Christ—"to the Jew first, but also to the Greek" (1:16)—breaks down those divisions. This insight not only supports the harmony that Paul wants to see among the Roman followers but also supports his mission to the Gentiles. As a Jew, Paul sees no conflict between his Jewishness and his mission. In fact, his mission is the necessary response to God's faithfulness to the Jews.

To support the point that the servant of the circumcised is also for the uncircumcised, Paul quotes Scripture (15:9–12). Following a common rabbinic pattern of "chain quotation," Paul cites several passages that come from the Law, the Prophets, and the Writings.[43] Paul is quoting the Greek (LXX) translation of Psalm 18:49 (LXX 17:50), Deuteronomy 32:43, Psalm 117:1 (LXX 116:1), and Isaiah 11:10, but it is not the original meaning of the passages in their original context that matters in this chain of citations. Rather Paul uses the language of Scripture to convey his own point. Jewish Scripture itself recognizes that the Gentiles will worship God, so Jesus Christ confirms this assertion made in Scripture by extending mercy to the Gentiles and giving them reason to praise God. Paul's own mission receives strong support from Scripture itself; and the Roman followers of Jesus, Jewish and Gentile, have scriptural reasons to work through their differences so that they may live and praise together.

Even as Gentiles glorify God, they may also, as followers of Jesus, hope to share in the glory of God (see comments on 5:1–5, pp. 87–93). The grafting to the olive tree that Paul described in chapter 11 allows Gentiles to hope to participate with the original people of God in the life of their God. This shared hope does not come because one people have won out over the other. Contrary to the idea of winning, in which Romans accustomed to military conquest would be steeped, the shared life with God that Paul has described comes from growing together. We do not hope by ourselves in the God of hope, but rather we hope together.

> **Truth and Mercy hold together Jew and Gentile, Church and World. Who here is strong? Who here is weak? Above, before, behind every human endeavour stands—The God of Hope.**
>
> Barth, *Epistle to the Romans,* 526.

Paul concludes his quotation of Scripture with a prayerful benediction (15:13). He asks the blessing of God on "you" in the plural, so it is the community together, not merely individuals, who may be filled with joy and peace and abound in hope. The power of the Holy Spirit acts in them all together. Taken with the benediction of 15:5–6, the hope for a faithful community that shares the mind of Christ in the dominion of grace leads to the hope that this community will be empowered by the Spirit

---

43. Ibid, 893.

and enjoy the Spirit's gifts. The hope for such a community further supports the hope that more, in fact all the nations, will come to live in this dominion.

Many theological commentators have interpreted the hope in this benediction as hope for the individual, that is, as hope of peace and joy in one's own personal life. Rarely has the communal dimension of this hope been conveyed. Paul's expressions of blessing call for us to recognize that it is in the community that each of us finds our hope for ourselves, and that it is as a community that we witness to what God can do for the world. A world looking for hope and peace and joy will look to where these things are evident. If they are not evident in the life of Christians together, they cannot be offered effectively to others. Fractious factions not only tear churches apart and cause pain to individuals in those churches, they also destroy the evidence of the dominion of grace as alternative to the dominion of sin. Christians must learn to talk about more than individual salvation in order to participate in the mission that Paul envisioned and to which he calls all of us.

15:14–16:27

Plans and Greetings

15:14–21

Paul's Work for God

After requesting blessing of the God of hope on the community, Paul begins the final portion of his letter. Following the style of letter writing in the ancient world, Paul includes the typical courtesies that would be expected, including expressions of confidence in the recipients. Even though he has identified and given instruction about a problem among them, Paul expresses confidence that the community will be able to work it out (15:14). He names qualities that would enable this outcome. Being full of goodness and knowledge and able to instruct may not have been evident in his description of the situation he has heard about, but they are qualities that belong to putting on Christ that Paul has called them to. There is perhaps a bit of flattery in naming these qualities before they have actually been in evidence, but his words also express a confidence that the hearers of his letter will take his words to heart. Paul's confidence may lie more in what he knows God can do than in what he knows about the situation in Rome. After all, he has just invoked the power of the Holy Spirit on their behalf, and he trusts that God will provide. Words that express this confidence are more likely to have a positive effect on his hearers than less flattering description would.

Paul's polite apology (15:15) for even broaching the subject follows. After all, Paul did not found this church and he has not yet visited it, so he is acknowledging that he has taken something of a liberty in addressing them as he has. Yet at the same time, the way he frames this apology reminds them of his authority. Paul opened this letter describing himself as a servant of Jesus Christ, and he now says more about that service. Paul is in this position because of the grace of God, and his particular task is to carry the gospel to the Gentiles (15:15–16). The word that Paul uses to describe his position is *leitourgon,* which is translated in the NRSV as "minister" (15:16) and was used in Paul's time for an ambassador.[1] Paul is not merely saying these things on his own behalf. Rather he represents Jesus Christ and the realm or dominion he has ushered in. Although he has spoken boldly, Paul has done so because his service requires him to speak on behalf of the God who rules the dominion of grace.

Paul's description of his service not only gently reminds the Romans of his authority to instruct them, but it also reminds them of his mission. He has been sent to the Gentiles, and he performs a "priestly service." This priestly service is not to make an offering on behalf of the Gentiles, nor only to collect an offering from them; it is rather to make the Gentiles themselves into an offering (15:16).[2]

> As if he had said, I have not snatched at the honour for myself, neither was I first to leap forward to it, but God commanded this, and this too according to grace, not as if He had separated me for this office because I deserved it.
>
> John Chrysostom, Homily XXIX, *The Homilies of S. John Chrysostom, Archbishop of Constantinople, on the Epistle of St. Paul the Apostle to the Romans,* 3rd ed., trans. members of the English church (Oxford: James Parker and Co. and Rivingtons, 1877), 463.

Just as a priest in a temple offers sacrifices to God, Paul offers the Gentiles to God. The Gentiles who would not have been allowed near the altar of the Jewish temple are now metaphorically considered as the offering placed on the altar. As an offering, they are acceptable to God. Although they do not live according to the works of the law, God accepts them and finds them well-pleasing. They are even sanctified, set apart as holy. Gentile followers of Jesus are certainly set apart from other Gentiles who fail to honor God, and they are called to be "saints" (1:7) as all followers of Jesus are.

If this is the work Paul has been given by God to do, then he also says he has reason to boast of it (15:17). Given his theological

---

1. Robert Jewett, *Romans: A Commentary,* Hermeneia (Minneapolis: Fortress Press, 2007), 906–7.
2. Leander E. Keck, *Romans,* Abingdon New Testament Commentaries (Nashville: Abingdon Press, 2005), 360.

objection to boasting previously in this letter, this boasting needs to be clarified. Ambassadors sometimes "boasted" of what they had done as a way of showing they were worthy representatives of the ones who had sent them.[3] It is, in a sense, a way of showing credentials. Living at the seat of government, the recipients of this letter would understand he was giving this kind of information. In adopting this rhetoric, Paul does not violate his theology against boasting. He is careful not to name these things as his own accomplishment but rather as what Christ has accomplished through him. The work that Christ does through Paul has gained the obedience of the Gentiles who have learned of Christ through what Paul has said and done (15:18). Paul's phrase "word and deed" would have been a familiar expression for Gentile hearers, and "signs and wonders" would have been familiar language of authentication for Jewish hearers. Whether expressed in language directed to Jewish or Gentile ears, Paul's work has been done "by the power of the Spirit of God" (15:19). His boasting, then, is ultimately about God's power, not his own.

Paul briefly describes the extent of what God has accomplished through him so far. He has reached as far as Illyricum, a Roman province of territory on the Adriatic Sea that includes what we know today as Albania and Bosnia and Herzegovina. When Paul says he has "fully" proclaimed the gospel (15:19), he does not mean he has preached everywhere in the area. Paul's typical pattern was to establish a church in cities and then leave local evangelism to the followers of Jesus in the area. Paul may mean that he has done all he can do to establish a center for the ongoing work in the region.

Having completed his duty in one region, Paul seems eager to move on. He does not want to go where someone else has already begun to build (15:20). To borrow from his metaphor in 1 Corinthians 3:5–6, Paul sees himself as the planter, not the cultivator. His particular ambition is to proclaim the gospel where Jesus Christ is not known at all. That he finds his task in Scripture (Isa. 52:15c–d) shows his ambition is not simply his own private desire to outdo others. When he moves on, it is not because he is refusing to cooperate with others. He simply understands his role as the prophet

---

3. Jewett, *Romans*, 909.

describes it, so he must go to new territory to carry out his specific task and trust others who follow after him to do theirs.

Barth finds Paul's habit of moving on to be strange and his boasting to be off-putting. He does, however, find in Paul's boldness to speak to the Romans an important model for theology and the church. Because its task is to speak about God, theology can never simply accept the conclusions of human beings about what has value and about how life should be lived. Even the best judgments of human thought fall short of the way God sees and understands. Theology plays an indispensable role when it raises questions about the security that human beings like to find in the knowledge they construct. The church can and should also play this role, but too often it brings the values of the culture into its own life. Theology that sees its purpose as serving this kind of church does no better. When the intellectual discipline and the institution that exist for the purpose of talking about God instead merely join the conversation that other disciplines and institutions are having about human life, then they may as well admit that they are bankrupt. Barth urges them instead to speak boldly, as Paul did, to have the courage to raise questions that will be considered inconvenient but which must be raised to expose the lack of finality in all that human beings do.

15:22–33
Paul's Plan to Visit Rome

Paul indicates that he has wanted to visit the Roman followers of Jesus for some time, but something has always kept him from doing so (15:22). Although Paul does not give any details about these hindrances, many examples of the trials he has faced are mentioned in his letters and in Acts. They include shipwreck, imprisonment, and distraction with conflict in other churches. Now that, as he has said in 15:19, his work is done in the region he has been in, he will be moving on to proclaim the gospel in Spain, and this plan for travel gives him both opportunity and reason to visit Rome. Not only can he pass through Rome as he travels west on his way to Spain, but he can also gather support for his mission while he is there. His hope for support in mission is signaled by his words about reaping a "harvest" among them (1:13) and being "sent on" by them (15:24). Scholars agree that the verb Paul uses in 15:24 implies the expectation of being sent with items necessary for the journey.

Spain was in some ways a suitable mission ground for Paul. No record of a substantial Jewish population exists for the time Paul wrote this letter, so it would be very unlikely the gospel could spread there through any Jewish mission. Spain was considered "barbarian" by the civilized world, and as a territory that lacks the common languages of the empire, Paul would have difficulty communicating the gospel to Spain's inhabitants. Paul has described himself as obligated to Greeks and barbarians (1:14), so he understands his work as apostle to include the "uncivilized" people in Spain. The gospel may have no other way of reaching them than through Paul. Furthermore, the way maps were drawn at the time, with the Mediterranean Sea in the center, Spain extended the arc of Paul's work quite naturally.[4]

Paul speaks of passing through Rome, spending time with the Romans, as the NRSV says, "for a little while" (15:24). He thus signals to them that they are important enough for his attention but that he will not stay long. As he has made clear, his work is not to build on what others have done but to lay new foundations for others. For the moment he has one more delay. He needs to go to Jerusalem, which is not on the route to Rome, to deliver a collection for the followers of Jesus in Jerusalem. This delivery is in response to the request of the other apostles that Paul records in Galatians 2:10. The way Acts tells Paul's story, it is while he is in Jerusalem that he is taken into custody because of a public disturbance. Eventually he does arrive in Rome, but as a prisoner. Tradition holds that he died there.

The collection that takes Paul to Jerusalem is mentioned in his letters to the Corinthians (1 Cor. 16:1–4; 2 Cor. 9:1–5). In 2 Corinthians, Paul refers to it not simply as funds but as ministry or service (*diakonias*) In the letter to the Romans, the word Paul uses for the collection in 15:26 is *koinōnian*, which implies much more than

---

4. Ibid., 924.

money or even service. It conveys fellowship and communion with one another. By using this word for the generosity the Gentile churches are showing to the poor among the Jewish saints, Paul is underscoring his point about how the strong and weak relate to one another. One of the ways that the powerful demonstrate their wealth and influence is to give money to charity, but the followers of Jesus are not giving with a sense of superiority. Rather, they are sharing with one another out of what they have. Paul uses the language of social obligation (*ophelein*) again in 15:27. Through this gift, the churches are fulfilling their duty to their brothers and sisters in Christ. Far from being a burdensome obligation, this duty is well-pleasing (*eudokein*) (15:27). Paul stresses the reciprocity of this duty. The Gentiles share (*koinōnein*) what the Jewish saints have spiritually. As Paul described in 11:18, the roots nourish the branches that have been grafted on. It is fitting that the Gentiles provide service for the physical needs of the Jewish saints. The strong are not merely benefactors of the weak. Instead each has something to offer to the other. Although Paul mentions this trip to Jerusalem to explain his delay in visiting Rome, it also serves as a concrete example of the lessons he wants the Roman followers to hear about how to live together.

> **Paul in this passage reminds us what we owe to the teachers of the Gospel, a matter about which he speaks frequently and more fully in his other epistles.**
>
> Philipp Melanchthon, *Commentary on Romans*, trans. by Fred Kramer (St. Louis: Concordia Publishing House, 1992), 294.

Although Paul has spoken in a matter of fact way about how the delivery to Jerusalem may delay his visit to Rome, he betrays concern in 15:30–33. Paul's mission to the Gentiles was not uncontroversial, and he faces the possibility of strong resistance in Jerusalem from Jews who do not follow Jesus, and even the followers there may not want to be associated with his ministry, perhaps not even accepting the gift he brings. Paul does not go into detail about the potential problems he faces in Jerusalem. Perhaps the followers in Rome know something of the situation there; they certainly were familiar enough with the tensions in the relationship between Gentiles and Jews to have an idea about how the Jews in Judea might react to Paul's way of presenting the gospel to the Gentiles. Or perhaps he simply does not feel it necessary for them to know details. Instead of giving explanation, what Paul does is ask for their prayers. This is not a request to be merely "remembered" in prayer. The word Paul uses (*synagōnisasthai*) (15:30) comes from military and athletic settings. He is asking them to struggle (*agōn*) with (*syn*) him through their prayers. Paul expects danger, perhaps physical and perhaps spiritual, and the prayers of the followers of Jesus in Rome can aid him in what he has to face. According to the record in Acts, Paul's concerns were well founded. Even if the prayers of the Roman followers did not prevent trouble, the knowledge they were praying for him must surely have supported Paul.

The stakes of this journey were high not only for Paul personally but also for the long-term relationships between Gentile and Jewish followers of Jesus. To be welcomed in Jerusalem would signal acceptance of his mission and his vision of how Gentiles and Jews could be one in Jesus Christ. A negative reaction to Paul among Jews who did not follow Jesus could influence negatively his reception by the Jewish followers. Jerusalem's openness to Gentile followers was already somewhat precarious, and not finding Paul and his ministry "acceptable" (15:31) could threaten to undo the solidarity across ethnic boundaries that Paul was working for. It is no wonder that Paul felt anxious about this journey.

Despite his apprehension, Paul is still hopeful he will be able to travel to Rome as planned. A successful trip to Jerusalem would certainly explain how he would arrive in Rome with joy, but whether or not he would be "refreshed" there might well depend on the resolution of tensions in the community (15:32). His prayer to the God of peace is not mere formality. He truly desires God's peace to be among them.

16:1–2

Introducing Phoebe

Letters in the ancient world typically ended with greetings from people where the letter is written to people where the letter is received. Before Paul starts his greetings he speaks of Phoebe and asks the followers of Jesus in Rome to welcome her. Paul's commendation of Phoebe to the Romans provides some information about who she is. Her name indicates that she is Gentile. Paul's reference to her as "sister" certainly conveys to the Romans their familial relation to her through Jesus Christ. It may also suggest a special connection to Paul. Of particular note is that Phoebe is not identified by way of relationships to other men or gender role (as wife, sister, etc.) but rather by her position and function in the church.[5] She is a deacon of the church at Cenchreae, which is a seaport near Corinth. Deacon (*diakonos*) was not yet the title for a formal office, but it does signal that Phoebe has a role in service or ministry in her church, more likely to be performed in leadership than in some subordinate function. For Paul to call her "benefactor" suggests even more strongly a leadership role in Cenchreae. She must have been a woman of wealth and high standing, so it is likely that she hosted the gathering of followers in Cenchreae in her home.

> See how many ways he takes to give her dignity. For he has both mentioned her before all the rest, and called her sister. And it is no slight thing to be called the sister of Paul.
>
> Chrysostom, Homily XXX, *Homilies*, 477.

What we know of Phoebe only leads to further questions. Did she deliver the letter Paul wrote to the Roman followers? If so, she would have been expected to read and interpret it to them. Did she go to Rome on Paul's business, or did she have her own business there? Jewett suggests that as benefactor to Paul, Phoebe was supporting his mission to Spain.[6] If Phoebe was in Rome to prepare for his mission, Paul's instruction to the Roman followers to welcome her and help her may not have been merely requesting hospitality but also asking for them to begin organizing support for his work.

It may not be possible to know precisely why Phoebe is

---

5. Elisabeth Schüssler Fiorenza, "Missionaries, Apostles, Co-workers: Romans 16 and the Reconstruction of Women's Early Christian History," *Word & World* 6, no. 4 (September 1986): 420–33.

6. Jewett, *Romans*, 945–48.

> For the women of those days were more spirited than lions, sharing with the Apostles their labours for the Gospel's sake. In this way they went travelling with them, and also performed all other ministries.
>
> Chrysostom, Homily XXX, *Homilies*, 488.

commended to the Romans as she is, but what we do know about her from what Paul says shows that he accepted and trusted women in leadership roles. The mention of other women in his greeting (about one-third of the twenty-six names he mentions are women's names) only supports his regard for what women contribute to the faith.

16:3–16
Personal Greetings

The number of people Paul greets is quite large, and because he has not yet visited the followers of Jesus in Rome, he must have met them or heard of them in his travels. Many are greeted by name, others are mentioned as a group ("the church in their house" 16:5). The individuals he greets bear names that are either Greek or Roman. Although Paul gives little information about each of them, their names allow scholars to infer something about their lives. For instance, scholars can tell from ancient records that a number of the names, such as Ampliatus, were names given to slaves. The people bearing these names were then probably slaves or former slaves.

Paul speaks of a few of the named persons as his "kin" (*syngenē*) (16:7, 11). This is the same word Paul uses in 9:3 to speak of the Jews as his kinsfolk, so rather than using the word the way we would for someone like a cousin, Paul probably means they are Jewish. The first people identified in this way are Andronicus and Junia, who deserve mention because of scholarly debate about them. Junia is the name of a woman, but because Paul identifies them as "prominent among the apostles," an alternate interpretation of this name arose. With the prevailing assumption that no woman could be an apostle, the suggestion arose that "Junia" in the manuscripts was a shortened form of the name "Junianus." A number of English translations use "Junias" to make the name refer to a male. Recent scholarship has shown there is no evidence to support the presumption of a male name, and to the contrary, evidence shows that feasts in the church celebrating Saints Andronicus and Junia acknowledged her as "the admirable woman Junia."[7] In fact, Chrysostom recognizes that Junia is a woman and says in his homily on these verses, "Oh! How great is the devotion of this woman, that she should even be counted worthy of the appellation of apostle."[8] Even though he sounds surprised at this honor, he does not deny her the title. Andronicus and Junia were probably a married couple who worked in mission together. The recognition of a woman apostle does much to dispel assumptions that women never had and should never have positions of authority in the church.

The other married couple that Paul mentions is Prisca and Aquila. This couple is also mentioned in Acts 18 and in other epistles (1 Cor. 16:19; 2 Tim. 4:19). Acts 18:2 makes clear that Aquila is a Jew but does not say the same of Prisca. It would ordinarily seem safe to assume that a Jewish man would marry a Jewish woman, but with a faith that is breaking down the barriers between Jew and Greek, the idea of marrying outside one's ethnic group becomes plausible. The lack of comment about Prisca's ethnicity in Acts 18:2 has provided an opening for a few scholars to suggest that she may have been Gentile, perhaps coming from a noble family. Some wealth and a high social status would explain how the couple could have a house large enough to host a church.[9] It would not explain why they worked as tent makers when they were living outside of Rome. Whether or not they share an ethnic background, Prisca and Aquila have worked together and with Paul "in Jesus Christ," they risked themselves to help Paul, and they are well known and praised among the Gentile churches. Prisca is not greeted as Aquila's wife but as coworker. They both are significant leaders, missionaries, and teachers, and Paul honors all they have done by greeting them.

When Paul refers to working together with Prisca and Aquila, he means working together in mission. In other letters, Paul uses

7. Ibid., 961.
8. Chrysostom, *Homilies*, 489.
9. Jewett, *Romans*, 955.

"work" or "labor" or "toil" to speak about missionary leaders (see, for instance, 1 Cor. 16:16 and 1 Thess. 5:12). When he uses such language to greet Urbanus, Mary, Tryphaena, Tryphosa, and Persis, he may be indicating their function and status as missionary leaders. It is significant that the last four of these named persons are women.[10] Prisca, then, would not be the only woman missionary leader among the Roman followers of Jesus.

The meeting of the followers of Jesus in Prisca and Aquila's house is the only one Paul calls "church," but the greetings suggest other groups who might be worshiping together. Paul mentions two households where some, but apparently not all, are followers of Jesus: the household of Aristobulus (16:10b) and the household of Narcissus (16:11b). In neither case is the named head of household greeted, suggesting that they are either not followers of Jesus or are perhaps no longer living. The greeting is very likely intended for slaves in the household rather than family members. Historical records and inscriptions do not have many instances of the name Aristobulus, but there is an Aristobulus who was brother to Herod Agrippa and was educated in Rome with Claudius (who later became emperor). The name Narcissus was more common. There was one freedman named Narcissus who worked for Claudius and another for Nero. There is at least some possibility that Paul is referring to one of these households. Slaves in these two greeted households would have been near the center of power and privilege in Rome. Although it is not possible to be sure of the identity of the people Paul was talking about, the potential for these connections provides a suggestive background for the "strong." Because slaves gained some status according to the high status of their masters, the taste for power and privilege in those households could be influencing relationships among the followers of Jesus in Rome.

Two other groups of followers are suggested by the greetings. Paul speaks of "the brothers and sisters" who are with Asyncritus, Phlegon, Hermes, and Patrobas (16:14) and "all the saints who are with" Philologus, Julia, Nereus, and Olympas. Many of these

10. Schüssler Fiorenza, "Missionaries," 430.

names were commonly used for slaves or freedpersons. In contrast, then, to the possibility of connection to privilege in the previous two households, these groups of followers were likely to have been made up of slaves and freedpersons of much lower economic and social status. They may have lived in the crowded and squalid tenements in the city. Worshiping together under those conditions would have been difficult, and the common meal they shared may have been an important source of nourishment. It is not hard to see how tension could arise among followers of Jesus with such different life experiences as these four households may have had. Vast difference in privilege and resources can raise barriers in a worshiping community in our own time as well as in theirs.

The range of people that Paul greets by name should not be missed. Not only do they include Jewish and Gentile persons, but they also include male and female as well as slave and free. The followers of Jesus in Rome have the potential for being the community in Christ that Paul envisions in Galatians 3:28. The theology Paul has explained to them throughout this letter has been to help them understand and realize this community. The greetings at the end of the letter highlight the diversity of the community, and Paul honors them all equally.

> It could not but encourage the poor especially, to be saluted by name, who perhaps did not know that the apostle had ever heard of them.
>
> John Wesley, note on 16:14, *Explanatory Notes upon the New Testament* (London: Epworth Press, 2000), 581.

When Paul admonishes them all to greet one another with a holy kiss (16:16), he is encouraging a concrete action that would demonstrate their solidarity and equality with one another. In the ancient world, kisses were shared primarily among family members as an expression of familial affection and intimacy. Paul's command to all the named persons and households to greet one another with a holy kiss makes them circulate beyond self-imposed barriers of distinct groups in the community and express their family relation to one another in Christ. This action would be particularly important if the holy kiss was normally given as part of the liturgy, when congregations gathered. Paul might in this command be encouraging them yet again to welcome each other to their common meals.[11] At the very least, the greeting Paul has in mind reminds each small group that it does not exist by itself but is connected to the others. His final comment in this section that all the churches of Christ greet the churches of Rome extends the reminder of that connection yet further.

16:17-20

Further Instruction

The instruction found in 16:17-20 seems an awkward insertion at the close of the letter. Although many scholars find it merely a strange place for Paul to say these things, others think it is an interpolation—that is, an addition made by a later editor to the letter. Although there is no manuscript evidence, reasons for thinking these verses were added later by someone other than Paul include that they interrupt the flow of the greeting, the vocabulary is different from what Paul ordinarily uses, and the content seems contradictory to what Paul has said throughout the letter. For instance, he has instructed the people in this community to welcome each other, not to avoid each other. Whether Paul or someone else wrote these words, is there a lesson in them that can be instructive in light of what Paul has been saying all along?

Even if these verses are likely an interpolation, their presence in this text now prompts reflection on the difference between disagreements that present barriers within the community and ideas that threaten the community itself. If an interpolation, these words were probably added at a time when communities eventually recognized as heretical were proclaiming competing versions of the meaning of Jesus Christ. To be avoided are teachers and teachings that distort the understanding of who Jesus Christ is, as early gnostic versions of the story of Jesus did. Paul instructed the Roman followers to work out their differences by appealing to the Jesus who was brutally executed, a physical person who was humiliated and shamed, who took

11. Jewett, *Romans*, 973–74.

on weakness, but who was vindicated by God in resurrection (see comments on 5:6–11, pp. 93–98). Other versions of the meaning of Jesus Christ that arose fairly early in history erased the pain and humiliation in favor of presenting only a powerful figure. The community should surely avoid this reversal of understanding.

Followers of Jesus can bear differences within the community that arise from different convictions about how to honor God. Teachers who are the source of dissent and offense, on the other hand, do not honor God or serve Jesus Christ but rather serve their own appetites (or bellies). Although Paul has addressed a food problem in this letter, one should not take the reference to bellies to be connected with that problem because Paul presumes that both groups in Rome are trying to honor God through their eating. Instead, the reference to bellies (*koilia*) in 16:18 more likely picks up on the understanding of the abdomen as the center of desire. Paul has been clear in 6:12–14 that primarily serving our own desires is evidence that we still live in the dominion of sin. Those who follow self-interest and their own pleasure (see 15:2–3) cannot be trusted to teach the truth of God because they are not living under God's rule. They will manipulate others to serve their own desires. Such people surely should be avoided.

The connection between 16:18 and 16:19 is not clear, but the writer seems to want to stress the integrity of the followers of Jesus, knowing and seeking the good and not confusing it with what is evil. Such integrity requires the ability to dis-

> Take care lest ye be deceived, especially by those who are nearest to you and most plausible.
>
> Karl Barth, *The Epistle to the Romans*, trans. from the 6th ed. by Edwyn C. Hoskyns (London: Oxford University Press, 1968), 536.

cern what is worth knowing and what needs to be avoided. Although followers of Jesus imitate Jesus by being welcoming, they do not blindly accept everything and everyone into their lives. Discernment matters, so "guileless" (16:19) cannot mean completely naive. One needs to know enough to be able to make a good judgment. Paul wrote about discerning the will of God in 12:2, and the key is having the mind of Christ. This discernment is to be done under an eschatological horizon, in 16:20a depicted not as the judgment of people (as in 2:1–11) but as the defeat of Satan. Know and avoid what is evil because it will fully and finally be crushed.

Whether or not this portion of the letter is an interpolation, the way to allow it to add to our understanding of this letter is to keep in mind all that Paul has said up to this point so that interpretation is guided by the overall message of the letter.

16:21–23
Further Greeting

Eight persons send greetings to the followers of Jesus in Rome at the close of this letter. Of those, the first four are identified as "relatives" or as Jews. Because Paul is apostle to the Gentiles, and because he has named himself among the "strong," Paul, by including these greetings in his letter, may be showing to the Jewish followers in Rome that he has not abandoned his people and in fact has good working relationships with other Jews as he pursues his mission.

Tertius and Quartus are names meaning "third" and "fourth" respectively, and they were common names given to slaves. Despite their depersonalizing names, they have significance among the followers of Jesus. Gaius may be the Gaius named in 1 Corinthians 1:14. As host not only to Paul but to the whole church, Gaius must have been a wealthy patron, either hosting gatherings of followers in his home or providing hospitality for other followers like Paul who traveled. As a public official, Erastus also would have wealth and standing in the community. Like Paul's earlier personal greetings, these final greetings show how social barriers were being broken down in Christ. Jew and Gentile, depersonalized slave and persons of high social standing come together and work together.

16:25–27
Final Doxology

Many scholars think that, like 16:17–20, the closing verses of this letter are an interpolation. Not all of the surviving ancient manuscripts contain the closing doxology, and some that do contain these verses put them in a different place in the letter. Vocabulary and content also raise questions. Of particular concern regarding content, the doxology speaks of God's revelation as having been kept secret, but it is now disclosed to the *ethnē* (nations), which is the word commonly used to mean Gentiles. Such a statement implies that the Jews did not understand what they had in their prophetic writings but that the Gentiles now possess this knowledge. The doxology gives priority to the Gentiles over the Jews, whereas Paul has spoken consistently through the letter of the Jew first and then also the Gentile.

Because it has a place in the lectionary, this text cannot be ignored even if it is correct that the verses were added later by another hand. The praise of 16:25–27 needs to be carefully interpreted to counter supersessionism in light of the overall message of Paul's letter. Acknowledging that Jesus and Paul were Jews, that the first people to understand the "secret" disclosed in the prophets were Jews, and that the community to which Paul wrote was made up of followers of Jesus who were both Jewish and Gentile could all be a part of this interpretation. We give praise not for how God reveals to Gentiles what the Jews did not understand but rather for how God used the revelation in Jesus Christ to open up a way for Gentiles to also become people of God.

If the doxology is an interpolation, it may have been written after the Jewish revolt against the empire beginning in 66 CE resulted in defeat by Rome, the shattering of the Jewish people, and the destruction of the temple in Jerusalem. Supersession is built on the idea that God was done with the Jews and replaced them with Gentile Christians as the people of God. At the time, given what had happened to the Jews, that idea must have seemed to Gentile Christians quite plausible. In our time, it is clear that the Jews, despite continuing persecution even to the point of genocide, are still a vital people with a living faith. God has not dismissed them, and Christians do not bring glory to God by acting as if we have taken their place as God's people. To interpret this doxology to bring glory to God, we cannot elevate Gentile Christians at the expense of Jews.

The doxology has many important parallels with the opening of the letter. John Wesley points out the following parallels: the power of God at work, the gospel of Jesus Christ proclaimed, the prophets, the obedience of faith, and the nations.[12] The doxology intends to praise God for all those things Paul affirms and uses to introduce himself at the beginning of the letter. The God who called and sent Paul will strengthen all of us who follow Jesus Christ. The revelation in Jesus Christ continues to be made known to the nations, and it is displayed in our faithfulness. When believers respond to this revelation by sharing and showing the good news of Jesus Christ, we bring glory to God. Paul's letter still speaks to us today to instruct us in how to respond to what God has done in Jesus Christ in such a way that we honor and bring glory to God.

12. Wesley, note on 16:25, *Explanatory Notes*, 583.

Postscript

Context is everything: This lesson from my time studying Greek exegesis as a Master of Divinity student has stayed with me. The lesson was reinforced for me as I worked on this commentary. The new perspective on Paul calls attention to Paul's context so that we may understand him better. When we understand him better, we are better equipped to think with him—not merely to repeat his ideas, but to allow his voice a place in shaping our ideas—about how to understand and proclaim the gospel in our own context. Preaching requires nothing less.

As I began working on this commentary, I taught a study on Romans in the local United Methodist congregation that I attend, the Church of the Messiah in Westerville, Ohio. I taught this study in part to make myself begin to focus on a task that seemed impossible, so I did not yet have the full benefit of all I read and learned in the writing that followed. Even so, as I conveyed what scholars of the Bible wanted to say about the text, as well as how these ideas were developed later by theologians such as Luther and Barth, the people who attended the study were energized by both. They could see the value of knowing what Paul said and also the value of learning from later interpreters. Both had meaning and relevance for their daily lives. We shortchange the potential for God to speak powerfully to the people if we deny one or the other.

Of course, learning to think with Paul requires us to learn to distinguish what Paul said in his context from the way Paul was interpreted by major theologians in their own contexts. One of the real values of the new perspective on Paul is that it helps the process of "thinking with" Paul by calling attention to our tendency to conflate Paul and his interpreters. Our deep formation in traditions that arose centuries after Paul wrote this letter may make such distinction difficult, but the exercise of making the attempt will no doubt be illuminating. It has been my intent to suggest that our formation in later readings is also important, but when we avoid taking that formation simply as the obvious reading of Paul, Paul may be able to help us understand our later traditions in fresh ways.

As someone born and reared in the Methodist tradition, I have not been formed to be constantly alert to ways that works might compete with faith, as perhaps some others have been. Still, my own tradition has been just as deeply influenced by the notion of imputed righteousness to overcome guilt as other Protestant traditions have. Behind this idea of imputation, I suspect, lies a particular tendency toward how to understand atonement. In addition, the doctrine of original sin sets the stage for the need for atonement. If theologians take seriously the idea of reading Paul from a new perspective, some really basic, familiar theological categories will come under scrutiny. To be honest, they already come under scrutiny for other reasons, so perhaps the convergence of pressing questions raised by our time and new ways of reading Paul might lead to helpful and perhaps even more biblical understandings of the human problem and how God acts to overcome it.

So many later readings of Paul took shape in polemic that we do well to pay particularly close attention to the ways our assumptions about what Paul is saying may have been formed in polemic. It is historically tragic that interpretation of Paul's letter, which was itself written to unite the original community to which it was addressed, has so often divided people. One of the important reasons for learning to distinguish Paul from his later interpreters is to allow this letter once again to address Christians as brothers and sisters who must remember their connection in Christ.

Context is everything, but one of the things we learn from putting Paul into his sociocultural context is that he did not let his own sociocultural context determine the content of the gospel. He exercised his freedom in Christ to borrow language and images from his culture, but he put them in service to the rule of the new dominion.

The word "gospel" itself is an example of how he did so. When we listen to what Paul has to say to our own context we must be careful not to distort the message to fit the old dominion but rather to examine our own comfortable ways of thinking and acting according to the new dominion.

If Romans is not a theological treatise but rather a letter, then it serves its purpose best when it allows Paul to speak to us as he did to the original recipients. This requires an act of imagination about how we are like and unlike the original recipients. The great distance between Paul's time and ours means our questions will not always be exactly his, or his ours. Because of changes between Paul's situation and ours, thinking with him sometimes means using his theological commitments to guide us to different conclusions than he may have held himself. It may also mean that thinking with him can sharpen our own questions so that we consider our own context in new ways. How might our situations be similar to the situations the followers of Jesus faced in Rome? Given what Paul said to them, what might we learn from him now?

My imagination has been caught by the way Paul speaks of dominions and allegiance to the people who lived at the heart of the empire. Paul's theology is an important challenge for any tradition that remembers nostalgically the days of numerical health when its churches were almost indistinguishable from the culture. Fueled by worry of decline, we ask too rarely, what makes us different? Paul's central image of a monarch ruling in a dominion may not communicate well for those of us who live in a country that threw off monarchy. Yet we need to find some way to raise his questions now. What does it mean to be loyal to the God of Jesus Christ instead of controlled by sin? How do we remain loyal not only as individuals but also as a community? How do we show our loyalty to God's authority while still living peaceably among others who may not recognize that authority? Paul cannot give us the specific responses needed for the circumstances of our time, but he reminds us to think about the theology of our response so that we do not settle for being pragmatic Christians only but also strive to be truly faithful ones.

I have also found questions about the relationship between Jews and Christians to be urgently pressing. None of us as Christians can hope to consider these questions free from the influence of our formation in our own faith, but we must approach them with humility to try to see ourselves as others see us. Because his time was so different from ours, Paul cannot give us the answers we need to our questions. We need to be reminded, though, of his commitment to his people and God's faithfulness to them as vital condition for thinking further about the questions we face in understanding this relationship. Thinking with Paul requires us to have a deep commitment to the well-being of the Jewish people. This commitment needs to be stated openly and often in worship, Bible study, and other places where people who do not have access to high level interfaith dialogue have a chance to think about these questions.

At many points as I worked on this commentary, I asked myself, "What was I thinking when I agreed to write this?" At times, the awareness of the controversies surrounding this letter was almost paralyzing. Nothing about writing it was easy; and yet, as I worked, I began to feel often that the time I could spend on this commentary was the best part of my day. The questions Paul raises are important. His insight into what it means to live in relationship with God and with each other is profound. His challenge to us today is relevant. The struggle to try to think with him about what it means to follow Jesus Christ is worth the effort.

For Further Reading

Barth, Karl. *The Epistle to the Romans*. Translated from the 6th ed.
by Edwyn C. Hoskyns. London: Oxford University Press,
first issued 1968. Barth's classic work takes interpretation
beyond the "first step" of historical criticism to theological
commentary on the Bible.

Christian Classics Ethereal Library. www.ccel.org. John Calvin's
Commentary on Romans is available on this site.

Furnish, Victor Paul. *The Moral Teaching of Paul: Selected Issues*.
Third edition. Nashville: Abingdon Press, 2009. This book
examines moral issues that Paul spoke about with the intent
to find moral guidance from him without giving up our own
critical thinking about these issues. It includes, but is not
confined to, issues in Romans.

Grieb, A. Katherine. *The Story of Romans: A Narrative Defense of
God's Righteousness*. Louisville, KY: Westminster John Knox
Press, 2002. Rather than moving verse by verse in the style of
a commentary, Grieb presents the story that Paul is trying to
tell in his letter.

Jewett, Robert. *Romans*. Hermeneia. Assisted by Roy D. Kotansky.
Edited by Eldon Jay Epp. Minneapolis: Fortress Press, 2006.
This comprehensive commentary provides much critical
detail about text and sociohistorical context.

Joint Declaration on the Doctrine of Justification. http://www
.vatican.va/roman_curia/pontifical_councils/chrstuni/
documents/rc_pc_chrstuni_doc_31101999_cath-luth
-joint-declaration_en.html.

Keck, Leander E. *Romans*. Abingdon New Testament Commentaries. Nashville: Abingdon Press, 2005. This compact commentary covers literary, sociohistorical, and theological/ethical concerns.

Kee, Howard Clark, and Irvin J. Borowsky. *Removing Anti-Judaism from the Pulpit*. New York: Continuum, 1996. Essays and sermons by Catholic and Protestant scholars and preachers explore how to preach without being anti-Jewish.

Luther, Martin. *Commentary on Romans*. Translated by J. Theodore Mueller. Grand Rapids: Kregel Publications, 1976. Prepared for a popular audience, this translation of Luther's commentary presents the main ideas that Luther developed as he studied Paul's epistle.

The Paul Page. http://www.thepaulpage.com. This website pulls together materials that demonstrate and explain recent trends in Pauline studies. It is a good place to get an orientation to the new perspective as well as specific topics, such as Paul and empire or Paul and Judaism.

Westerholm, Stephen. *Justification Reconsidered: Rethinking a Pauline Theme*. An alternative view on the new perspective/ old perspective debate that seeks to show how traditional theologians have been more faithful to Paul's ideas than revisionists have been.

Wright, N. T. *Justification: God's Plan and Paul's Vision*. Downers Grove, IL: InterVarsity Press Academic, 2009. Wright offers an account of Paul's understanding of the place of justification in his overall view of God's plan for our salvation. This account does not focus only on Romans but also draws from his other letters.

Wright, N. T. *Paul for Everyone: Romans, Part 1* and *Paul for Everyone: Romans, Part 2*. Louisville, KY: Westminster John Knox Press, 2005. Nontechnical and pastoral, these commentary books share information about the letter along with explanations that invite imaginative engagement. Glossaries explain key terms.

Index of Ancient Sources

Index of Subjects